SLOUCHING TOW

Slouching Towards Big Pink

Essays on Bob Dylan and The Band, Woody Guthrie,

and Franklin Delano Roosevelt

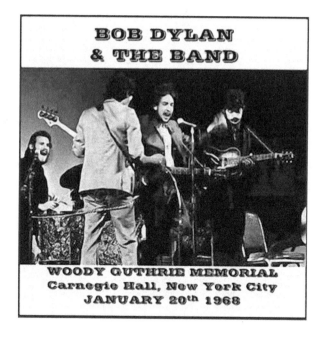

Adrian Smith

This edition published 2020 by:
Takahe Publishing Ltd.
Registered Office:
77 Earlsdon Street, Coventry CV5 6EL

Copyright © Adrian Smith 2020

ISBN 978-1-908837-14-1

TAKAHE PUBLISHING LTD.

2020

To Mary, to Georgia, and again – above all – to Adam

Adrian Smith is Emeritus Professor of Modern History at the University of Southampton. His books include three biographies, a history of the early *New Statesman*, and *The City of Coventry: A Twentieth Century Icon*. He supports Coventry City FC, Coventry RFC, and Warwickshire CCC. For half a century he has considered Richard Thompson England's greatest songwriter and guitarist. Year on year he waits forlornly for Jay Farrar and Son Volt to abandon the Midwest honky-tonks and tour Europe.

CONTENTS

Slouching Towards Big Pink

My son's serve was a triumph of coaching, a thing of beauty. On the rare occasions he played tennis as an adult I marvelled at his default textbook delivery. The same applied to sailing. Once qualified, he never took to the water again. Yet that capacity to handle a dinghy in even the roughest conditions was instinctive – you just knew there survived a residual confidence, quiet and enduring. He had natural ability, and at a young age was a disciplined and willing student. An effortless absorption of technical skills translated from the tennis court and the tideway to the studio and the workshop: the sinuous serve matched by subtle and confident line drawing, the seamanship paralleled in leftfield solutions to sculptural conundrums. In truth Adam was never a sportsman. He was always an artist, a craftsman, a creator.

Yet, with great patience and generosity of spirit, Adam invariably indulged my passion for sport. He was always great company, even when quietly bored by the apparent lack of action. The only occasion I saw him genuinely excited was county cricket's one-day final in 2012, when Hampshire narrowly defeated Warwickshire. I treasure the memory of that day, and not our return to Lord's in September 2016, by which time Adam was seriously ill. To my intense relief, a dismal match ended early. Was there an unstated assumption by us both that this was the last time we would sit in a stand side by side, the son quietly amused by the father's undimmed loyalty to the city and the county he was born into but had long since left? I don't know is the honest answer.

What I do know is that the true meeting of minds was in music, and on Adam's birthday six weeks later a spur-of-the-moment present arose out of my fear for the coming year: was it conceivable that we might be here, in Brighton, twelve months from now sipping champagne and eating cake? No, it fucking well wasn't. I looked down at the records stacked by the Scandinavian-style 'seventies stereo system. Like so

1

many in their late twenties and early thirties, Adam and his wife Georgia had enthusiastically embraced the renaissance of vinyl. The albums were mostly mine, passed on secure in the knowledge that they would be well treated and properly appreciated. For this reason I hadn't hesitated to hand over every LP by The Band that I bought between seeing them at the Isle of Wight in August 1969 and a New York screening of *The Last Waltz* nine years later. *Music from Big Pink* lay on the turntable, and I knew Adam played it time and again, day after day. Exhausted by the effort of building a fiendishly complicated helix ladder for the sculptor Kath Campbell, he saw it installed in Cambridge and then made his way home. The realisation of Campbell's testing design confirmed Adam's remarkable capacity to translate a basic concept into an engineering triumph. He never went back to work, and soon after he could no longer make his regular appointment at Bart's. The world contracted to Five Dials, and a soundtrack courtesy of Hudson, Manuel, Danko, Helm, and Robertson. There are probably several tenuous connections between Brighton and Woodstock, but none so sad as this one.

Music from Big Pink constituted a genuinely fresh sound, as confirmed and amplified by its brilliant successor. For reasons lost in the mists of time I had never owned The Band's eponymous second album on vinyl. I now felt strangely guilty that such a plangent, powerful, and near-perfect record was absent from Adam's collection. In other circumstances the omission of *The Band* from the LPs passed on to my son would have been a cause for regret, but no more than that. But to me on 7th November 2016 its absence appeared yet another cruel irony in a never-ending succession of cruel ironies – only on this occasion I could do something about it. I slipped out of the flat, made my way down to The Lanes, and bought a copy of *The Band* in Vinyl Revolution. I'm looking at the record as I type: it's exactly the same as the gatefold sleeve album released in September 1969, but it cost well over ten times as much. Nevertheless, for me and my wife Mary, and of course for Adam and Georgia, this was money well spent. From now on *Music from Big Pink* alternated with *The Band* on the daily playlist, their-pre-eminence challenged only by *Harvest*.

This late appreciation of Neil Young was another cruel irony, although I always admired Adam's ability to discriminate. There was no adolescent dismissal of all his parents' heroes, for example he loved Tom Petty; but neither was there an uncritical embrace: repeat playing of The Band did not extend to Bob Dylan. Adam had eclectic tastes, and as a teenager displayed an indifference to the commercial mainstream worthy of John Peel – although in later years he did regret opting for an Algerian hip hop cooperative instead of REM on his first visit to Glastonbury.

These were the years when he experimented with dreadlocks, discovered tattoos (referencing a mighty combination of William Blake and Joe Strummer), and briefly dallied with piercing. 'Spig' played bass with his schoolmates in Forty Foot Fall, a punk rock band which recorded its own material and progressed from local pubs to bottom billing at Southampton's best known venue, The Joiners. Always his own man, from an early age Adam demonstrated the self-resilience and fixed purpose so typical of an only child. Thus he kept me, and his mother, at a distance from his band, only calling on my services as a chauffeur when no other parent was around. This was – and is – to my deep regret. Yet looking back now I can understand why he acted in the way he did.

Adam knew that, for all my enthusiasm and encouragement, I didn't really like the music. Here was a loud, brash, gloriously raucous sound that I thought had more in common with thrash metal than my clearly dated concept of what constituted punk rock. Musical osmosis (Burritos, Band, and Buffalo Springfield in the kitchen/Byrds, Beach Boys, and Beatles in the car) meant Adam knew my preferences and prejudices better than I did myself: without a word being spoken, it was made clear to me that my services as a de facto roadie were not required. This tough yet considerate response was consistent with a conscious avoidance of appearing ungracious if given a present he would never wear, use, or listen to: from Crazy Horse to the Red Sox, how many T-shirts were gratefully received and never seen again? The end of sixth form signalled the end of Forty Foot Fall; after that Adam played bass only a handful of times. Not that he ever wholly turned his back on industrial-strength punk rock, whether tracing an obscure Brooklyn outfit to the back room of a south London pub or resurrecting at full volume a long forgotten '45.

Adam never discriminated between old and new, his compilation CDs ranging from Kings of Leon to Jackson Browne. For him his favourite artists carried no baggage – for example, he loved David Byrne but knew almost nothing about Talking Heads. Billy Bragg was seen only in an immediate political context, and not as a survivor of late 'seventies and early 'eighties challenges to blatant racism and class oppression. In this respect my son was at one with a succeeding generation's embrace of context-free streaming and a default shuffle play.

In late 2014 I went with Adam to hear Old Crow Medicine Show play at the Roundhouse in Islington. I was amazed to find the gig sold out, with nearly two thousand fans singing along to every song. Given that Ketch Secor's band was at the time almost unknown in Britain why and how were so many millenials so knowledgeable? Adam pointed to the band's prominence on YouTube, and the degree to which social media coverage compensated for minimal radio exposure on Radio 2 and 6 Music. By this time I no longer referred in seminars to 'the digital revolution,' an undergraduate having pointed out that his generation had known nothing different.

Although born into the dying days of an analogue age, Adam's relationship to the internet and the smart phone was no different from that of my gently subversive student. He could effortlessly embrace new technology, while at the same time be drawn time and again to the worn and antique, from esoteric leather luggage to specialist tools long since dispensed with; his library was a unique combination of cutting-edge literature, novel sequences (Patrick O' Brian, Olivia Manning, and Evelyn Waugh, but no Anthony Powell as I told him he needed to wait for middle age), and faux tooled leather volumes from the golden age of Edwardian popular fiction. No wonder he loved the sepia-soaked, bourbon-stained, post-civil war aesthetic of *The Band*'s album sleeve – it complemented his own immersion in the gothic and the confusion of a world gone wrong. The penultimate track is 'Unfaithful Servant' – Adam's dystopian landscapes reveal people who clearly have taken that fatal turn, have experienced that terminal moment of betrayal. These are arresting, disturbing, and above all, beautifully executed pictures.

The parish church packed, Adam's funeral took place a week before Christmas. Georgia chose music with a special place in her heart, indeed in both their hearts. The next morning we sat in the crematorium chapel awaiting the cortege. This would be a short, stripped down, unstructured ceremony, and as such a test of emotional resilience far harsher than the previous day's service. This time I chose the music, a solitary song. As Adam's coffin arrived the chapel filled with the sound of 'The Weight'. Levon Helm's voice rang out: 'I pulled into Nazareth, was feeling 'bout half past dead…'. In my mind I could hear Adam – 'The Band…nice choice, Dad' – and pictured the wry smile, the brief gesture of approval. Delivering the eulogy in church had called for controlled emotion – there was a job to be done, and only after that could the crying come. Now I was far more exposed, far more vulnerable, and hearing 'The Weight' was a plaintive power punch that left me near helpless. Mary spotted this straightaway, and now the roles were reversed from twenty-four hours earlier: could I handle this, and should she oversee proceedings? Tearful but insistent, I stood up and waited for Richard Manuel to lead the all too familiar chorus ('...Take a load off Fanny, and you put the load right on me) and then deliver the fourth verse; for a brief moment I found myself thinking, 'What a voice, what a waste.' Then the music faded away and I took control of myself, control of events. I echoed my remarks of the previous day, that Adam was a kind and hugely generous person, a fair-minded and compassionate human being, for ever on the right side of the barricades. I read from the *Four Quartets*, where Eliot in 'Little Gidding' tells us that, 'Here, the intersection of the timeless moment/Is England and nowhere.' A final moment of contemplation and reflection – the past two terrible years raced through my mind in a compression of anger and pain. Then we bid our darling boy goodbye.

That night the Dodge Brothers dedicated the band's Christmas gig to Adam. It was an end-of-an-era party in The Thomas Tripp, the Lymington pub where Mike Hammond and Mark Kermode had started playing together twenty years before. What once was a happy festive reunion for family and friends now attracted fans from far beyond the New Forest: with national radio exposure and their latest album laid down at Sun Studios, Mike, Mark, Aly, and Alex had outgrown their spiritual home. The pub was packed, thus ensuring a hefty donation to Macmillan Cancer Support. I had asked Mike if near the end of the evening I could join the band in singing 'The Night They Drove Old Dixie Down'. For Mary, Georgia, and I this had surely been the worst week of our lives – *nothing* before or after could ever match the experience of losing the person we loved most. That morning we had witnessed a formal farewell, but mere ceremony could never constitute a genuine goodbye: would we ever really say goodbye, or would Adam be a constant presence for each of us? The answer to that, three years on, is an emphatic yes – he's with all three of us all the time. If there is a healing process then it's long and painful, and, rather than seeking to forget, it embraces individual and collective memory. Back in December 2016 all this was still to come. That night we needed – *I* needed – some form of emotional release, however temporary.

Thus the day began and ended with Robbie Robertson's best known and most enduring compositions: 'The Weight' a mystery, a plea, a lament (but for what? to whom – who are these people?), and 'The Night They Drove Old Dixie Down' a mournful statement fixed in time, stirring but stark, evocative and yet free from sentiment and romance. The power of both songs never fails to impress me. I remember around twenty years ago teaching an undergraduate course on the 1960s, and screening clips from *The Last Waltz*. An obvious choice was Scorsese's close camera capture of Levon Helm's passionate, unaided, heartfelt rendering of 'The Night They Drove Old Dixie Down'. When Helm finished the song I was astonished to see a class raised on rave and rap bursting into spontaneous applause.

Back in The Thomas Tripp I was summoned on stage by the Dodge Brothers, and duly joined in both the chorus *and* the verses, all inhibitions lost in the emotion and the power of the moment. Yes, there was immense sorrow, but at the same time I rejoiced in the sight and sound of so many people – many of course family, friends, and neighbours – chorusing an anthem I knew had meant so much to our son. This was his local, in which as a student he had served behind the bar. How many Christmases had Adam, invariably a reluctant dancer, finished his pint and to the surprise of all thrown himself into a form of quasi jiving? I could picture him standing with old school friends home for the holidays, listening to the Dodge Brothers and once or twice nodding to me on the far side of the room: this is the music from the heartland of America that you love, and you must know that I do too. As Mike Hammond brought the final cacophonous chorus to an end, I remembered my mad dash to the record shop only five weeks before. How many times had Adam listened to *The Band* between his birthday and leaving Brighton for the last time? Was there any solace, pleasure, or relief every time he laid the LP on the turntable? I have no idea, but I hope that to some degree, however small, the music served as a distraction. Hope – it's all we can cling to.

'Don't forget the motor city!' – my parents and pop

By the start of the 1960s Britain's premier car city – the Detroit of the West Midlands – was riding a wave of consumer affluence, its most popular dance hall and record shop both suitably positioned in the Precinct, civic and commercial symbol of post-Blitz reconstruction. Unlike Liverpool, Manchester, Newcastle, and Birmingham, Coventry couldn't boast a roster of pop groups riding the 'sixties zeitgeist, an exception being the Sorrows with their 1965 Top Twenty single 'Take A Heart'. Soon forgotten in the UK, the Sorrows enjoyed a long after-life in Italy, re-recording their songs in Milan to satisfy local fans (thus setting an example to another apparent one-hit wonder, David Bowie, whose 'Ragazzo Solo Ragazza Sola' refashioned 'Space Oddity' as a stunning psychedelic *balata*). Proto-garage rock, a resurrected, hard rockin' 'Take A Heart' is today a final encore for the Richard Thompson Band, but sadly not in its Italian version, 'Mi Si Spezza Il Cuore'.

The Sorrows signalled that, like any other city of comparable size, Coventry enjoyed a beat boom, with local lads growing their hair, saving hard for the fake Fender or the second-hand snare, and chatting up the neighbourhood Dusty or Cilla. There were plentiful outlets for music and dancing, the principal venues being the Locarno in the city centre and the Matrix further out. In its heyday the Matrix boasted an impressive array of show bands and pop groups, including one of Ringo's earliest gigs with the Beatles. The Locarno Ballroom was an impressive example of postwar glass and steel architecture, its Precinct tower still on show today as the entrance to Coventry's central library. Along with the Leofric Hotel in Broadgate, the Locarno was the showpiece of a new and confident Coventry, rooted in full employment, consumer affluence, and municipal interventionism. Sixties sporting success, courtesy of Jimmy Hill's 'Sky Blue revolution' and an all-conquering rugby club, was the icing on the cake.

By the end of the decade, with the Matrix no more, the Locarno reigned supreme, its commercial-minded DJs sharing the stage with mainstream good-time acts like Geno Washington and the Ram Jam Band – this wasn't quite the venue Kevin Rowlands had in mind when writing Dexys Midnight Runners' breakthrough hit, but for his many Midlands fans Geno was the main man. Jerry Dammers did memorialise the Locarno in the Specials' B-side to 'Ghost Town', 'Friday Night, Saturday Morning'; as did Chuck Berry in his hit live recording of the dreadful 'My Ding-a-Ling'. While the fame of the Who and the Pink Floyd had seen them play gigs at the Locarno, by 1969 the principal venue for 'progressive music' was the Lanchester Polytechnic, today's Coventry University. The polytechnic's union building stood opposite what was then Coventry's newly consecrated cathedral, and in the late 'sixties and early 'seventies it was one of the biggest student venues outside London, capable of matching Leeds University in attracting famous names from both sides of the Atlantic. Earnest, serious-minded sixth-formers of my generation, too young to have posed as provincial mods high on soul, Tamla, and God knows what else at the Matrix or the Locarno, and currently in thrall to what music weeklies labelled 'the underground', served our rock fan apprenticeships every Friday night at 'The Lanch'.

For my parents mention of the Matrix prompted memories of before I was born, while their rare visits to the Locarno were for civic functions such as the crowning of the carnival queen (providing a low-loader for the procession qualified my father as a judge). For all my mother's heroic efforts to understand and appreciate Dylan or the Beatles, neither she nor my father was especially interested in popular music, let alone classical. The only occasion in the year that they saw a singer perform was the Christmas pantomime – year on year the Coventry Hippodrome would convince a fading star that his or her career could be revived courtesy of a six-week stint in doublet and tights. Local boy Frank Ifield was always a big attraction, apart from the Sorrows his native city's only claimant to chart success until the arrival of Two Tone. When courting my parents had attended variety shows at the Hippodrome, with comedian Max Miller a guilty pleasure. Dad clearly preferred the risqué joke to the cheesy love song – beneath the veneer of puritanical respectability he was remarkably relaxed about drinking, long(ish) hair, late nights, and the keys to his car (for ever the platoon commander, trusting those in his charge to act responsibly). He could well afford to acquire a radiogram, but chose not to do so. In consequence there were no 78s or 45s in the house, let alone LPs, until I bought my first record-player.

There was no generational antipathy towards rock 'n' roll, just indifference. Hostility might easily have been the case given that my father had reached forty by the time 'All Shook Up' gave Elvis his first transatlantic chart-topper. Dad's musical tastes were shaped by wartime experience and competitive ballroom dancing. Like an inveterate hippie insistent that Quicksilver Messenger Service's first live album constitutes the acme of rock music, my dad never moved on from Vera Lynn. The adolescent mind has little understanding of time as a relative concept, and my father's favoured artist seemed someone from the dim and distant past – that distancing exaggerated by the permanent revolution in popular music taking place for much of the 1950s and 1960s, and the consequent emergence of a recognisable youth culture. Vera Lynn was scarcely middle-aged when the Beatles first lodged themselves in the national psyche. Today, for anyone over thirty the music of twenty years ago retains a degree of contemporaneity, think hip hop or grunge (Brit Pop was already a fading force); but no teenager in 1965 listened approvingly to the songs our parents had treasured when a similar age.

Not that their generation's preferred music had gone away, as the Top Ten confirmed week on week – Cliff Richard had long since swapped 'Move It' for 'Congratulations', and for every Procol Harum or Pink Floyd there was a Ken Dodd or Englebert Humperdink: in terms of cool the BBC's *Top of the Pops* could never match ITV's *Ready, Steady, Go* as programme content was determined by record sales. The generation gap was never more visible in the Smith household than when teatime coincided with *Top of the Pops*. Commercial television at seven o'clock on a Friday night offered a very different viewing experience. I had no clear memories of Jack Good's pioneering programmes for hep cats of the skiffle era, *Six-Five Special* and *Oh Boy!*, so for me Manfred Mann's 'Five, four, three, two, one...' signalled the start of a show like no other. My mum and dad never disparaged the mods strutting their stuff on the studio floor as the Tamla or Stax headliner rendered *Ready, Steady, Go* compulsory viewing – they simply didn't get it.

I don't think my mother and father ever danced other than as one half of a pair locked in each other's arms. They loved the music of ballroom dancing for one simple reason – they were both exceptional dancers. Even I, observing the adults through the prism of my half-pint lemonade shandy, could see how good mum and dad were when compared to most other couples. My parents made every dance, especially the waltz and the quick step, look effortless. They fulfilled every cliché of gliding across the dance floor, the one knowing instinctively the other's steps and intentions. My father's prowess as a county-class cricketer ensured similar success as a dancer. The lightness of touch, acute peripheral vision, and speedy footwork which rendered Alf Smith such a formidable batsman were equally evident whenever the Midlands' answer to Henry Hall lifted his baton and set the orchestra swinging. My dad taught my mother to dance, and he was clearly a superb teacher. However, he never danced with her competitively. My mother had no problem with this as on an early date her future spouse introduced his dance partner. Here was a couple interested only in winning trophies, so jealousy was never a problem, and all involved became lifelong friends. By the time my father and his partner began their winning streak war was on the horizon, cutting short their success in the same way that Hitler put paid to 'Tiger' Smith's cricketing career.

If, as Alison Abra has chronicled, the 1920s were a formative decade for British ballroom dancing, the late 1930s saw consolidation of the five standardised, strictly codified foundational dances. These dances had been sanitised and rendered sexless, witness the tango's rapid displacement by the fox trot. Needless to say, if the lights were low, and the ballroom crowded, then couples rightly disregarded any attempt to stifle romance. My dad was obsessed with getting his technique right, but with regard to medal-winning not sex. He was first on the floor for the fox trot, but if invited to tango would have been first out the door. Little wonder any sight of *Ready, Steady, Go*'s amphetamine-fuelled army dancing the watusi to the sound of Zoot Money or Georgie Fame and the Blue Flames would send my dad straight out the room to do the washing up. Nor was my mum inclined to take up presenter Cathy McGowan's suggestion that she try out London's latest dance craze on the lounge carpet.

Yet, to their credit, my parents were remarkably relaxed about my own musical adventures. They let me frequent folk clubs in my mid-teens, and from seventeen sanctioned my hitching alone to music festivals. Over ten years before, my mother had happily left me all day with boys far older than myself – they were the sons of close neighbours, and she trusted them to look after me. Needless to say, neither of my parents noted that – for my age – I boasted an impressive knowledge of rock 'n' roll and American folk music. This was not a consequence of pre-adolescent precocity but the result of my primary school years being spent next door to a teenager with impeccable musical taste.

Lew and Cis Palmer's son was a rock 'n' roll evangelist whose enthusiasm overcame any reluctance to spend time with a little boy eager to listen. Watching television and listening to the radio at the start of the 'sixties reinforced a firm belief that pop music was mostly rubbish. That insight into the world of Susan Maughan and the Karl Denver Trio was rooted in the deep impression made by John Palmer and his mates a few years earlier when letting me sit in the corner while they listened to records. Was the evangelism so deep-rooted that John deemed it vital to drag the little lad away from his Meccano set and subject him to a diet of music unimaginable on the then Light Programme? While the big boys played the board game Scoop, pausing only to change the 45s, I sat there mesmerised by the sounds of Buddy Holly, the Everly Brothers, Duane Eddy, Eddie Cochran, Gene Vincent, and, glory of glories, Chuck Berry.

Richard Hoggart, in his recently published *The Uses of Literacy*, saw such an experience as a passive, corrosive exercise in cultural displacement, famously encapsulated in the book's milk bar scenario (where what today we would label American 'soft power' has wiped out any distinctively British aspect of young people's lifestyle activities). What Hoggart failed to see was the way John Palmer's generation weaved American popular music into the nation's cultural DNA: adaptive and creative, they revitalised R and B and rock 'n' roll to such an extent that the best British bands – the Beatles, the Animals, the Rolling Stones, the Yardbirds, and the Kinks, had they been allowed to tour – forced white audiences in the States to comprehend what black music was all about. Billy Bragg, in *Roots, Radicals and Rockers: How Skiffle Changed the World*, makes the point that this trans-Atlantic recharging of the musical batteries was by no means unprecedented, with mid-century collectors like Alan Lomax bringing over from America field recordings of Appalachian ballads and Irish laments that dated from the earliest years of colonisation and the great wave of migration which followed the Famine.

No doubt John Palmer and his mates played Elvis and Little Richard, but my clearest memory is of hearing those artists who were especially popular in Britain long after rock 'n' roll peaked in the States. In his bathroom studio Joe Meek – 'Britain's answer to Phil Spector' – cannily exploited this residual transatlantic affection for lately departed rock 'n' rollers, with one-hit wonders Mike Berry and Heinz recording vinyl tributes to Buddy Holly and Eddie Cochran. The bathos of Cochran dying, and Vincent nearly dying, in a village outside Chippenham (in the words of one US newsreel, 'beside a lonely Wiltshire highway') left a lasting impression upon young British blokes. Bequiffed teds and black leathered bike boys were fiercely proprietorial about their dead heroes; but they weren't alone, witness John Peel and Ian Dury both flying the flag for their 'blue gene baby.'

Flying the flag for rockers this side of the Atlantic was of course the Shadows, their erstwhile leader restricted to his first two singles: a now neutered Cliff Richard and his Brylcreemed peers were all stoutly condemned as third-rate imitators of the real thing – as was made abundantly clear to me as I sat far from the Scoop board mesmerised by the sound of first generation Fenders, Gretschs, and Gibsons emanating out of the Dansette.

The Beatles also paid homage to their heroes, but they were clearly the real deal; as our young neighbour recognised the moment he saw their first nationwide TV appearance on 'Thank Your Lucky Stars'. Not that he was unique in acknowledging the dark ages were over – aged eleven, even I could see that great music was back. Within days John Palmer had signed up to the Beatles fan club, and his love of the Fab Four never waned. I would soon be my own man, looking beyond Liverpool to New York and the West Coast. John Palmer would also be looking westward, starting a new life in Torquay with a young wife and a plumbing certificate. Before then he inspired me one last time: in the late spring of 1963 he called over the garden fence, summoning me and

Slouching Towards Big Pink

my freshly acquired four-track recorder. In the Palmers' front room John told me to tape his latest acquisition, an LP with a cover shot of a scruffy looking bloke and his girlfriend walking down the street. An hour later I was back home, pressing the play button. Almost immediately my mum was in the lounge shouting above the sound of a song which within weeks would be ubiquitous, 'What an awful voice – who is that?'. '*That* is Bob Dylan, and *that* is 'Blowin' in the Wind''.

16

Finding Woody Guthrie

'Song To Woody' was – and still is – the stand out track on Bob Dylan's debut album. On a rough and ready record it sounds great, it's easy on the ear. Most Dylan fans know that the song uses the tune of Guthrie's '1913 Massacre', and that it rewrites a line from the better-known 'Pastures of Plenty' ('we come with the dust, and we go with the wind'). I first heard 'Song To Woody' when I was about twelve, and immediately I wanted to know more about him. Somebody good enough for Bob was surely good enough for me. He sang about Cisco and Sonny, but I had no idea who they were. Somehow or other I did know that Lead Belly had written 'Goodnight Irene'. This was curiosity, not precocity – finding out about Woody Guthrie was no different from, say, wanting to know more about what John, Paul, and George got up to in Hamburg. I'd seen a picture of him in a library book, and he looked great (in fact he looked really cool, but 'coolness' was a concept unfamiliar to me in 1964). My mum and dad had never heard of Woody Guthrie, and neither had anyone else I knew. I assumed he was dead, and Bob's tribute did nothing to deny this.

Predictably, it was John Palmer next door who facilitated my pre-teen embrace of folk music. His impressive record collection included LPs by Bob Dylan and by Joan Baez. What's more the Baez albums included songs by Woody Guthrie. We were a long way from Bleeker Street, and if truth be told we spent a lot more time listening to the Beatles, but John Palmer convinced me that New York was just like Liverpool, but without the electric guitars. He told me to listen to the Light Programme just before ten on a Saturday morning, and, astonishingly, I could hear an American folk singer – it was Paul Simon filling the 'God slot'.

By now I had a clear and simple idea of what constituted 'folk': it was something played in America by young women with long hair, notably Joan Baez, and young men with peaked caps, like Tom Paxton

– another discovery next door. I had no idea how Woody Guthrie fitted in to all of this as there appeared to be other folk singers who were a lot older, or by virtue of their clean-cut appearance seemed a lot older. They appeared to have nothing in common with Bob Dylan, but their wholesome music enjoyed far more airtime on the radio. I hated happy-clappy anthems such as 'If I had a Hammer', sung by the likes of the Kingston Trio, and sing-along songs 'for the kiddies' by Burl Ives or Pete Seeger – had I known so much of this stuff was by Woody Guthrie then that would have been it. My view of Seeger was jaundiced for many years, and still, whenever I read of Peter, Paul, and Mary's centrality to the Greenwich Village folk scene, I hear in my head 'Puff the Magic Dragon'. Seeing the Coen brothers' *Inside Llewellyn Davis* confirmed all my old prejudices.

Thus, the boundaries of what I understood to be 'good' folk music were ridiculously narrow, and rooted in ignorance. Being far too young to know about an underground folk scene focused upon London, Glasgow, Edinburgh, Sheffield, and Hull, I presumed that all folk music this side of the Atlantic was dire, whether that be the White Heather Club's insipid interpretation of Highland jigs and reels, the Third Programme's high art version of English murder ballads, or the Clancy Brother's sanitisation of Irish rebel songs. For anyone unfamiliar with the embryonic revival, televised folk music meant bearded men in Arran sweaters singing jaunty songs as a current affairs programme's painful form of light relief. At least once a week on *Tonight* the relentlessly upbeat Robin Hall and Jimmie Macgregor sang 'the songs of jolly Scotland' to a prime-time audience – the collateral damage to a fragile folk scene must have been enormous, with every viewer's residual prejudice regularly reinforced. Pioneers like Martin Carthy, Davy Graham, and Shirley Collins were scarcely known, so folk musicians on TV were mostly fading skiffle stars or family-friendly, home-spun versions of the Kingston Trio. 'Traditional music' seemed to entail plucking a banjo or sticking your finger in your ear – how could that compete with the Rolling Stones?

Embracing the English – or indeed any other – tradition clearly had to wait, not least as I was yet to understand that enjoying music wasn't an either/or experience. Within a few years I would come to recognise that eclecticism was something to be embraced, even if I couldn't as yet articulate why appreciating a wide range of music was of itself a good thing. I could enjoy both Bob Dylan and the Beatles, but that was about it – and once the former started playing electric music then the compatibility was that much greater (with the Byrds a convenient bridge). The excitement and raw appeal of mid-sixties pop rendered folk music the poor relation. For the moment Woody Guthrie remained a nebulous concept rather than a real person. I was in no rush to hear any recently released folk records, let alone music from America in the 'thirties and 'forties – Woody Guthrie was still on hold.

Enlightenment came with Coventry's newly opened record library. It was largely frequented by impoverished lovers of classical music, and jazz buffs on the lookout for that legendary Charlie Parker performance so long missing from their voluminous collection of Bird recordings. No-one ever seemed to consult the library's folk section, which, in an era of municipal munificence, was bulging with old and new releases. I spent very little time listening to the Argo recordings of the BBC *Radio Ballads*, produced for the Third Programme by Charles Parker, Ewan MacColl, and Peggy Seeger from the late 'fifties onwards. They sounded stolid, ponderous, and frankly boring; I was too young to appreciate their value as a unique record of a fast disappearing industrial Britain. Thankfully, also available were the complete catalogues of British folk's foundational record labels, Topic and Transatlantic. At last I got to hear Bert Jansch and John Renbourn, and I discovered another of Transatlantic's big names: the Johnstons. They hailed from County Meath and their early LPs – along with Finbar and Eddie Furey's debut album – constituted a hot-house training in Irish traditional music. By an immense stroke of luck the Johnstons were the first act I ever saw in a folk club. Whether singing solo or in close harmony, Paul Brady and the two Johnston sisters were a thrilling act; leaving me with the naïve belief that folk nights must always be that exciting.

I now knew something about Irish music, and, thanks to Dylan, Baez, Paxton, and Phil Ochs, I was already familiar with contemporary and traditional folk from the far side of the Atlantic. Yet I had a wholly warped view of Scottish folk, and I still knew almost nothing of the English tradition. Enlightenment came courtesy of Carthy and Collins, their albums the pride of the record library stacks. Even at the age of fifteen I knew how important Martin Carthy was – hadn't he passed all his best tunes on to Dylan and Paul Simon? Not so, Shirley Collins – and yet here was someone equally vital to the folk revival. I didn't know it at the time, but this was a woman who had criss-crossed the pre-civil rights southern states with folklorist Alan Lomax recording unknown blues singers like Mississippi Fred McDowell, laid down a ground breaking jazz-folk LP with Davy Graham, and in a sequence of pioneering albums captured the essence of rural life across southern England on the eve of the Great War. Originally on Topic, Shirley Collins and her sister Dolly, maestro of the portative organ, were later signed by Harvest, EMI's ostensibly 'underground' label. Like encountering Kate Bush or the Unthanks for the first time, I was stunned by Shirley Collins's voice, and the unique stripped-down sound created in tandem with her sister – this was unlike any form of music I had ever heard.

Perhaps it was the prohibitive price of imported albums, or the record librarian's prioritising of modern jazz, but American labels like Folkways were poorly represented in the municipal vinyl collection. I eschewed Pete Seeger, my original prejudice reinforced by reports that at the 1965 Newport Folk Festival he had tried to cut the power supply when Dylan strapped on his Stratocaster and led Mike Bloomfield and his brother bluesmen into an ear-splitting rendition of 'Maggie's Farm'. Working through the list on Bob's homage to his mentor ('Cisco, and Sonny, and Lead Belly too...'), I found nothing by Cisco Houston; and a solitary record by Sonny Terry and Brownie McGhee. The duo for some reason always included Coventry in their UK tours, across the decade playing a variety of local venues from the Hippodrome to the Lanchester Polytechnic, which is where I saw them in 1969. They rated highly in terms of authenticity and entertainment, which is why promoters and audiences always wanted them back. I loved the sheer unadulterated joy of the Terry and McGhee work songs, not least 'Midnight Special', and this probably explains why Lead Belly suffered by comparison. The record library's only Woody Guthrie album was a recent compilation, permanently on loan. However, as luck would have it I discovered the Guthrie mother lode in the fullest, the filthiest, and frankly the foulest of the three junk shops to be found in Gosford Street.

Regeneration has belatedly restored civic pride, but in the late 1960s Far Gosford Street was already acquiring a somewhat seedy image. I spent hours rifling the record bins in each of the three junk shops, looking out for rock 'n' roll and rockabilly 78s and 45s dumped by ex-teddy boys on the day they walked down the aisle. Mike Hammond, film historian and frontman for the Dodge Brothers, reckons mid-sixties visits to stores holding second-hand vinyl or even specialist record retailers was a rare experience for white American kids on the lookout for fresh sounds: his own experience in a southern California suburb saw him buying records at the 'five and dime' – he and his peers lived too far from the downtown record stores, making it that much harder to come across music not heard on AM radio stations. More compact cities and towns in Britain meant one or more specialist shops were never more than a bus ride away, leaving Woolworths to play the same chart-focused role as in America.

One Saturday morning in Far Gosford Street I found not one but two original Folkways albums. This was well over twenty years before the Smithsonian Institute bought Folkways following the death of its founder, Greenwich Village's legendary music promoter Moses – Moe – Asch. The first was a 1964 reissue of *Dust Bowl Ballads*, which Asch initially released in 1950. This had followed RCA's refusal of Guthrie's request to collect on a single LP the songs subsidiary label Victor Records had put out as 78s ten years earlier – Asch broke copyright law to support an already ailing Guthrie, and shamed RCA into backing down when they threatened legal action. The second album was a mid-fifties anthology bearing the same title as Guthrie's 1943 autobiography, *Bound For Glory*. Asch had released the record following a benefit concert he organised for the Guthrie family in March 1956. Its eleven songs were introduced by Will Geer, the LA actor and political activist who in the late 1930s had worked with Woody Guthrie on staging agitprop shows for migrant workers. Geer read extracts from his old comrade's memoirs, just as he had at the concert – and as he would again at the memorial concerts in Carnegie Hall on 20th January 1968. Of course I knew nothing of this, nor that it was Will Geer who introduced Guthrie to New York fellow-travellers after the singer followed his friend east in February 1940.

The Folkways albums boasted sturdy cardboard covers as yet unknown in Britain, and, when taken together, they constituted an impressive collection of Woody Guthrie's finest anthems – including the two songs that accompanied the near unknown 'Dear Mrs. Roosevelt' when Dylan played his Carnegie Hall sets in January 1968: 'The Grand Coulee Dam' and 'I Ain't Got No Home'. Sadly, these deeply scratched and well worn LPs sounded terrible on my Murphy Majorette. They were in such an awful condition that it was easier on the ear to experience Woody Guthrie courtesy of intermediaries like Joan Baez and the Byrds.

Both Baez and the Byrds recorded 'Deportee (Plane Crash at Los Gatos)', supposedly Guthrie's last song, circa 1948 – in late 1976 when the Rolling Thunder Revue took to the road, Baez would regularly duet with Dylan on 'Deportee'. If this really was Woody's final farewell, then the Byrds' plangent delivery seemed suitably poignant. Ostensibly, the pathos of the song lay in its composer unknowingly ending his career with such a masterly fusion of melody and political intent. In due course I discovered that 'Deportee' was written as a poem, which Guthrie performed as a chant, and that a schoolteacher called Martin Hoffman had added a musical accompaniment towards the end of the 'fifties. This then raised the question as to what actually was Woody Guthrie's last complete composition. It would be well into the present century before I found an answer to that particular question.

Looking back, I realise that I acquired my two monumental records not long after Woody Guthrie died, in October 1967. This was a month before the release of *Alice's Restaurant*, the success of that album focusing attention on Arlo Guthrie. It was at this point, early in 1968, that I found out Woody Guthrie had died of a hereditary condition. The following year's film version of *Alice's Restaurant* included a heart-wrenching scene of Arlo visiting his father, lying in a hospital bed his mind and body shredded by a freak of genetics. Director Arthur Penn's not so subtle sub-text was the very real possibility of the carefree, innocent, Svejk-like son one day falling victim to the deadly Huntingdon's disease (a possibility, thankfully, as yet unrealised). I hadn't been alone in assuming that Woody Guthrie was long dead. This was a common assumption in both Britain and the States. For example, when Dylan played the Royal Albert Hall in May 1966 one ill-informed heckler screamed out, 'Woody Guthrie would have turned in his grave.'

As I found out more about Guthrie the man, so I found out more about his politics. Buying the Folkways albums had prompted me to delve into the history of the Dustbowl and the Depression. These inquiries, combined with the discovery of George Orwell, initiated a much-needed political education. I was never a teenage rebel. Aged fifteen or sixteen I was conscious of what was going on in the wider world but knew little of domestic politics – I registered events, but not their implications. Radical ideas and actions took place elsewhere, for which read the United States, such that any interpretation of what was happening closer to home was still influenced by my conservative-minded, *Daily Express*-reading parents. I would have vehemently denied this, but it was horribly true. Thus, over half a century later I shudder when recalling a classroom discussion where I spouted utter nonsense about immigration – and can only apologise to anyone in the class offended by my comments.

Guthrie, Orwell, a student subscription to *The Times*, and at least a modicum of maturity, shaped my political thinking. I was never a sixth-form *soixante-huitard*, but, from Paris to Pretoria, San Francisco to Saigon, there was a call for political engagement – by the time I left school my low-key activist CV included marching in opposition to the 1969-70 Springboks tour and the war in Vietnam. On the cusp of a new life, far from Coventry, these were formative years – the years when one's moral compass is set for life. Family, friends, fresh ideas, and a myriad of other influences go to moulding a personality at an impressionable age, but I like to think Woody Guthrie – *what he stood for, rather than the man himself* – in some small way helped set that compass.

Early exposure to Bob Dylan and Joan Baez had opened my mind to the notion that folk music was more than hearty chaps in pullovers and wholesome girls in gingham skirts singing songs you last heard in primary school. From that moment Woody Guthrie was a presence, however dimly perceived, within my musical consciousness. At the age of sixteen, courtesy of my vintage Folkways albums, I could at last hear the original compositions, as opposed to the saccharine (Seeger) or respectful (Baez) interpretations. In a pre-bootleg era no gritty Dylan

24

covers were available – on his LPs Bob didn't sing Guthrie, he sang about him.

Bob Dylan famously mythologised Woody Guthrie. Guided by veteran folkies in Minnesota, he discovered the man from Okemah by himself, and for himself. Once famous Dylan became the conduit through which his own generation, and then mine, first heard Guthrie's music. The likes of Pete Seeger had laboured for years to resurrect Guthrie's reputation, and with cruel irony it took a young Jewish boy from Hibbing to succeed where McCarthyite survivors in New York and LA had repeatedly failed. It's worth remembering that until Robert Zimmerman reinvented himself and took Greenwich Village by storm, the desperately ill Guthrie was an ever present in the minds of a surprisingly small circle of east and West Coast progressives. As we've seen, many one-time admirers assumed he was dead, while others dismissed his songs as dated.

Yet in many respects mainstream liberals' insistence that Guthrie's homespun leftist philosophy was scarcely relevant to contemporary America acted as a spur to both older and younger architects of the folk revival: in persona and performance Dylan traced a direct line back to the Dustbowl, but – as Phil Ochs always maintained – among singers of his own age he was by no means alone. Ochs was an unrepentant polemicist, insistent that this gave him an authority and authenticity which Guthrie would acknowledge were he able to do so. Ever more loudly he denied Dylan's debt to Guthrie: despite family protests Dylan had aped his hero's appearance and mannerisms, while failing to adopt the same uncompromising attitude towards poverty and discrimination. When in the summer of 1964 his *bête noir* veered sharply from the political to the personal, on *Another Side Of Bob Dylan*, Phil Ochs felt vindicated. As shown later in the book, where Dylan denied his public standing as a 'protest singer', Ochs posed as the nation's conscience. He considered himself the true heir of Woody Guthrie, delivering clear unambiguous messages on inequality, impoverishment, racism, corruption, colonialism, and militarism.

Dylan revelled in ambiguities. He avoided the sloganizing of radical politics, and dealt only in moral complexities. However much he drew upon Woody Guthrie at the onset of his career, he quickly moved on. Yet he never turned his back on Guthrie, eschewing his politics or denying his music. Ochs believed this to be the case, as did Pete Seeger until Dylan recorded *John Wesley Harding* and signed up for the Carnegie Hall concerts. Only on the surface did Dylan distance himself from politics, deceiving fans and commentators in much the same way as the eighteen months following his motorcycle accident in July 1966 was a period of intense activity and not, as popularly assumed, convalescence and isolation. Decades would pass before he went into the studio to record a Woody Guthrie song ('Pretty Boy Floyd' on *Folkways: A Vision Shared*, the 1988 all-star tribute to Guthrie and Lead Belly); but the spirit of Guthrie prevailed when on a 1971 single he denounced the death in prison of George Jackson, and on a 1975 release alleged the wrongful incarceration of boxer Rubin 'Hurricane' Carter. These were in essence 'protest songs', dismissed by Dylan sceptics but embraced by the faithful, not least veteran Guthrie admirers seeking fresh vindication of the faith once played in young 'Bobbie', tyro scourge of the liberal establishment.

Whether claiming that Carter was 'falsely tried' or that prison guards 'shot George Jackson down,' Dylan was intent on making a statement, unequivocal and with no hidden sub-text. It was that same clarity of intent and expression which in late adolescence attracted me to the songs of Woody Guthrie – do we ever feel as passionately about right and wrong as in late adolescence? For me at that time there was no back story, as all that I knew about Guthrie's life was drawn from liner notes and articles about Bob Dylan. For example, I had no knowledge of the appalling way Woody treated the women closest to him. Thus, everything seemed clear cut, and black and white, not least in the sentiments expressed via his music. I wasn't necessarily hell bent at the age of seventeen on bringing down capitalism, but I could recognise crude and cruel exploitation, not least when Guthrie bemoaned the fate of Okies uprooted and desperate for work in the fruit fields of California. It wasn't difficult to see that Guthrie was in his own ornery way a patriot, desperate for his country to pull itself out of the Depression and proud of grand New Deal projects like the taming of the Columbia River. Listening to Woody Guthrie, and then reading George Orwell's *The Lion and the Unicorn*, I learnt early on a key distinction, too often misunderstood on the left: the difference between nationalism, invariably reactionary, destabilising and illiberal, and patriotism, in the right hands a progressive phenomenon of huge promise.

If this vital lesson was all I learnt from Woody Guthrie then that's more than enough to justify the long hours in my bedroom listening to every song on the two Folkways albums and endeavouring to decipher the lyrics. Today I have an informed, suitably nuanced view of Woody Guthrie, as later essays will confirm, but I can still appreciate the essence of his appeal – he was a man full of faults, but any teenager instinctively sympathetic to change, and the means to secure that change wherever they might be found, can recognise Woody Guthrie as a force for good, a guy you would always find on the right side of the barricades. There is thus a simplicity of appeal, but that simplicity, that naivety, should not be dismissed – all adolescents need heroes and role models, and, for all his faults, Woody Guthrie still offers the same inspiration that he provided for me over half a century ago.

The Isle of Wight, 31st August 1969

Looking back to the late 'sixties it's striking how little even the most dedicated followers of Bob Dylan knew about their absent hero. This applied both sides of the Atlantic, reflecting the gulf between passive consumers of a newly commodified counterculture – the ordinary fans, remote in every way from the metropolitan centres of chic and cool – and what might loosely be termed an alternative establishment. In Britain a parochial music press, overly reliant on PA reports and record label press releases, reinforced a misleading image of Bob Dylan, the reclusive convalescent. Contrast this fog of misinformation and speculation with how much we now know about Bob's 'lost' years, from his motorcycle accident in July 1966 through to the release of *John Wesley Harding* nearly eighteen months later. These days students and devotees enjoy an encyclopaedic knowledge of Dylan's life in Greenwich Village, New York and Byrdcliffe, Woodstock.

In the United States, especially on the eastern seaboard, Dylan's day-to-day activities were common knowledge among New York's hippest cognoscenti – he stepped out of the limelight, but the embrace of family life brought him and his wife Sara a degree of normality. This was no Howard Hughes scenario, and whether upstate or in the city Dylan went about his daily business, often unrecognised given the wispy beard and down-home mode of dress. Once his Woodstock and Manhattan addresses were in the public domain then invasion of the Dylans' domestic privacy was deemed fair game.

In Britain, however, it did feel very much as if Dylan had gone into hiding, with rumours of a broken neck and a career prematurely ended. Again, those in the know soon found out that, even if a recluse and in recovery, a recharged Bob Dylan was busy making music – and busy making music with the Hawks, his backing band from the tempestuous 1966 world tour. By the spring of 1967, when sessions relocated from the Red Room at Byrdcliffe to the Hawks' rented house, 'Big Pink', Dylan was on a creative – and a comic – high, resurrecting a host of near forgotten folk songs and throwing into the mix a succession of dazzlingly surreal or subversively heart-wrenching self-compositions – songs full of crazy characters like Tiny Montgomery, Skinny Moo, and Quinn the Eskimo, all of them brought to life in the 'Billy McCarty' [Richard Gere] section of *I'm Not There*, Todd Haynes's brilliant 2007 film featuring multiple Dylans.

A wider awareness of the newly named 'Basement Tapes' came in June 1968 when Jann Wenner devoted the cover of *Rolling Stone* to demanding that Columbia release the sample acetate of Woodstock recordings sent to select artists and record companies in London and LA. At that point Wenner's Bay Area vanity project was unavailable in large parts of the United States, let alone the United Kingdom. Needless to say, back in 1967 Bob Dylan fans in the West Midlands knew nothing of a fledgling *Rolling Stone*, let alone the assemblage of Americana captured on a Nagra four-track in a West Saugerties basement: the mystery of our man's absence merely encouraged anticipation and expectation of a return to stage and studio in which he offered up a bigger and better version of what went before – a revisited *Highway 61 Revisited*. In reality, of course, nothing could be further from the truth.

An all-pervasive air of mystery worked to Bob Dylan's advantage, both artistically and financially. His absence from the full glare of publicity was not the commercial disaster Columbia/CBS may have anticipated, at a time when labels expected their artists to generate a stream of LPs and singles year on year. The four albums released in the period 1968-70 achieved higher chart placings than their immediate predecessors, and yet critics judged all but *John Wesley Harding* to be inferior. In the spring of 1970 Columbia felt confident enough to advertise *Self-Portrait* with a simple strapline below a nameless cover: 'In four weeks this portrait will be in one million homes.' Greil Marcus

The Isle of Wight, 31ˢᵗ August 1969

has noted the degree to which prolonged absence made the global heart grow fonder: 'It was one thing to be a pop star; it was another to be a legend, and that, a year before he reached thirty, was the situation Bob Dylan was trying to fight his way out of...'

Dylan's manager, Albert Grossman, learned the lesson that less is more when transforming the Hawks, longstanding rock 'n' roll sidemen old beyond their years, into a bunch of enigmatic upcountry music makers still close to Dylan but busy forging their own distinctive identity – The Band really were like no other band, as I was soon to find out. Barney Hoskyns, in his biography of The Band, showed how after the release of *Music from Big Pink* Grossman created a mystique around what in their previous incarnation had been a 'volcanic powerhouse, an amphetamine-driven explosion of electricity.' Backing veteran Canadian rock 'n' roller Ronnie Hawkins and later Bob Dylan, or plying their trade alone in seedy clubs from Toronto to Tupelo, the Hawks had craved publicity – in *Testimony*, guitarist and principal songwriter Robbie Robertson remembered just how much they yearned success. Transformed from tight R and B bar band to enigmatic explorers of rock music's new frontier, The Band were discouraged by their manager from giving interviews or from playing all but a handful of gigs prior to their eponymous second album appearing in September 1969. By accident or by design a late night performance at Woodstock did not feature in the festival film – for Robertson, playing to the Hawks' new-found sons of the soil image, the audience at Yasgur's Farm looked, 'like a ripped army of mud people. We felt like a bunch of preacher boys looking into purgatory.'

From Woodstock through to their epoch-ending all-star finale seven years later, The Band invariably rose to the grand occasion. Yet they were also woefully inconsistent, with a whole host of factors, not least group dynamics and degrees of individual substance abuse, determining the success of every performance. Bassist Rick Danko and pianist

Richard Manuel consumed drugs and alcohol in alarming, and ultimately fatal, quantities. So much, therefore, depended upon the reliability of Robbie Robertson and organist Garth Hudson, and on the leadership of Arkansas drummer Levon Helm. The Band's authoritative performance at the Isle of Wight festival confirmed what was obvious from their debut album: Helm's powerful presence gave the group an added dimension, not least as a foil and inspiration to Robertson. Amid the mayhem of 1966 he'd quit the Hawks, and only when the touring stopped had he made his way to Woodstock, where he would remain for the rest of his life. It's hard to imagine The Band without Levon Helm, his drumming and above all his singing central to their success on stage. When Helm was on form then he was magnificent, by dint of personality and example driving on his Canadian comrades in arms.

Music from Big Pink would in due course complement *John Wesley Harding*, even though Dylan relied on Nashville's finest session men not the Hawks to capture the austere, stripped-down sound which announced his re-emergence into the public arena: he seems to have written the songs, and facilitated their recording, in a parallel creative process, wholly separate from the music-making at Big Pink. The recording sessions for *John Wesley Harding* took place over three days in the late autumn of 1967. The first person to hear Dylan's dream-like, Bible-based, heritage-drawn collection of ciphered stories and guileless love songs was producer Bob Johnston. Robbie Robertson knew nothing about them until Dylan came back to the Catskills with master tapes. When asked if the songs were unduly stark and severe, Robertson rightly advised against any overdubbing – he kept his Stratocaster in its case.

John Wesley Harding enjoyed a low-key release, with no promotional single (Jimi Hendrix more than compensated, with his eviscerating cover of 'All Along the Watchtower'). Knowing nothing of the Woody Guthrie memorial concerts in January 1968, and unaware just how much time Dylan spent recording material which wouldn't see the light of day for nearly half a century, I assumed that he was back home walking the dog and reading the generally positive reviews of his latest record. He surely took pleasure from confounding the critics by releasing an all-acoustic country-flavoured compendium of fantastical frontier tales and counter culture parlour songs.

I was too young to carry any baggage when it came to Bob Dylan. Hence I was as relaxed about Bob rediscovering his roots in folk and country as I had been when he took to playing, in his own oft-quoted words, 'thin wild mercury music.' Frankly, I lacked the necessary critical skills to discriminate and appreciate when it came to the Dylan oeuvre. I had no expectations and no fixed opinions. As a self-proclaimed folk fan I really liked *John Wesley Harding*, even if I couldn't say why. After all, half the lyrics were lost on me, and some of them still are. Similarly, as – courtesy of *Sweetheart of the Rodeo* – a convert to country music, I 'got' *Nashville Skyline*; even after my mum said how much she liked 'Lay Lady Lay'. (She probably took to the song because of its lush romantic arrangement, and because the singer didn't sound at all like Bob Dylan even though he most certainly was Bob Dylan. I've always liked the story that a heavy cold left him with a rich baritone voice for just long enough to record the album).

Dylan was a rare visitor to the British charts, and the success of 'Lay Lady Lay' was a direct consequence of all the publicity surrounding his first proper gig since the motorcycle accident three years before. In the summer of 1969 you didn't have to be a Bob Dylan fan to know he was coming to England: Woodstock's loss was the Isle of Wight's gain.

If I'm honest I don't remember much about the 1969 Isle of Wight festival, other than the headline performances on the last night. I have a blurred recollection of chaotic organisation, sleep deprivation, little to eat, and Richie Havens reprising his Woodstock mega-set from a fortnight earlier – and that's about it. I do on the other hand have a crystal clear recollection of coming home from school two months earlier clasping a copy of *Melody Maker* and announcing my intention to see Bob Dylan and The Band. My mother, to her eternal credit, agreed that I had to go: by teatime plans had been laid for my parents to take me to Portsmouth and to meet me off the Ryde ferry three days later (teenage solipsism meant my never asking where they spent the bank holiday weekend). None of my friends fancied going, so I went to the festival on my own. There was no hesitation or apprehension, or even disappointment at the absence of a companion. In this respect I was a classic example of the only child, gregarious and yet at the same time a solitary soul. Even today, I'm still happy in my own company, the cat that walks alone.

I went to see Dylan and The Band, and all the other acts were a bonus but nothing more. Had say the Byrds or Fairport Convention been billed to play then I would no doubt have paid more attention to who was on. The Who brought the first night to a close, and the set list suggests a towering performance. Yet it's clear that Townshend and co left no lasting impression on me – I was there for Bob. I had no expectations, and in consequence I was less likely to be disappointed. Dylan's appearance had been hyped up so much that his older fans were preparing for something just short of the second coming. More sceptical observers, not least Fleet Street's seasoned show biz correspondents, looked back to previous tours and anticipated an arrogant, amphetamine fuelled rock star riding for a fall. Neither the Dylan devotee nor the cynical hack got what they wanted: a genial Gibson-strumming crooner in a Hank Williams suit bore no resemblance to the snarling iconoclast who'd led his rewired bar band on a coruscating audio assault of our most august halls a mere three years before (albeit, three years in the 1960s constituting a lifetime – the distance between 'She Loves You' and 'A Day In The Life').

The Isle of Wight, 31st August 1969

Sitting alone in a densely crowded field near Woodside Bay on the evening of Sunday, 31st August 1969 I was a blank canvas – do to me what you like, Bob! Ever the optimist, I anticipated a positive experience, my expectations for Dylan's performance heightened by what came before. The Band were a revelation. They boasted three lead singers, a technically brilliant guitarist with a highly distinctive sound, an astonishing array of instruments, a standard of musicianship rarely seen on the British college circuit, and above all, a genuinely timeless collection of songs which carried the crowd to somewhere south of Roanoke. *New York Times* correspondent Nik Cohn rightly judged The Band to be, 'terrific. Their harmonies half-country, half-gospel and the beat good hard rock, they made the endless succession of English bands that had gone before seem like so much Mickey Mouse.'

In an era of post-psychedelic bombast and faux blues, Cohn was spot on. Only at a festival as eclectic and unfocused as the Isle of Wight could The Band be on the same bill as long forgotten, self-indulgent mediocrities like Blodwyn Pig and the Edgar Broughton Band. The same weird juxtaposition of the brilliant and the banal applied to Pentangle. They were a star attraction on the Sunday afternoon, but time and location rendered their performance strangely sterile. The fact that this was the first time I saw Bert Jansch and John Renbourn, and yet all I can remember is being a bit bored, signals an emotional vacuum – where was the sense of awe, the keen awareness that here were masters of their craft, the surge of joy and excitement, and the acknowledgement that music could be simple and visceral and hugely complex at one and the same time, which I unconsciously felt as I listened to The Band?

A counterfactual version of Bob Dylan at the Isle of Wight would see The Band end their set to huge acclaim, and the man himself walk on stage in a charged atmosphere of high anticipation, collective goodwill and good vibes – a quick nod to his sidemen, and whoosh, they're away... Except of course that the reality was very different. The long wait was deflating and dispiriting, and thank God the field was bone dry and the weather fine. Dylan's much delayed arrival was both untheatrical and downbeat – festival folklore has him either crippled by stage fright or upping his price. It required a display of Springsteenesque energy to resurrect audience excitement, and that demonstrably was not Bob's way. It's not surprising, therefore, that I felt a tad underwhelmed by Dylan's performance. Whereas I had travelled to the Isle of Wight happy just to see Bob, by the time The Band signed off I wanted a show: a continuation of what I had just seen and heard but with the added bonus of Bob Dylan centre stage – not that I knew of their existence at the time, but a rave up akin to the sets played at the Guthrie benefit concerts eighteen months before.

I was equally ignorant of the fact that only a month before Dylan and The Band had played in that same rackety country-soul style at the Mississippi River Festival in Edwardsville, Illinois: the set within a set comprised Appalachian murder ballad 'In The Pines', Little Richard's 'Slippin' and Slidin'', and a reprise from the Woody Guthrie concerts of 'I Ain't Got No Home'. In *Testimony* Robertson claims Dylan turned up out of the blue, but this away from the limelight gig offered useful rehearsal time ahead of the trip to England. Not that Dylan intended replicating his mid-west embrace of The Band's 'Muscle Shoals lilt' once the eyes of the world were upon him.

How many in the waiting crowd at Woodside Bay knew of the Edwardsville prelude to the night's proceedings? Scarcely anyone I would suggest. Among the audience were the disciples, the true Dylan believers, many of them veterans from the 1966 tour with the Hawks. They divided between the 'Judas!' endorsing purists, who applauded the reappearance of an acoustic guitar, and the apostles of amplification, who deemed their hero far too laid back when airing his post-protest anthems. Playing alone The Band had somehow transcended the limits of analogue technology, although anyone on the edge of the crowd might not have agreed. It was demonstrable to all – or almost all – just how good they were. Regrettably, when The Band returned with Bob Dylan a collective experience became a myriad of experiences, depending upon where you were in an arena lacking all the advantages of today's Glastonbury-size festival, not least giant screens and crystal clear sound systems.

Dylan's deceptively nuanced and stylish set reflected Robbie Robertson's description of what The Band-to-be and their mentor had been trying to achieve a year earlier in West Saugerties: 'Subtleties came into the music: it had this kind of timeless spirit.' At the Isle of Wight the further you were from the stage the more those subtleties were lost – this was an exhausted audience, eager for an injection of energy and excitement, and what they got was a lo-fi set which would have sounded brilliant in a bar, or indeed a basement. If you were sitting in the VIP area or immediately outside then you could appreciate at once how well the six men worked together. Here was a tried and tested combo comfortable with their sound. Not surprisingly, admirers and collaborators like George Harrison and Eric Clapton enthused over the discipline, musicianship, good humour, and inventiveness (even Nik Cohn qualified his jaundiced festival report by conceding that Dylan's 'deep-toned and lazy and romantic style' was 'impressive'). For less privileged festival-goers, already disgruntled by having to wait so long in ever greater discomfort, a primitive and grossly over-stretched PA had muffled the sound: the unconverted and sceptical half a mile back saw simply a man in a white suit going through the motions.

To appreciate the variety, wit, clarity, vocal power, and pure musicianship, this was a performance that had to be heard in its entirety. Not surprisingly, the four poorly-mixed songs from the festival which appeared on *Self-Portrait* the following year did little to persuade anyone not present – or even many who were – that Dylan's hour-long set had been a success. The track selection seemed random, with 'Like A Rolling

Stone' inevitably suffering by comparison with the studio version; given the nature of the album why not substitute the set's one traditional song, 'Wild Mountain Thyme'? Today *Self Portrait* is seen as a critical stage in Dylan's ambitious blending of contemporary composition and America's disinterred musical heritage (as he told the *New York Times* in 1997, 'You can find all my philosophy in those old songs.'). Back in 1970 the record's critical reception ranged from faint approval to damning dismissal, most famously by Greil Marcus in *Rolling Stone*. The incongruity of a best-selling album attracting mixed reviews paralleled Dylan's experience at the Isle of Wight festival. Context was everything, and only those with full knowledge of all that had taken place since July 1966 could interpret Dylan's laid back, laconic style and his career-spanning choice of material as a statement of how far he had travelled, and in what direction he was heading. Here was a wilfulness of intention three decades ahead of the Never Ending Tour. A recasting of the collective memory, and a de facto redemption, would come only when a later generation revisited the tapes.

The digital remastering of Dylan and The Band's Isle of Wight set, when released on the 2013 box set *Another Self Portrait (1969-1971)*, proved a revelation. Its clarity of sound revealed to all but the initiated the warmth and enthusiasm of Dylan's engagement with the audience and with his fellow musicians. Here was a partnership as powerful as that forged three years earlier and tested to near destruction in venues from the Sydney Stadium to the Royal Albert Hall. The cleaned-up tape from the festival mixing desk confirmed what was already evident from the remastered and expanded version of The Band's *Rock of Ages*: that album's added tracks included Dylan joining his erstwhile partners on stage in New York as they led their festive fans into the first hours of 1972. Here was a natural fit, with a rawness and directness markedly absent from *Before The Flood*, the over-blown, over-hyped record of Dylan and The Band's 1974 coast-to-coast tour.

The Isle of Wight, 31st August 1969

New Year's Eve 1971 took Bob and his band of brothers back to Edwardsville, Illinois, on 22nd July 1969 and to Carnegie Hall on 20th January 1968 – but not to Woodside Bay on 31st August 1969. Their performance that night was in every respect a one-off. No two Bob Dylan performances are the same, but his appearance at the Isle of Wight was both unique and unusual. Unique in that it bore no resemblance to any other appearances with The Band before or after, let alone their previous incarnation as the Hawks; and unusual in that if anyone triumphed that night it wasn't Bob: it took 44 years for us to acknowledge his Isle of Wight set as a quiet achievement, but only a matter of minutes to appreciate that The Band were as disciplined, rooted, and life-affirming on stage as in the studio.

Coda

Parental approval extended beyond the Isle of Wight to both the Bath festivals, the second perversely staged at Shepton Mallet over the Whitsun weekend 1970. The only reason for spending a bank holiday in the Somerset countryside getting thoroughly soaked and surviving on a diet of yogurt, apples, and flat Coca Cola was to see the Byrds. Thanks to the likes of Led Zeppelin playing on and on and on, the one band I really wanted to hear was pushed back from Sunday evening to the early hours of Monday morning, by which time my friends and I were on our way home. Missing the Byrds at Shepton Mallet ('Britain's Woodstock!') confirmed Dylan and The Band at the Isle of Wight as the high point of my teenage festival-going. I did in due course see the Byrds at the 1971 Lincoln Folk Festival on a sunny day and stormy night that started with Tim Hardin and ended with James Taylor, a scheduling which surely should have been reversed. Four festivals across three years was more than enough – for me, that was it.

From then on, eight hours in a football stadium was my limit. Only once did I unroll my sleeping bag in anticipation of a second day listening wearily to a wide range of music, most of which I could have lived without. This was at *La Fête de Lutte Ouvrière* in 1978. France's Trotskyists staged their festival next door to Le Bourget Aeroport, where the Paris Air Show was taking place. Every aerial display that weekend generated a chorus of boos from the party faithful – for music-loving plane-spotters it was a vision of heaven and hell. Headlining the *fête* was the indestructible Little Bob Story, Le Havre's answer to Dr Feelgood. To the accompaniment of F16s and Super Etendards screaming skywards, a diminutive Bob bared his soul and an anorexic Cambodian bassist bared his chest, both mesmerising the audience. They exuded a rock 'n' roll authenticity Johnny Hallyday would have killed for.

Following in the footsteps of Bob and Woody, summer '76

With Bob Dylan and Woody Guthrie as my guides, I spent the summer and early autumn of 1976 in the States and Canada. It was the first time I crossed the Atlantic. I left home with a vague idea to visit places familiar to Guthrie and Dylan, mostly on the West Coast. This wasn't *Bound for Glory*. I never slept outdoors, nor did I leap aboard a freight train – nor, perversely, did I visit Oklahoma. It wasn't *On the Road* either. No-one offered to take me from New York to San Francisco in a rusting 'fifties sedan, with the Bird ever present on the car radio; or put me up in a sleazy, sweaty tenement where the couple in the next room smoked and screwed all night long.

I had just enough money to avoid travelling à la Woody or Jack. A modest budget covered food, accommodation – and records. My travel arrangements involved a Greyhound bus pass, the occasional train trip on Amtrack, and as a last resort, hitching a ride. If truth be told, finding myself in places familiar to Dylan and Guthrie proved largely serendipitous. With travel plans so haphazard, this could scarcely be labelled a musical pilgrimage. Twelve months earlier, of course, Dylan had been planning his own road trip: although, unlike me, the Rolling Thunder Revue had travelled north, into New England, in the fall of 1975. My intention was to travel south by Greyhound as far as the Gulf of Mexico, and then head west all the way to LA.

The original art deco Streamline design could still be seen in the four thousand buses that made up the Greyhound fleet. They offered leg room, padded seats, air conditioning, and luggage space unknown in Britain at the time: however comfortable the coach, travelling hundreds of miles day and night, with only short 'comfort breaks', was bound to be a muscle-numbing experience – and yet, crossing the continent by

Greyhound remained a key element of the American dream, the romance of the road.

Songwriters from Robert Johnson to Andrew Choi have namechecked Greyhound buses. While on sabbatical Bob Dylan got in on the act with 'Get Your Rocks Off', a throwaway blues from Big Pink. Greyhound deserves better of Bob – he was born in Hibbing and so was the company, on the eve of the First World War. Back in 1963 Dylan was a white poster boy for the civil rights movement, but among African Americans he meant little or nothing – he wasn't a Sam Cooke or a Chuck Berry: 'Promised Land' remains one of the great Greyhound anthems, with a segregation sub-text. Like the 'poor boy' en route to California I've caught a bus out of Norfolk, Virginia; but thankfully mine didn't break down and leave me stranded in downtown Bir-ming-ham. It's scarcely surprising Chuck had to get out of Alabama fast – in 1964 civil rights campaigners across the south were still risking their lives day after day.

The building of multi-lane inter-state highways after the war had rendered travel across the United States that much easier, enabling Americans to drive long distances by car. Greyhound and its competitors could provide a faster service, but, like the railroad companies, they saw a dramatic drop in passenger numbers. By the 1960s most people who travelled by bus were young, invariably students, or black and poorly paid. Chuck Berry knew how the passive resistance of the Freedom Riders had quickly spread from segregated bus services in the southern states to the trans-continental coach lines, where local white drivers sent black passengers to fill up the rear seats. The campaign for civil rights had relied on the federal courts to outlaw segregation on the buses, and in the stations of major operators like Greyhound and Trailways.

Invariably, Greyhound terminals or shared stations were located in the poorest part of town. At any time, night and day, queues of African

Americans could be seen waiting to board the bus or to use the available facilities (washrooms, lockers thankfully large enough to hold a rucksack, and bizarrely, coin-fed mini TVs to sit down and watch). Grim, grimy, and long overdue for renovation, the big city terminals were uncomfortable places, which you wanted to get out of as soon as possible. Yet outside awaited an even less congenial setting, with passengers exiting into poor neighbourhoods with high levels of social deprivation and crime. Washington's bus station was only a few blocks from the White House, but the immediate neighbourhood was blighted by poverty and gun crime. Tom Waits captured the atmosphere perfectly in his early ode to the LA Greyhound terminal, 'Depot, Depot'. Nor was this a wholly black phenomenon, as I remember stepping out of the San Francisco bus station late at night and being bundled into a patrol car by a couple of cops who asked, 'Are you crazy? Nobody walks the Haight at this hour!'.

Travelling through the southern states on a Greyhound bus in the summer of 1976 I was often the only white passenger. This was an election year, and my trip took place against the backdrop of the presidential primaries and the start of the campaign. The night the Republican convention chose its candidate our black driver pulled off the highway so we could all hear the final vote over the radio: his passengers feared that if Ronald Reagan usurped Gerald Ford, the unelected incumbent in the White House, federal support for the poorest sections of society would be cut. To their obvious relief Ford narrowly won the nomination. The following November President Ford lost to the Democratic candidate Jimmy Carter, a politician too honest and well-intentioned to survive longer than a single term in office. Carter was governor of Georgia, his credentials as a retired naval officer rendering him ideally suited to facilitate conflict resolution – as quickly became evident after he left the Oval Office, but sadly not while he was still there.

Inevitably Dylan and his sidemen have a place in this story. Governor Carter first met Dylan in January 1974, at his official mansion in Atlanta. It's never been easy to impress Bob Dylan, but Jimmy Carter clearly did. The Band shared Dylan's enthusiasm for a southern Democrat with strong liberal instincts who entered the primaries a long shot for securing his party's presidential nomination. Richard Manuel's silky smooth rendering of Hoagy Carmichael's 'Georgia On My Mind' was a staple of The Band on stage, and in 1976 the song was released as a single. A pre-poll performance on *Saturday Night Live* gave The Band welcome publicity at a point when their popularity was clearly on the wane: for every stand-out track on recent albums there were three fillers, while drugs, drink, and an absence of crowd-pleasing new material rendered concert performances lifeless and predictable. In California at Thanksgiving, just three weeks after Carter's election victory, The Band rose to the occasion one last time, their grand all-star finale filmed by Martin Scorsese.

In *The Last Waltz* the Winterland Ballroom displays a grandeur far from the reality of its everyday appearance. The Band chose to bow out in San Francisco, but Toronto or New York would have been more fitting. Given its close association with Bob Dylan, and with The Band, one possible venue was Carnegie Hall, in mid-Manhattan: as early as November 1961 Albert Grossman staged a breakout gig in the upstairs concert room, perceived by many at the time as premature; in October 1965, courtesy of the Hawks, a very different show took place in the main auditorium; and in January 1968 The Band-to-be backed their mentor at the Woody Guthrie benefit concerts.

In the early summer of 1976 I paid a visit to Carnegie Hall. From my cheap and decidedly seedy hotel in the Flatiron District (not a flophouse worthy of Woody, but the kind of place a youthful and newly named Bob Dylan might have checked in to fresh off the bus), I walked up 7th Avenue to two blocks south of Central Park. There stood Carnegie Hall, solid and grim. Inside and outside, the stern brick-built building looked much as it had at the time of its construction, in the early 1890s: the sixty-floor skyscraper that now towers over the original venue was yet to be built, and a planned renovation of the baroque foyer and the eighty-year old auditorium remained on the drawing board. This was a venue designed to house a symphony orchestra, and with space to spare. Gazing down the long aisles towards the vast stage I could see why a riotous Rolling Stones gig had ended the concert hall's brief flirtation with pop music; and yet at the time I was there Alice Cooper would have been greeted with open arms if he promised to fill the place. The building had only just escaped demolition at the start of the 'sixties, and by the mid-1970s property developers saw the money-making potential of a prime location in the heart of Manhattan. Not that demolition was a real possibility: Carnegie Hall has a symbolic importance for New York Democrats and progressives, which we'll return to in the essay on Guthrie's farewell to FDR, 'Dear Mrs Roosevelt'.

In 1976, oblivious to the fact that CBS had released *A Tribute to Woody Guthrie Part One* in the UK, I was yet to hear music from the benefit concerts staged at Carnegie eight years before. I was now familiar with the venue, but not the music – it would be 1982 before I first heard Dylan's set, including the near unknown 'Dear Mrs Roosevelt'. I wasted hours in dingy record stores in Greenwich Village and Soho, picking up the odd Dylan picture sleeve single while failing to find a copy of the Guthrie tribute album. I tipped my hat to Gerde's Folk City in the West Village, although its current location was a block away from where Dylan played his first proper gig in April 1961, five months before Robert Shelton dropped in to hear him and promptly dashed off a rave review for the *New York Times* – the rest is history.

Knowing nothing of New York's proto punk scene I missed out on CBGB, while Max's Kansas City – which I did know about courtesy of the Velvet Underground – had already closed. I did, however, frequent the newly opened Lone Star Café, on 5th Avenue. 'The finest honky tonk east of Abilene' boasted a giant iguana on the roof, a banner over the door insisting 'Too much ain't enough', and – in both the menu and the music – a direct line to Austin, Texas. In the 1980s, until its closure at the end of the decade, Dylan became a familiar face in the Lone Star Café. The remnants of The Band regularly played there after Robbie Robertson refused to countenance carrying on: *The Last Waltz* really was the last waltz, and the group's creative force set his eyes on Hollywood.

From Manhattan I rarely ventured into the Bronx or Queens, and only occasionally took the ferry to Staten Island. My trips across the bridge into Brooklyn were more frequent, but I never thought to visit the south side of the borough. Joe Klein's authoritative biography of Woody Guthrie was still four years off (and Norah Guthrie's tour guide to New York a further thirty-two!). Thus I knew nothing of the Guthrie family home from November 1943 to September 1950: 3520 Mermaid Avenue, Coney Island; an address which in 1998 became the title of a Wilco and Billy Bragg collaborative project, the first of a series of albums which have seen established artists forge new songs from lyrics for which Guthrie's music was lost or never existed. Not that I would have found 3520 Mermaid Avenue had I tried. The three-storey block of apartments just a short walk from the beach was demolished in 1972. It was replaced by a much larger apartment building, similar to the one which Woody and his third wife Marjorie moved their family into after leaving Mermaid Avenue: appalled that black tenants were subject to blatant discrimination, an ailing Guthrie took on his new landlord, the openly racist Fred Trump (a Woody-White House connection discovered by Joe Kaufman, expat and Guthrie expert).

I never took the train to Coney Island, but I did buy a one-way ticket to Washington DC. Penn Station was the poor relation of Grand Central, a brutal restoration project in the 1960s having destroyed the last vestiges of Gilded Age glamour. The terminal's sorry state summed up New York at one of the worst moments in the city's history. Today the Acela Express, Amtrack's flagship service, rides the length of the eastern seaboard, but back in 1976 the rolling stock, if not the locomotive, was of an earlier age. I could picture Woody Guthrie and Cisco Houston setting off to join their ship in Norfolk Roads, or Lead Belly reluctantly taking the train south, back to that 'bourgeois town.'

Although African-American, Lead Belly enjoyed wider recognition than Woody Guthrie in the 'thirties and 'forties: Huddie Ledbetter was the rock-hard former convict with a twelve-string guitar who wrote 'Goodnight Irene', and popularised the ever-evolving prison songs 'Rock Island Line' and 'Midnight Special'. Ironically, Lead Belly was dead and Woody Guthrie in hospital when the Weavers popularised their music. Between them, Pete Seeger and Lonnie Donegan made Guthrie and Lead Belly songs the mainstay of skiffle group repertoires on both sides of the Atlantic. In 'Bourgeois Blues' Lead Belly castigated prewar Washington's segregation and discrimination. Woody Guthrie would have heard the song first-hand, about the time 'Bourgeois Blues' became a Communist theme tune and the FBI started taking an interest in the man who wrote it. Bob Dylan probably first heard the song on a Pete Seeger protest LP from the mid-1950s. Guthrie associated the capital with meeting folklorist Alan Lomax, and a mammoth recording session for the Library of Congress. For Huddie Ledbetter it was just another southern town, where white folks could throw a black man and his wife out of a hotel room he'd already paid for.

Lead Belly's description of life inside the Beltway was spot on: Pennsylvania Avenue was only a few blocks from a sprawling black neighbourhood beset by problems of acute poverty and violence-fuelling social deprivation. This de facto ghetto was a legacy of the days when servants and manual workers in the federal capital had been overwhelmingly black. Wandering around the city well over a century after the end of the Civil War it felt as if not that much had changed. Although the Folkways label wasn't taken over by the Smithsonian until 1987, this surely was the time to explore the museum's music collection. The same was true for the Library of Congress. The truth of the matter was that I didn't have time, and on my first visit to Washington there was too much to see. After a week staying with friends I got on the Greyhound and headed south.

The bus crossed North and South Carolina on a wearying, muscle-aching day-night journey. This trek across the southern states took me as far as Atlanta. I left the coach terminal in a suitably dishevelled state, only to find an oaf in a bright red pick-up was waiting to run me over. Even without the assassination attempt, I hated Atlanta. After a peremptory down town tour, I got back on the bus for a second epic expedition: a more leisurely journey through Georgia, Alabama, southern Mississippi, and eastern Louisiana to New Orleans – the southernmost city on Highway 61.

In New Orleans all the music I heard was out on the street. There was no listening to Doctor John or Professor Longhair live on stage in the French Quarter. Instead, I would wander around Tremé, taking in cajun, zydeco, blues, trad jazz, and a whole host of street sounds which defied description. The quality of New Orleans buskers must be unmatched anywhere in the world, except possibly for Clarksdale, the home of the blues back up the Delta. Day after day I walked and walked, covering huge distances around the city. Not that I was following in the footsteps of Woody Guthrie. He had little if any contact with New Orleans, although it's easy enough to picture him hanging out in harbour bars, or in cafes around the cathedral, all in the giant shadow of the levee. It doesn't take much imagination to see how New Orleans might easily have been Woody's kinda town. It's certainly Bob Dylan's kinda town. He wrote a talking blues about the city early in his career, took mark two of the Rolling Thunder Revue there, included it on his 1981 'Born

Again' tour, and went back in early 1989 to record *Oh Mercy* with Daniel Lanois and the Neville Brothers. If you want to know why Bob Dylan won the Nobel Prize for Literature then read his paean of praise to the Big Easy in *Chronicles*. He loves the place: 'There are a lot of places I like, but I like New Orleans better.'

In due course I was back on the bus. Having cut across the bayou from New Orleans, through Baton Rouge, to Lake Charles and the border with Texas, I found myself on the Gulf of Mexico, and thus a good six hundred miles south of Woody Guthrie's home state. Not that it made sense to go there, as at that time I didn't know where in Oklahoma he was born – it is in fact Okemah, and you won't find a town that small on a Greyhound road map. Apart from the eponymous state capital the only towns I could name in Oklahoma were Tulsa and, courtesy of Merle Haggard, Muskogee. By not taking the more northerly route westwards I also missed out on the Texas panhandle, a vast area of high plains and canyons stretched between Oklahoma and New Mexico. This is cattle country, and at its heart is Lubbock, birthplace of the Crickets. A detour to visit Buddy Holly's home was tempting, but the distance there and back was too much. My intended destination was far to the south: Austin, the state capital, and by the mid-seventies already one of the hippest places in America.

Unfortunately I arrived in Austin just as a week-long festival of 'outlaw' music came to an end – all the big names had played, including Guy Clark, Jerry Jeff Walker, Townes Van Zandt, Waylon Jennings, and of course Willie Nelson. Largely thanks to Nelson, the state capital would in due course hand its country festival over to Luckenbach, an even hipper focal point for alt-country. Austin was now free to stage every spring America's most ambitious celebration of new music, the South by South West Festival. The ten-day SXSW Festival, thirty years old and complemented by an equally ambitious film festival, takes place in and around the Austin Convention Center. Among the break-through acts there are always a few old stagers, including in 2007 Son Volt, with leader Jay Farrar singing songs from his Guthrie-inspired album *Okemah and the Melody of Riot* – it's somehow reassuring to know that among the assorted indie, hip hop, and electronica acts the voice of Woody still rang out. The same was true five years later when Guthrie's centenary was marked by Bruce Springsteen singing 'This Land Is Your Land' to end his speech on why 'Woody's gaze was set on today's hard times...he's a ghost in the machine – a big, big ghost in the machine.'

Both the convention centre and the festival(s) reflect the transformation and growth of Austin across the past forty years. Today's sky-scraper strewn conurbation is scarcely recognisable from what was once a quietly dignified focal point for both respectable conservatism and home-grown radicalism; the two world views amicably bumping along side by side in a manner scarcely conceivable today. Austin as a city fulfils a dual function: as home to the state's judiciary, legislature, and executive, and as a major centre of scholarship. In the mid-seventies it felt as if the whole community was built around the Texas State Capitol and its surrounding buildings. Built of red granite in a grandiose late-Renaissance style, this sprawling centre of government dominated a then tower-free landscape. Beside it stood an unequivocal statement of modernist campus architecture, the University of Texas at Austin.

It may seem strange that an epicentre of 'British Studies' lies in the heart of Texas, but Austin's university boasts a vast collection of private papers, unmatched on any native campus outside of Oxford, Cambridge, and London: the Harry Ransom Center is a cornucopia of Anglophone archival delights which every modern British historian finds hard to leave. Whether on campus, in a down town bar, or exploring a myriad of museums and galleries, Austin was a place you couldn't help but like – a feeling shared by Bob Dylan.

In September 1965 Dylan and the Hawks arrived in the state capital full of foreboding. This was only their fourth gig together, and they anticipated the now familiar hostile reception. To their amazement they found an open-minded audience which oozed good will. Stadium shows elsewhere in Texas saw Austin miss out on Dylan's 1974 tour with The Band, but two years later the Rolling Thunder Revue took over the Municipal Auditorium: a setting scarcely in the spirit of the original enterprise saw a grandiose performance, unrecognisable as the good-time, all-star medicine show of the previous fall. In late 1978 Dylan returned, filling the University's vast new sports centre…and, as decade follows decade, he keeps going back.

Over the past half-century Bob Dylan has played most cities in southern Texas, including San Antonio. I took the bus there from Austin, spending an hour or two in a near empty Alamo. I wondered if Dylan had toured the site four months earlier, when the Rolling Thunder Revue passed through the city. Poor ticket sales necessitated switching that night's show to a smaller venue. Every gig in Texas faced the same problem: in Austin two shows became one; while in Houston Willie Nelson was brought on board, and yet still the seats stayed empty.

It's a long drive down Highway 10 from San Antonio to El Paso. The Greyhound sped west through a drab semi-desert landscape interrupted only by characterless one-street towns – Kerville, Junction (it was), Sonora, Ozona, Sheffield (the Pecos river valley a far cry from that of the Don), Fort Stockton, Van Horn, Fabens. Some of these places I only saw in the dark, but no matter as every bus station and diner seemed the same. These were Cormac McCarthy's 'Cities of the Plain', each with a story to tell. Every bar boasted a John Grady Cole or a Billy Parham, but I was speeding through the border country so fast I never had time to tip my hat and share a beer.

Like Austin, El Paso then was very different from El Paso now. No doubt there was crime on every corner, but the cross-border tension and the narco-driven violence was less visible. Illegal migration was an issue, but not in such a way as to define individuals' or whole communities' ethnic *and* political identities – no-one, not least the Border Patrol, was looking to build a full length wall. I felt relaxed walking around the city, in a way I feel certain would not be the case today.

These days El Paso and Ciudad Juarez have multiple musical associations, ranging from Ry Cooder's much-covered 'Across the Borderline' (a Dylan favourite) to just about anything by the city's adopted son, Tom Russell (from the eerily prescient 'Who's Gonna Build Your Wall' to the regretful 'Leaving El Paso'). In October 2017 the all-star Lampedusa tour rolled in to town, raising funds for child refugee charities: Joan Baez sang 'Deportee', which resonated powerfully with the local audience.

El Paso is of course synonymous with Marty Robbins' maudlin gunfighter ballad, a top ten hit in 1959. Bizarrely, Dylan and the Heartbreakers covered the song at a New Mexico gig thirty years later – it's never been sung since. It was an El Paso radio station which in 1968 banned Bob Dylan on the grounds that his lyrics were incomprehensible; yet perversely, DJs could still play Dylan songs if performed by other artists. Dylan clearly doesn't harbour a grudge as he regularly visits El Paso on the Never Ending Tour. For all that, the Lone Star state has never been a natural home for Bob Dylan – you sense that he's happier the far side of the Rio Grande, and never more so than in the 1970s, from *Pat Garrett and Billy the Kid*, through 'Romance in Durango', to 'Señor (Tales of Yankee Power)'. As Dylan described to Cameron Crowe in 1985, "'Señor' was one of them border type things...Nuevo Laredo, Rio Bravo, Brownsville, Juarez' – fertile territory for *corrido* balladeers like Bob and Tom Russell.

From El Paso the Greyhound continued west on Highway 10 into Arizona. We passed the turning for Tombstone and rolled on to Tucson, from where we switched north, heading for the state capital. The intensity of the raw heat that hit me the moment I stepped off the bus in Phoenix ensured a short stay. Within a few hours I was travelling across central Arizona to Flagstaff, gateway to the Grand Canyon.

Wisely, neither Bob Dylan nor Woody Guthrie have tried to capture in song the size and scale of the Grand Canyon. In April 1963 Dylan prefaced his first major concert in New York with the monologue, 'Last Thoughts on Woody Guthrie'. The poem placed God in the Grand Canyon at sundown, with the man from Okemah lined up alongside him. Guthrie preferred monuments made by man – more likely he and his maker could be found astride the Grand Coulee Dam, a towering concrete wall greater than 'the seven wonders that the trav'lers always tell.' Yet, criss-crossing Arizona on his travels, Guthrie surely stood on the edge of the Grand Canyon. Picture him in a vast national park as yet unspoilt by mass tourism, dumping the Marxist dialectic and spinning a suitably homespun philosophy re love, beauty, and nature. Then, stupefied by a landscape no words can adequately describe, he would have declined a descent to the canyon floor, picked up his bag, and caught the first bus west – I did the same.

Crossing the state border into California saw a gentle and painless version of the welcome which had awaited Guthrie and his fellow Okies. Instead of bullying 'vigilante men' the bus was boarded by inspectors from the food regulatory body, based up in Sacramento. Curt but courteous, they removed anything eatable and then sprayed passengers with a suitable scented disinfectant. Unlike Woody Guthrie and the Joad family we were the sweetest smelling travellers who ever entered the Golden State.

Los Angeles was home to Woody Guthrie in the late 1930s, and Bob Dylan's choice of residence forty years later. When he wasn't having fun down on the border, or hanging out somewhere between Bakersfield and Sacramento, Guthrie lived close to Griffith Park in Glendale – it could scarcely be called a family home given how little time Woody spent there. The same could said of the newly divorced Bob Dylan's beachside house and recording studio, hidden among the gated communities of Malibu. My seaside preference was somewhat less salubrious: Venice Beach. Paul Beatty's description in *The Sell Out* of his hero's bus journeys to the Westside has echoes of my trips to the beach in the summer of 1976. Thankfully, I wasn't stopping in the fictional district of Dickens, but south-west of Downtown in University Park. It was here that a bicentenary conference and concert were held in 2012, with academics joining the likes of Tom Morello and Jackson Browne to argue that LA not New York was crucial in the moulding of Woody Guthrie's world view – this after all was where he first found fame as a broadcaster, with 'The Woody and Lefty Lou Show', became active politically with the Communist Party, and wrote several of his best known songs when out on the road with Will Geer.

The USC campus – home to the all-conquering Trojans football team – reflected the considerable wealth of an LA private university; but despite its central location I rarely felt secure and relaxed. Feeling unsafe at night, especially when in east LA waiting for a bus, was one reason why I stayed less than a fortnight. Watching *La La Land* four decades later brought home to me just how little of Los Angeles I saw on my first visit. Like Woody Guthrie in 1937, I assumed that the best way to discover the 'real' City of Angels was by foot. In truth LA was too spread out to explore, other than by car; and in any case walking was clearly seen as an alien practice. This was most apparent in Beverley Hills, where I was stared at by passing drivers, and questioned by the neighbourhood police.

Without a vehicle I rarely ventured far in the evening, let alone go to a club and see a band. If not on my own I would surely have taken in The Troubadour. This was no musical pilgrimage, but at least I lingered a while outside the Capitol Records Tower on Hollywood and Vine – the sound of the Beach Boys not Sinatra going around in my head. The next day I said goodbye to USC, heading south via Long Beach. Like Guthrie in early 1938 I spent a few days in San Diego; but unlike Woody I stayed at the state university, and I stayed sober. Guthrie was en route to Tijuana, and a riotous, short-lived career as a variety show host on renegade station XELO. In contrast, I headed back to LA, and then on to Santa Barbara. Tom Waits' depot on Sixth Avenue had become like a second home, and from there I caught the Greyhound express up Interstate 5 to San Francisco.

In the Bay Area I took a room at San Francisco State, but initially stayed with distant relatives from Galway. Living in the western suburb of Parkside, a lengthy tram ride from the heart of the city, Julia and Martin were extraordinarily kind, generous, and hospitable. They took me to mass on Sunday morning and the Irish club on Saturday night. Woody Guthrie would have loved the Irish club, but for an Englishman in 1976, surrounded by unreconstructed republicans, an invitation to discuss the political situation 'back home' was always going to be an uncomfortable experience.

Downtown, a different kind of identity politics was alive and vibrant. Martin never introduced me to Armistead Maupin and Harvey Milk, but then almost certainly he had no idea who they were. From his Castro Street base Milk was energetically campaigning for gay rights and plotting his eventual election as city supervisor. A few blocks away Maupin was crafting for the *San Francisco Chronicle* the serial stories which two years later formed the first of five volumes, *Tales of the City*. Of course I had no idea who Maupin and Milk were, but I did recognise that most people treated gay couples in a matter-of-fact fashion inconceivable at that time back home. Where San Francisco led, Brighton followed.

Having sampled both trams and cable cars I walked everywhere, from the Presidio east to North Beach, and from Mission Bay west to the Castro. Very quickly I formed a mental street map of what seemed a surprisingly compact conurbation. By this time Haight-Ashbury was starting to look seedy and run-down, its 'head' shops and cafes busy offering out-of-towners an ersatz summer of love. At night it was very different, with bars boasting the likes of Chris Hillman and Ben Sidran (the Byrd/Burrito unexpectedly disappointing, and the keyboard maestro surprisingly uplifting). While dutifully taking in the art galleries, museums, and would-be honky tonks, I checked out the record and book stores. San Francisco boasts the only bookshop in America, and possibly the world, where multiple copies of Dylan's impenetrable 'novel', *Tarantula,* are readily available for purchase. City Lights sits on the corner of Columbus Avenue and Broadway in North Beach. It's been there since avant-garde poet Lawrence Ferlinghetti and friends gave the burgeoning Beat movement a base in 1953. Today City Lights and its publishing arm is a very twenty-first century operation. In the 1970s, however, the store constituted a quiet, calming environment where you could mooch round the shelves, pick out a book and start reading it without looks of disapproval from the staff, and pour yourself free cups of coffee from a percolator brewing since breakfast. I can't recall ambient music, but if there was then it was surely a soothing Indian raga.

Countless books and learned articles have explored the influence on Bob Dylan of Beat writers, notably Allen Ginsberg and Jack Kerouac. Only Tom Waits owes more to that small but vocal band of taboo-breakers who in both literature and lifestyle spurned the conventions and social mores of postwar American society. Needless to say, in their attitude and behaviour towards women and ethnic minorities, not least African Americans, the Beats were never as revolutionary and enlightened as they thought themselves to be. Waits, no stranger to City Lights, built his early career around a barfly image rooted in jazz, improvisation, displacement, and the rootlessness of America's poorest and most excluded. His second album is an homage to Jack Kerouac: *The Heart of Saturday Night*'s title song channels the experimental novel *Visions of Cody*, written around 1950 but not published until 1972.

'Cody' was Neal Cassady, Kerouac's hell-raising companion, ever ready to betray his long-suffering and forgiving friend for the promise of a beer or a blow job. Like Waits, the young Bob Dylan saw Dean Moriarty, Cassady's alter ego in *On The Road*, as one more heroic subversive in a long line leading back to Huck Finn: however outrageous their behaviour we uncomprehending slaves to bourgeois convention stand ready to forgive. For Dylan, 'this made perfect sense to me.' Talking to Cameron Crowe in 1985 he acknowledged the depth of his debt to the Beats, capturing the excitement and exhilaration of reading *On The Road* and Ginsberg's *Howl* in a Minneapolis garret while listening to Charlie Christian and John Coltrane, Brownie McGhee and Thelonius Monk. This formative experience is revisited in *Chronicles*, itself a text heavily indebted to Kerouac and his fellow adventurers in experimental prose.

In fiction and in reality San Francisco was the closest Neal Cassady had to a home, whether by choice or as a result of incarceration. City Lights was a rare place of calm in a crowded and chaotic life, although I doubt if his visits entailed any literary engagement. By the time I was whiling away an hour or two in the store Cassady had been dead eight years. In that time the legend had grown, strengthening his status as underground America's go-to muse (there's a long list of Cassady-inspired music, but, given that Tom Wait's tribute sounds laboured, only the songs of Bob Weir and King Crimson really stand out). Nick Nolte's disturbingly convincing portrayal in the well-received bio-pic *Heart Beat* was still four years away. Tom Wolfe in *The Electric Kool-Aid*

Acid Test, his front-line report on the acid-drenched adventures of Ken Kesey's Merry Pranksters, dutifully records Cassady's dual role as manic bus driver and role-model renegade. Standing in the North Beach temple of Beatdom I speculated on whether Ginsberg had ever engineered a meeting between Bob Dylan and Neal Cassady (less than a year before, the Rolling Thunder Revue had paused to visit Kerouac's grave in Massachusetts; Sam Shepard's *Rolling Thunder Logbook* portrays Ginsberg orchestrating the literary pilgrimage to Lowell – a painful scene captured in the tour-based feature film *Renaldo and Clara*). I suspected any such meeting would not have gone well. Like Holden Caulfield, Dylan is quick to spot a 'phoney' when he sees one: would he have labelled Neal Cassady, the man not the myth, an extraordinarily shallow and self-centred individual?

Don't Look Back, the documentary Don Pennebaker filmed during Dylan's 1965 tour of the UK, shows Ginsberg two years after he first heard 'A Hard Rain's A-Gonna Fall' and, in his own words, knew straightaway that 'the torch had been passed.' Ginsberg cuts a forlorn figure when either talking about Dylan or deferring to him and his obsequious pill-popping retinue; he was far happier hosting the *wunderkind* in San Francisco at the end of the year – his VW camper van briefly served as an alternative tour bus. Pennebaker's film displays all too vividly Joan Baez's shabby treatment in London, so it's no wonder she gave Anthony Scaduto, Dylan's first biographer, a scathing assessment of how swiftly Ginsberg fell from hipster icon to fawning acolyte. It's equally unsurprising that Dylan, stoned out of his mind in Big Pink eighteen months later, chose to bash out a raucous and suitably disrespectful 'See You Later Allen Ginsberg'.

Nevertheless, for thirty-five years Bob Dylan and Allen Ginsberg maintained a close personal relationship rooted in mutual respect and admiration, and deep affection. Ginsberg confirmed this in his sleeve-notes for *Desire* and assorted fragments of verse, and Dylan on the dust jacket of Ginsberg's collected poems – the work of 'the single greatest influence on the American poetical voice since Walt Whitman.' Ginsberg was always there for Dylan, and it's no exaggeration to say he loved the man. He often spoke nonsense about his midwestern Prometheus, most vividly while on tour with the Rolling Thunder Revue ('For Dylan to reveal his heart completely [singing 'Sara'] is for me a great historical event...'), but every plaudit was from the heart.

Allen Ginsberg always looked first to Walt Whitman, then to William Blake; and then perhaps to Robert Zimmerman. Was John Steinbeck an influence given that Ginsberg named a 1972 anthology of his early poems *The Gates of Wrath*? Maybe Steinbeck provided a necessary bridge, but Woody Guthrie does seem an unlikely hero. (Or – unlikely as it may seem – did Ginsberg find a connection via Ramblin' Jack Elliott, another Depression-era Jewish boy from the furthest edge of New York City?) Guthrie and Kerouac had more than a wander lust in common, so maybe Ginsberg considered the man from Okemah an honorary Beat. Ginsberg attended one of the two memorial concerts on 20th January 1968, but, given the line-up, he was bound to be there. It was at the actor Robert Ryan's post-performance party in the Dakota Building that Ginsberg saw Bob Dylan for the first time in two years – for both men the spark was re-ignited.

Like Ginsberg, Whitman is Bob Dylan's muse and touchstone, and *Leaves of Grass* his ur-text. Here is a man marinated in the poetry and prose of mid-nineteenth century America, not least the Civil War years – newly arrived from Minnesota, Dylan the autodidact spent hours in New York Public Library digesting ante-bellum newspapers, and for light relief he would dip into Clausewitz or Thucydides. Dylan revealed in *Chronicles* how much he immersed himself in contemporary accounts of the Civil War before writing ''Cross The Green Mountain', commissioned for the 2002 film *Gods and Generals*. It's the perfect scene-enhancing song, and deeply moving. Walt Whitman, volunteer nurse in the Army of the Potomac and transcendentalist voice of the Union cause, was a very different person from Bob Dylan. Whitman was an intensely private and sensitive man, for whom the war proved a searing experience. He was a witness to history, and for us Dylan stands beside him, transcending time. It's Whitman's voice we hear in "Cross The Green Mountain', the lyrics echoing the [divided] state-of-the-nation poems in *Drum-Taps*, published in 1865 and a stark chronicle of suffering, sacrifice, honour, and righteousness.

Scanning the poetry shelves at City Lights it dawned on me that Dylan could have teamed up with a very different poet from Allen Ginsberg. Somewhere in Haight-Ashbury lived Thom Gunn, a man who, although gay, English, and a Cambridge graduate, shared Dylan's love of French Symbolists, the Beats, second generation Romantics, Triumph motor cycles, and rock 'n' roll. Gunn wrote of the sexual energy Elvis exuded, even via the juke box; and his Brando-inspired biker paean 'On The Move' unintentionally foresees jazz and rock's relentless demand for regeneration; the concluding lines could easily apply to Miles Davis, Bowie, and most obviously Bob Dylan: 'At worst, one is in motion; and at best,/Reaching no absolute in which to rest,/One is always nearer by not keeping still.' Gunn must surely have known Christopher Ricks. The poet and the literary critic had much in common, from a mutual admiration of F.R. Leavis to a shared connection with Stanford University. I can imagine them in regular correspondence re the most arcane and obtuse aspects of Dylan's lyrics. Similarly, I like to think that Gunn, listening to *Blood On The Tracks* for the first time, heard echoes of his own work in songs such as 'Tangled Up In Blue' and 'Simple Twist of Fate'. In a counterfactual world where Bob Dylan looked first for a versifying role model to Thom Gunn, not Allen Ginsberg, he would soon have been reading Ted Hughes, leading to endless speculation about songs such as 'Girl From The North Country', and the inevitable compilation of a Dylan bestiary.

One hot day in August I took the BART under the Bay to Berkeley. I had been encouraged to steer clear of Oakland and to enjoy the good vibes of Berkeley: the former, original home of the Black Panthers, was blighted by social deprivation and racial tension, while the latter had seen yesterday's student protestors become today's liberal establishment. On the University of California's Berkeley campus the victories won over Vietnam and Watergate were seen to justify a more relaxed atmosphere, with the focus now largely on lifestyle and cultural discourse. No holds barred discussion of gender politics, postmodernism, structuralism, and the latest theory to have arrived from the Sorbonne might on occasion be unedifying, but it was a lot less violent than the mass protests of the Johnson and Nixon years – or indeed, the stand-offs between 'Antifa' antifascists and the Alt Right triggered by President Trump's election. These days, ironically, there is less violence in the plazas and shopping malls of downtown Oakland than on the streets and parks surrounding University Avenue.

If Berkeley today constitutes a chilling reminder of how deeply divided America once was, and is again, back in the mid-1970s it was a blissed out hippy redoubt. Counterculture veterans took pride in the enthusiastic reception given to Dylan and the Hawks when they played two nights at the Berkeley Community Theater in December 1965. The concerts were covered by the founding father of *Rolling Stone*, Ralph Gleason – the same age as my dad but still the Bay Area's hippest pop and jazz critic. Gleason reported the front row presence of Beat aristocracy, accompanied by a select guard of Hell's Angels: Ginsberg, Ferlinghetti, and Ken Kesey all signalled their enthusiastic approval of Bob's new direction. Cool members of the academic community were also present, presumably without a biker bodyguard.

Both students and staff frequented an off-campus club called the Keystone. In the 'seventies the Keystone was a popular music venue, at which Jerry Garcia provided the de-facto house band. He drew on past, present, and fringe members of the Grateful Dead to make up the numbers, and his repertoire drew heavily on Bob Dylan. Garcia playing guitar at the Keystone had an obvious appeal, but I feared a lengthy improvisation based around 'Knockin' On Heaven's Door' might prove a test of patience. The reality would have been far from the case, with Jerry Garcia a masterful interpreter of the Dylan oeuvre. Admiration was two-way as Bob Dylan made clear when his friend, collaborator, and 'big brother' died in the summer of 1995: 'There's no way to measure his greatness or magnitude as a person or as a player…He really has no equal.'

In the spirit of Guthrie, or even Jerry Garcia, I planned a break-out expedition, not north over the bridge to Marin and into the wine country, but beyond the Bay Area to Santa Cruz – and then on down Highway 101. I caught the bus to Palo Alto and San José. For mile after mile we passed second-hand car dealers, motels, low-tech industrial estates, fast food outlets, and suburban shopping malls. Silicon Valley was still decades away, and the never-ending, featureless edge-of-town landscape reflected an analogue world that today has gone for ever. The same is true for Santa Cruz, but forty years ago it was a remarkably unspoilt seaside town, built around a Spanish-style high street that led down to the beach. I stayed in the cheap hotel at the top end of the street and ate in the cantina at the bottom. In the woods behind the town, and looking down on the Pacific, was the stunningly beautiful campus of the University of California. UCSC was only ten years old, and famous for its interdisciplinary curriculum, and a progressive approach to teaching and assessment – its approach to assessment was so progressive in its early, radical days that there wasn't any.

It was hard to leave Santa Cruz, but after a few days I moved down the coast to Monterey. This was the heartland of colonial California, and Monterey had served as its capital until Spain finally relinquished control in 1821. On arrival I headed straight for what was once called Ocean

View Boulevard, but which twenty years before had been renamed Cannery Row in honour of John Steinbeck's novel. Published in 1945, *Cannery Row* is set in the most industrialised part of town, where until the mid-1950s competing canneries ensured a small but steady income for packers and fishermen. In a series of vignettes Steinbeck portrayed a dynamic and vibrant community, peopled by interesting and idiosyncratic personalities; but once the sardine fishing grounds became exhausted, and the canneries closed, the area became derelict and run-down. More recently Cannery Row has undergone gentrification, with the spectacular Monterey Bay Aquarium a motor for regeneration and an influx of tourists.

All that was in the future when I walked along a rain-soaked and strangely empty Cannery Row. For the adolescent Robert Zimmerman, reading *Cannery Row* in high school prompted a high school obsession with Steinbeck. In due course this obsession was reinforced when Dylan connected Woody Guthrie with *The Grapes of Wrath*. One of the many verses that make up 'Sad Eyed Lady of the Lowlands' starts, 'With your sheet-metal memory of Cannery Row' – not even the combined talents of Michael Gray and Christopher Ricks could work that one out. Given all the formative books that are listed in Bob Dylan's 2016 Nobel laureate lecture the absence of John Steinbeck comes as a surprise. The two men could conceivably have met as Steinbeck didn't die until 1968, six years after he too had won the Nobel Prize for Literature. A lasting affection for *Cannery Row* – or the presence of Joan Baez at Carmel – may explain why in 1963 and 1964 Dylan travelled all the way to Monterey for the annual folk festival, but once there played sets of just two or three songs. Appropriately, one song he did play was 'Song To Woody'.

Woody Guthrie spent time in Monterey, but it was in Los Angeles that he met Steinbeck. Will Geer, a tireless campaigner, brought the two men together in the spring of 1939. For the next eighteen months Geer and Guthrie performed together at benefits for the John Steinbeck Committee To Aid Farm Workers. In public Steinbeck lauded Guthrie as someone who 'sings the songs of a people and I suspect that he is, in a way, that people,' but in private he refused to see the ballad of 'Tom Joad' as anything other than a straight steal from *The Grapes of Wrath*.

I caught the tourist bus out of Monterey, through Pacific Grove, and along 17-Mile Drive to Carmel. Not long before I had been walking down Desolation Row, but now I found myself riding through millionaires' row. Inland were long drives leading to hidden mansions, magnificently maintained golf links, and private parkland suggestive of gentle walks and a stiff gin and tonic at the end of a hard day's birdwatching. Cormorants and shags seemed to cover every outlying rock, competing for space with sea otters on alert for the next high tide and a fresh invasion of sand bass and mackerel. After an hour or so we arrived in Carmel, at that time the home of Joan Baez, Mike Nesmith, and the Monterey Symphony Orchestra – and, of course, jazz aficionado Clint Eastwood. With the rain pouring down, the palm trees bending in the wind, and the cafes shuttered, I walked out of Carmel to take my chance hitching on Highway One. There then followed a series of adventures in and around Big Sur worthy of Woody Guthrie's tallest tales. Suffice it to say, that two days later I hitched a succession of lifts to San Luis Obispo bus station, from where I took the Greyhound bus back up the coast to San Francisco.

It was time to head north, to follow the northern stretch of Route 101, and to spend some time in Canada. The bus rolled over the Golden Gate Bridge, through the wine country of northern California, and on to Eureka and the Redwood National Park. We crossed into Oregon with the Pacific on our left and the sequoias to our right. Overshadowed by more famous settings below San Francisco, the Oregon coastline remains stunning, and surprisingly unspoilt. Back in 1976 it was striking how few tourists there were, and in later years numbers never matched those heading for Big Sur. Leaving the coastal route at Lincoln City, the Greyhound cut inland to Portland, where sensibly I broke my journey. At this point the true Guthrie devotee would have caught the bus to Spokane and then followed the course of the river back to the sea – 'Roll on Columbia'! It was in Washington state that at the start of 1941 Woody came to work for the Bonneville Power Administration, writing twenty-six songs in just four weeks. Instead I headed north through Olympia and Tacoma, and along the southern stretch of the Puget Sound to Seattle.

Seattle in the mid-seventies was very different from the fashionable city of culture we know today. Big-name sports teams were few in number, and visitors came mainly to enjoy the state-wide view from the Space Needle, erected in the heart of the city for the 1962 World Fair. With grunge not even on the horizon and experimental jazz awaiting Bill Frisell's arrival, Seattle was a long way from the musical powerhouse it became in the 1990s. Locals did, however, acknowledge their so far solitary contribution to the sound of electric guitars played in a suitably loud and spectacular fashion: staring out of the late dusk gloom as the Greyhound rolled into town was the giant face of Jimi Hendrix, painted on the side of a warehouse. The man who redefined 'All Along the Watchtower' (although another son of Seattle, Eddie Vedder, offers a creditable alternative on the soundtrack of *I'm Not There*) is the city's most obvious link with Bob Dylan. It's not always proved a happy relationship. In March 1966 Dylan and the Hawks were given a fiery reception when they arrived in Seattle from Portland – both shows in the north-west were bruising experiences. Eight years later Dylan and his sidemen returned in triumph, filling the Coliseum, a fourteen thousand seat sports arena. Since that time Seattle has seen Bob Dylan play in a succession of venues, sometimes brilliantly, sometimes sadly not.

From Seattle I took the ferry up the Puget Sound to Vancouver Island, where I spent a few hours in Victoria before crossing over to Richmond for a brief stay with a friend's ex-pat brother. Two days later I caught the bus into Vancouver. Lodged between the Rockies and the Pacific, here was a metropolis unlike any European city I had ever visited. Vancouver was clean, strikingly modern, and populated by people who seemed universally healthy, good-looking, and at one with the world. This was the far side of the country from The Band's home town, Toronto. Furthermore, Canada was never natural territory for Woody Guthrie, other than a stopping-off point for crossing the Atlantic. Although born close to the border, Bob Dylan has no close connection with and affection for Canada. So here, in BC, this story ends – except for an experience which Dylan could work wonders with.

After a week criss-crossing the Rockies, taking in Jasper, Banff, and Mount Revelstoke National Park, I was back in Calgary. I stupidly chose to travel overnight, meaning that I missed a fresh sight of the mountains. Around midnight we stopped for half an hour at what surely was one of the most isolated bars in North America. Truckers, lumberjacks, mountain men, bikers, bus drivers, passengers, barmen, and waitresses were all crammed in to a tiny hut, complete with pool table and juke box. The noise was deafening, but the atmosphere was incredible. It was like a fantasy All-American bar, and ironically it was in Canada. Two kids hit the beer hard in the time available to them, and they smuggled several bottles on to the coach. Booze and speed left these guys high as a kite and deaf to the driver's repeated warnings of what would happen if they didn't shut up and let the other passengers sleep: around 1 am the bus pulled up, the door opened, and two protesting young men were left on the side of a mountain road in the Canadian Rockies somewhere south of Lake Louise – you don't mess with a hard-hearted, twenty-year service Greyhound driver from Spokane who means what he says.

Wholly unsympathetic to the two teenagers' plight was my newly acquired travelling companion: 'He told those guys they would be off the bus if they pissed around, so what do you expect?' This was a friendship forged in desultory conversation leaving Calgary and loud shouting over a couple of Coors in the All-American bar. An ethereal dress worthy of Stevie Nicks disguised the tough persona of a woman around my age who for some impenetrable reason had relocated from Toronto to the Rockies. She had been nervous and edgy when talking to me in the queue, but once on the bus relaxed to the point where by dusk I knew her life story. At first I was sceptical when she claimed to have got the wrong side of a gang of drug-dealers in Calgary while working in the shop they used to launder money. But across the course of our conversation I became convinced that she really was on the run. At that point she asked me if I fancied spending a few days at her friends' house, located in woodland east of Kamloops. This was where she planned to hide until she felt it safe to look for work in Vancouver. I had time to kill until catching my flight home so, without reflecting on the oddness of the situation, I said yes.

The next time we stopped my new friend told me to retrieve my rucksack and, with the driver distracted, bring it on the bus; her massive tapestry bag was already squashed in the luggage rack. Just outside Kamloops she sashayed down the aisle, and whispered in the driver's ear. To my astonishment, half a mile later the bus stopped, enabling us both to get off. Whatever she had said to the hard-hearted, twenty-year service Greyhound driver from Spokane it worked – his only reward was a sweet smile, a blown kiss, and a desultory wave. We walked down a long track, the early morning sun streaming through the dense pines, until we reached a large ranch-style house. The occupiers were friendly but surprisingly indifferent to our presence. For the next two days we were largely left on our own, even at meal-times. It really did feel as if we were holed up in a rural hideaway, more Bonnie and Clyde than

Pretty Boy Floyd. So this was what it felt like to be on the run. When we weren't walking in the woods, chopping wood, frying hash browns, and doing whatever fugitives do, we listened to music. Time and again I played *Blood On The Tracks*, ever more convinced that we were living out a missing verse from 'Tangled Up In Blue'.

Needless to say the drug dealers never turned up, although I'm sure they did exist. We kept an eye out for strangers but the house was in a clearing surrounded by tall trees, with no indication of its existence out on the main road. This was no romantic tryst, so we played board games, drank a few beers, and confirmed the breadth of the culture gap between Calgary and Canterbury. My runaway friend smoked the odd joint, and looked at me with pity when I declined on the grounds that I was a lifetime non-smoker with an aversion to the smell of marijuana.

When, on my third morning in the woods, I walked back down the track to hitch into Kamloops there was no exchange of addresses and no promises to keep in touch. This had been a chance meeting, which livened up my stay in Canada even if I suspect it was soon forgotten by my erstwhile companion. In no time I was in town and boarding the Greyhound bound for Vancouver; a speedy switch to the airport bus, and by midnight I was somewhere over the Arctic en route to Heathrow.

When I came home, did I know anything more about Bob Dylan and Woody Guthrie? The honest answer is, probably not. But never mind Bob and Woody – did I know anything more about myself? Only that, for all the pleasure I gained from the company of others, I was still the cat that walked alone. Remarkably, not once did I experience a keen sense of loneliness. There were occasions, usually while listening to live music, when I wished close friends were present to share the experience; but that was different from a conscious yearning for company. Note the reference to friends not relatives. I wasn't especially close to individual cousins in the way that I am now, and I had no siblings. Thus friendship meant more to me than familial ties. If I'm honest, that's still the case.

Out there on the West Coast in the summer of 1976 I felt comfortable in my own company, while at the same time enjoying the conviviality of time spent with my hosts, and with the astonishing number of Anglophiles keen to make my acquaintance. There's no obvious smugness regarding my – in reality, scarcely challenged – capacity to cope adequately on my own. If anything, I feel a sense of embarrassment, verging on shame. I was so self-contained that only once or twice did I think to tell my parents where I was and what my plans were. Clearing the family home a few years ago I found a pile of letters and cards sent to my mum and dad across the course of the 1970s. There was no estrangement, and, conscious of being an only child, I telephoned them regularly. Dutifully, I never missed being back home for Christmas or Easter, and I returned regularly at other times in the year. Yet, astonishingly, I sent only one postcard from America in 1976 – and I don't recall sending many more on later visits.

Drawing on my own experience as a father, albeit in an era when phone and digital communication meant frequent contact, I can only assume my parents were worried sick by the lack of news: days turned into weeks, and weeks turned into months, with just a single update and a picture of Alcatraz to assure them that all was well. Then out of the blue a telephone call, and their son's matter-of-fact announcement that he was safely home, albeit feeling a bit jet-lagged. How could I be so insensitive? Was I more concerned about being tailed by heavy dudes from Calgary than my mother's mental state? Clearly not, but an indictment of my behaviour at the time is that a conscious awareness of my mum's emotional well-being was simply not there. Thus, while my adventures abroad demonstrated self-reliance and a certain mental toughness, my apparent indifference to the happiness or distress of those closest to me illustrated both the solipsistic perspective of an only child and an embarrassing lack of maturity given my age. This, of course, was the one thing I had in common with Woody Guthrie: being absent for a whole summer, and thoughtlessly failing to keep the family informed as to where you were and what you were up to.

There are in fact two things not one that I've in common with Woody Guthrie: suffering the death of a child. Guthrie had two children die before him, but in the case of his son Bill, killed in a car accident, he was too ill to be conscious of the tragedy. The same clearly did not apply when his daughter Cathy died of severe burns in 1947, aged four. Tragically, being caught in a deadly blaze was a constant in Guthrie's life, as of course was Huntington's – after his death two daughters died of the disease. He dealt with Cathy's death the same way he handled any other test of his credentials as a husband and father, by escaping responsibility. Guthrie's default response to any domestic crisis was to go back on the road. Yet I can't condemn him for wanting to get away when his daughter died. We all must deal with our loss in whatever way suits us best, and hopefully that's not by inflicting further distress upon the ones who share our despair.

How can any parent who has not experienced such grief understand how it feels – and the fact that the years pass but you never come to terms with the hole in your heart, the brutal fact that the child you loved so deeply, and would have done anything for, has broken the rules and gone before you? Nick Cave, another great songwriter who lost a child, writes of how he and his partner were, 'flung to the outer reaches of our lives. We were outlanders floating in deep space…surviving in exile on the perimeter of our lives, way beyond anything that mattered.' Cave identifies 'community and work' as redemptive forces, 'the lifelines thrown out to us as we floated in narcissism and self-absorption.' Are the words I write evidence of 'narcissism and self-absorption'? Should I be focused on Bob and Woody, and travels forty-odd years ago, with no acknowledgement of this single sad shared experience? Being 'outlanders floating in deep space', and not having worked your passage home, isn't evidence of emotional self-indulgence – it's the harsh reality. Cave is right to identify writing as cathartic 'and the key to get back to my life,' but work can only take you part of the way there.

Perhaps, to cut to the chase, the determining factor is how your child died. For Guthrie and Cave it was a catastrophic accident – one minute your child is here, and then he or she is gone. That's it – now deal with it. The raw truth is that our son Adam took two years to die. That was two years for him to deal with a terminal illness, two years for his partner to live with someone she desperately hoped could hang on far longer than his prognosis dictated, and two years for his mother and father to control their emotions given their only child's obvious need of parental comfort and support. No doubt Nick Cave and his wife could have provided just such support had it been required – fat chance Woody Guthrie could, notwithstanding the remarkable resilience and stoicism of Marjorie Guthrie.

Our son displayed a humbling courage and fortitude, from the moment his condition was diagnosed to the moment he died. Often I lie awake before dawn, my heart broken by the thought that night after night, in those final hours of darkness, Adam must have lain in bed fearful for the future, and rightly bitter as to how fucked up his life had become. His mother wrongly insists that I 'don't do empathy,' but by God I'm doing so at three o'clock in the morning. You look at photographs – those crude and brutal then/now shots – and you ask yourself how someone so fit, handsome, and muscular could be reduced to a shadow of his former self, a shaven-headed prisoner of a malign cellular gulag. There are obvious echoes here of Guthrie's cruel fate across the 'fifties. Of course what happened to Woody Guthrie was truly dreadful, but my son was only thirty-two for Christ's sake. Adam would have been the first to stand beside Guthrie on the barricades, but there

71

the similarity ends – for my boy there was always a fixed point on his moral compass.

If Nick Cave and Susie Bick feel they are on the path to a psychological accommodation of the awful tragedy inflicted on them then surely that is a good thing. Did Woody Guthrie arrive at a similar means of coping with the loss of his daughter? Who knows? Trying to delve beneath Guthrie's hard emotional carapace seventy years on is a task beyond even the shrewdest of biographers. Thankfully, this is one experience Dylan has never needed to embrace in his music (Cave, it should be noted, has done so – triumphantly – on successive albums, *Skeleten Tree* and *Ghosteen*). I'm not sure that Mary and I will ever feel any degree of calm resignation. I see the way in which we now live our lives, separately and together, as a ceaseless succession of coping strategies – some work, some don't. Stated so starkly, it sounds like a future which is unrelentingly bleak, forever flatlining. But reality is very different. We're not talking a simple, simplistic, monochrome, but endless shades of grey – to mix metaphors, the highs and lows of getting on with one's life, but with that same hole in the heart never to be filled.

As I made my way around the USA and Canada in the long hot summer of 1976 did I have any idea that I would be writing about Bob Dylan and Woody Guthrie so many years later? Of course not. Had, for some bizarre reason, the question arisen as to my mental toughness in dealing with the death of a son four decades into the future, did I have the imagination and empathetic power to anticipate the awfulness of such tragedy? Clearly not. Would anybody? I had a naivety, rooted in a lingering immaturity and the absence of genuine suffering and hardship in my life to date; this negated the knowledge of what it meant to be truly tested. There was also, I might suggest, a residual innocence – and what I would give, if only for a moment or two, to recapture that innocence: to be standing outside Monterey on Highway One, leaving

Following in the footsteps of Bob and Woody, summer '76

Bobbie and Joanie back in Carmel, and with Woody's ghost beside me on the roadside hopeful of Big Sur by sundown. Oh, what a time it was...

Slouching Towards Big Pink

Nashville – the ghost of Woody Guthrie

While he was still alive how many Woody Guthrie songs were recorded in Nashville? The country and western establishment invariably dismissed the man from Okemah as an unmelodious rabble rouser. He'd been dead six months when Music Row session players grudgingly gave the Byrds a bluegrass version of 'Pretty Boy Floyd': Chris Hillman's vocals and John Hartford's banjo playing confirmed what every self-respecting folkie already knew, that Woody Guthrie's songs were a gift to country music. The Byrds endured a torrid time on the Grand Ole Opry, but *Sweetheart of the Rodeo* gave the green light to the likes of Johnny Cash, Dolly Parton, Willie Nelson, and Waylon Jennings – almost overnight their repertoire embraced all of Guthrie's best known compositions.

In countless journeys from one coast to the other Guthrie always steered clear of Nashville, which was probably wise given the politics of pre-war Tennessee. Yet, when staying in the city some thirty years ago, it was Woody Guthrie who dominated my thoughts.

Nashville then was very different from Nashville today, but on and around Broadway not much has changed. One memorable Saturday night my friend and I moved from bar to bar listening to pick-up bands and anonymous singer-songwriters – the men and women who, in an increasingly desperate search for success, night after night take their guitars to a hundred different honky-tonks. Often extraordinarily talented, they attract boundless goodwill but not a hint of a recording contract. We fought for space on the sidewalk with out-of-town country fans fresh from the Grand Ole Opry and hungry session men desperate for a gig. Uniformly dressed in boots, neatly pressed Levis, and tailored plaid shirts, conservative-minded gentlemen of a certain age greeted their immaculately groomed and manicured companions as they arrived on the main drag in suitably expensive SUVs. Younger dudes in metallic painted pick-ups cruised up and down, their buddies bawling out unintelligible insults every time they came back down the block.

Even late on a Saturday the specialist record stores were still open, their outside speakers ensuring a cacophonous soundscape out on the street. The choice of albums was staggering, with customers painstakingly working their way through every section. By the early 'eighties cassettes were commonplace and compact discs the way of the future, but in Nashville vinyl was still king. Each store contained thousands of LPs, but the range of artists on show was deeply conservative. These days Emmylou Harris may be the 'Queen of Nashville', but at that time her albums were always somewhere on the back shelves. Texan songwriters such as Townes Van Zandt or Jerry Jeff Walker were nowhere to be seen, while rehabilitated 'outlaw' artists like Willie Nelson and Waylon Jennings languished in the shadows, still not fully forgiven in the eyes of the Nashville establishment. The executives and producers of major labels like RCA were obsessed with music as 'product' long before cultural commentators began bemoaning the commodification of popular music. If ever there was a conclusive case for quantity suffocating quality, then it was mainstream, commercial country in the 1980s.

Overwhelmed by sales promotions for Dolly Parton and Crystal Gayle, and haunted by racks of posthumous Jim Reeves albums that seemed to stretch for ever, we fled the record stores in search of yet another bar band and yet another beer. We soon found Beth and Doug, a Tulsa couple en route home to Oklahoma from two years working in the Bronx. In true Okie tradition they had thought about California, but – like Woody Guthrie in 1940 – calculated that they could make more money by heading for New York. Doug, a gangling and painfully thin man in his late thirties, with a ginger quiff delicately arranged to camouflage his receding hairline, explained how his savings from seven-day-a-week construction work would finance a last ditch bid for stardom. While her husband enthused over the new band he planned putting together in Tulsa, Beth smiled nervously and then added her support – he was a great guitarist, and he deserved a break. She scarcely sounded convincing, and I had the distinct impression that this wasn't the first time these ambitions had been aired in conversation with a stranger; albeit not an Englishman who furiously nodded his head in agreement every time Doug restated his firm belief that Guy Clark was one hell of a songwriter, and we should all raise our glasses to toast the great man. Meanwhile, the house band interrupted their set so the roadie could tour the bar stetson in hand. I had plenty of coins but no dollar bills, so I threw all my loose change into the hat. Three requests later, the steel guitarist dedicated his next solo to the poor son-of-a-bitch who could only afford seventy-five cents.

Not long after we left the bar. Doug, by now well-fuelled, whispered to Beth. Embarrassed, she asked us if we would hear Doug sing? Of course we would. Just down the street was a big blue Chevy, and Doug pulled out of the cab a beautifully crafted Gibson J-45 acoustic, paid for by long hours of overtime back at the building site. Traffic noise made tuning impossible but Doug insisted on singing Guy Clark's 'L.A. Freeway'. It's arguably Clark's finest composition, and in this instance the lyrics were especially poignant: for Los Angeles read New York. Beth was visibly nervous, more and more convinced that her partner's flamboyant gesture would end in tears. She was right as by now a crowd was gathering: young blacks, cops, drunks, and bemused tourists. Doug's impromptu performance was a car crash in the making, with his new found friends the unintentional instigators. Pathetically, I tried to maintain an atmosphere of good humour, posing as the naïve Englishman abroad. Meanwhile Doug persisted with his interminable tuning. Cursing, he conceded defeat and plunged into the first verse.

This was no Guthrie-style triumph over adversity, the crudity of delivery somehow compensated for by Okie chutzpah. Nor was it a consciously low-key performance of the kind favoured by Tulsa's favourite son (I once saw JJ Cale's band open in near darkness with two lengthy instrumentals, and only then did a shadowy figure step forward to murmur, 'After midnight, we gonna let it all hang down...'). Doug fumbled the chords, started to strum, and then stopped. This was a song he played almost every day of his life. At the second attempt he survived the opening verse, singing in a voice both shaky and husky. With the chorus, disaster struck. On the third line his memory went blank. Panic crossed his face, and he looked pathetically to Beth for help. She smiled and nodded encouragingly, lifting him to tackle anew the same stubborn refrain: 'If I can just get off of this LA freeway/Without getting killed or caught...' This time as he reached the third line Doug looked to me, in his eyes a clear plea for help. If Nashville was nirvana then a glorious joint rendering of Clark's much covered classic would in an instant have wiped away the preceding embarrassment. Perhaps some of the bystanders would have joined in the chorus next time around. But this was Nashville, Robert Altman style. I couldn't remember the words either. For the record, they are, 'I'd be down that road in a cloud of smoke/For some land that I ain't bought bought bought' – back at the motel I would remember these lines, but by then it was too late.

Humbled and suddenly sober, Doug returned the J-45 to its case. He renewed his invitation for us to visit Oklahoma, and with Beth desperate to comfort him in any way she could, headed back to the Chevy. The drunks were derisive, the black kids contemptuous, the tourists still bemused, and the cops all ready to run Doug in on a criminal charge of fraud and deception. Where was Woody when you needed him? OK, it would have been bullshit, but the man from Okemah would have known instinctively what to say to make sure Doug kept his dignity.

It was all too obvious that Doug was never going to be a country and western star; not even a cult hero known only to the keenest students of arcane Americana. He was driving home, not to fuse his best buddies into a slick country rock band which every A and R man south of the Mason-Dixon Line would kill to sign, but to endure a few weeks of delusion and a lifetime of disillusion. If he did not foresee his fate that night then he soon would. Beth already knew, but then she had known all along. To her immense credit, she didn't scold or patronise.

We went to find a cab. Neither of us said much – what was there to say? Behind the rhinestone glamour and the spurious romance, Nashville was a hard city where the stars acted out their real-life soap opera and the aspiring stars survived on a finite diet of hope and style. *Nashville*, surely Altman's finest film, offered a two-hour encapsulation of fragile fame, mental frailty, corporate calculation, controlled hysteria, and thwarted ambition: poor hapless Doug was the antithesis of the corrupting, amoral, and unscrupulous Tom Frank, the self-absorbed singer-songwriter played by Altman stalwart Keith Carradine. With a passing nod to his brother's performance in *Nashville*, David Carradine portrayed a less than angelic Woody Guthrie in Hal Ashby's 1976 bio-pic *Bound For Glory*. Great music and Haskell Wexler's camera work ensured favourable reviews, but empty seats contradicted United Artists' claim that, 'His life has touched all of our lives. This is his story.'

Clearly most Americans, not least the good people of Nashville, felt sure Woody Guthrie had not in any way touched their lives, assuming of course that they had heard of him in the first place. Unlike Doug, who learnt the hard way, Woody Guthrie had no desire to conquer Nashville – he left that ambition to his cousin, Jack, who played the Grand Ole Opry in 1946, a year before TB ended his career and then his life. Woodrow Wilson Guthrie knew that any artist arriving in Nashville, even for a one-off street show en route to Tulsa, has to sacrifice more than a little dignity. As Doug's Chevy C/K pick-up powered down Highway 40 the next morning I prayed that he still held his head high – it was after all a Sunday. Although in Nashville no sabbath can count as a day of rest, let alone a day for quiet contemplation on what might have been or what might still be.

Bob Dylan and Ricky Nelson, an unlikely combination

Twice over the past ten years I have ventured into Stereo Jack's, at 1686 Massachusetts Avenue, Cambridge, and inquired as to the availability of Rick Nelson's *In Concert at the Troubadour, 1969* (American Decca, USA, 1970). On both occasions the eponymous store holder's hysterical laughter could be heard as far away as Harvard Yard. Anthologised tracks confirm the album's reputation, but its scarcity is confirmation of how few copies were pressed at the time of release. At the end of the 'sixties Nelson haunted the counter culture, deeply unfashionable and yet desperate to play the coolest clubs on the Strip. Back at the start of the decade he'd been one of America's biggest stars, the child prodigy who grew up to become an accomplished TV and film actor and a phenomenally successful pop singer – when Elvis disappeared into the Army it had been Ricky Nelson who filled the vacuum. Between 1957 and 1962 he had thirty Top 40 hits in the States, several of which were in due course covered by Canada's Ronnie Hawkins and the Hawks, the backing band he bequeathed to Dylan. None of Ricky Nelson's rockabilly songs would in due course feature on The Band's R and B album, *Moondog Matinee*, but they still knew all the chords.

Nelson's success was largely a consequence of his good looks, and regular appearances on his family's high ratings comedy show. Yet from a young age he proved himself a serious musician, with a keen eye for talented songwriters, studio staff, and session players: his band boasted a teenage James Burton on lead guitar. Until his costly divorce Nelson was a wealthy man. This meant that long after the hits had dried up he could still recruit LA's finest sidemen. From the outset Nelson's records were quality products, scoring highly in terms of production and musicianship. For this, if no other reason, one fan stayed faithful long after Ricky became Rick, the TV appearances ended, the record sales dried up, and the concert halls shrank in size: Bob Dylan.

Unlike ex-Monkee Mike Nesmith, Rick Nelson singularly failed to distance himself from his pop star past. This was partly because he was an inferior songwriter, but primarily because he had enjoyed a higher profile – and therefore had far further to fall when the 'British invasion' abruptly ended six years of Top Ten hits and TV stardom. Unlike his great hero Carl Perkins, Nelson was never a role model, and he didn't have a back catalogue of self-composed rock 'n' roll classics which could see him through the barren years – no British beat group ever paid tribute to Ricky Nelson. In any case modest chart success, by comparison with say Buddy Holly or the Everly Brothers, left Nelson something of an unknown quantity in Britain: few fans this side of the Atlantic appreciated how huge he was in the States, or singled him out from all the other pouting one-hit wonders who came and went.

Nelson's strength was as an interpreter of successive generations of songwriters, from Hank Williams through to Bob Dylan, and beyond. He had impeccable taste, and by the mid-sixties was seeking out little known songwriters, such as Leonard Cohen, Tim Hardin, and Randy Newman. That search for genuinely fresh material was encouraged by James Burton. By now based in Nashville, Burton urged Nelson to focus on country music as a means of reviving his career. The Everly Brothers took the same advice, but their Kentucky roots gave them an authenticity which Nelson, the star of a long-running comedy set in a Los Angeles suburb, demonstrably lacked. He shortened his first name to gain credibility and cultivated a distinctive brand of country rock. Although promoting a genuinely fresh sound, Nelson lacked the hip persona of a Gene Clark or a Grams Parsons. A succession of albums failed to fire the enthusiasm of critics, let alone the record-buying public. On the review pages of *Rolling Stone* or *Village Voice*, Rick(y) Nelson was distinctly passé.

In the autumn of 1969 Nelson regrouped, going back on the road with a fresh bunch of musicians. Over four nights at the Troubadour the newly named Stone Canyon Band established their credentials as a tight, well-organised, crowd-pleasing blend of fresh-faced rockers and Bakersfield veterans, including Buck Owens' long time steel guitarist, Tom Brumley. Their LA show was everything which Chris Hillman wanted for the Flying Burrito Brothers live, and which Gram Parsons subverted almost every time he went on stage. Nelson's sets drew heavily on Bob Dylan, from the early years in Greenwich Village through to the Basement Tapes. The aforementioned live album, *In Concert at the Troubadour, 1969*, was well-received but then disappeared without trace. Dylan was on the other side of the country when Nelson enjoyed his momentary triumph in Los Angeles; although some of The Band could conceivably have been in the audience, nodding their heads in recognition every time Nelson and his sidemen drew on the Big Pink sessions.

Despite this minor triumph Nelson's career continued to flatline – the Stone Canyon Band was living on borrowed time. With cruel irony the only Top Ten hit for Rick Nelson, reinvented country rock artist, was the 1972 single 'Garden Party'. This self-penned composition was a wry observation on being booed off-stage at Madison Square Garden for playing 'Honky Tonk Women' at the annual Richard Nader Oldies Concert. The lyrics of 'Garden Party' report that in the wings that night were John Lennon and, 'much to my surprise, Mr. Hughes in Dylan's shoes wearing his disguise.' Dylan's presence wasn't that surprising given the retro show's impressive line-up, with Chuck Berry and Bo Diddley headlining. From his teenage years back in Minnesota Dylan was a great admirer, and this would continue long after Rick Nelson died in a plane crash on New Year's Eve 1985. It's no exaggeration to suggest Nelson built a fresh persona around the songs of Bob Dylan. He once described Dylan as 'My idol as far as a writer...really the spokesman for that period where the country was going through a lot of changes, politically...he was the poet of that era.'

That healthy respect was duly reciprocated. In 2004 Dylan wrote at length in *Chronicles* about how, even after arriving in New York, he identified with a similarly-aged but far more famous Ricky Nelson, and that, despite the obvious demise of clean-cut, good-looking pop stars, he still found him an inspiration. Nelson was clearly a cut above the Fabians and Frankie Avalons of this world – with Burton on lead guitar, he boasted a band which really rocked.

In an earlier interview Dylan applauded the way Nelson had played his songs so that they sounded, 'like they were his own, like he had written them' – a process of reinterpretation and reshaping of course all too familiar to Dylan himself. Following Rick Nelson's fatal plane crash Dylan's 1986 tour with Tom Petty and the Heartbreakers saw every concert include a tribute, and a respectful performance of the 1958 hit 'Lonesome Town' ('Ricky Nelson did a lot of my songs; I'd like to do one of his.') In an interview with Sam Shepard for *Esquire*, recast as a one-act play, Dylan named Nelson alongside Guthrie, Elvis, and Hank Williams in his reflections on mortality: following the motorcycle accident, 'I too heard the steady thrust of death that had been constantly looking over its shoulder at me.' Dylan had a choice, and he chose to live: 'I realized how much I'd missed.' That option clearly wasn't available when Rick Nelson took off in his antique DC3 one last time. Needless, to say in later years Nelson would crop up periodically on *Bob Dylan's Theme Time Radio Hour*, with suitable warm words to introduce the likes of 'Hello, Mary Lou'.

Bob Dylan and Rick Nelson maintained at a distance a strangely symbiotic relationship. I have no idea if, notwithstanding Dylan's shadowy presence at Madison Square Garden, the two men ever met. My sense is that if they did then, once the initial courtesies were over, it would soon have been obvious how little they had in common. At different times in their respective careers Robert Zimmerman wanted to be Ricky Nelson and Rick Nelson wanted to be Bob Dylan. They couldn't have been more different, a WASP idealisation of every mother's son and a Jewish kid from Hibbing en route to God knows where. It wasn't long before Bob Dylan wanted to be Bob Dylan (or to be more precise, Bob Dylans); but as young America's one-time heart-throb, Rick Nelson carried the heavier baggage.

There was a touch of Dorian Gray about Rick Nelson: sensationalist reporting saw his personal life shredded, and his professional career ended in disappointment and disillusion, yet twenty years after his career peaked he retained his good looks and he still sounded great on stage. Flying his band around the country in a Douglas Dakota looked cool, but in reality it was a means of saving money: an investigation into the DC3's final flight found a history of poor maintenance. When Bob Dylan was confronted with a huge alimony bill he called up The Band and embarked on a highly lucrative tour of the nation's stadia. Broke and broken, Rick Nelson took any gig he could get. In his final days he performed again as Ricky, resurrecting the old hits and delivering to loyal fans what they had always longed for. Dylan applauded Nelson's interpretation of his songs, but, had he slipped unrecognised into a sports hall show somewhere outside Shreveport or Sioux Falls, then you can be sure it's 'Believe What You Say' or 'Be-bop Baby' – and not 'She Belongs To Me' – he would have hoped to hear.

DYLAN, GUTHRIE, AND ROOSEVELT

THE STORY OF A SONG

An introduction …

Here's a story built around a single event in the life and career of Bob Dylan, and his backing musicians in what soon became The Band; at a time when neither they nor anyone else had any notion of what would happen next. On 20th January 1968 Dylan and the Hawks-that-were/The Band-to-be, played a three song, thirteen minutes set at the matinee and the evening shows staged in tribute to the recently deceased Woody Guthrie. Scarcely anyone who heard them in New York's Carnegie Hall perform one of those songs at the Guthrie benefit concerts – 'Dear Mrs. Roosevelt' – knew of its existence. This was – and is – a uniquely anonymous composition, rarely performed at the time of its inception, and resurrected by Bob Dylan for one day only. So this story is all about that song – a song wreathed in mystery for over half a century. Such intensive treatment of one obscure piece of music may seem way over the top, but the history surrounding 'Dear Mrs Roosevelt' tells us much about American progressive and radical politics in the middle decades of the past century. It tells us much about Woody Guthrie, and the likes of Pete Seeger and folklorist Alan Lomax, but it also tells us much about President Franklin Delano Roosevelt and his First Lady, Eleanor Roosevelt. Above all, it tells us a great deal about Bob Dylan, at a critical moment in his crowded life.

Over half a century later no Dylan set has included 'Dear Mrs. Roosevelt': hundreds of shows, embracing hundreds of songs, and yet Guthrie's lament for President Roosevelt has never been sung again. For decades most Americans knew only a sanitised version of 'This Land Is Your Land'. Today the one Guthrie song lodged firmly in the national psyche is invariably sung in its entirety. 'Dear Mrs Roosevelt' is more politically sensitive, which no doubt helps explain its anonymity. Although Guthrie's complete lyrics had appeared in print – and today are available on his archives' website – in 1968 the song was resurrected only in its censored form: Dylan dropped those verses he deemed politically embarrassing. Knowing only Dylan and his sidemen's censored version, it was the shorter song which a handful of minor artists later made their own. This is Bob Dylan's least known performance, and Woody Guthrie's most obscure composition – it's also the last complete song that he wrote.

The focus is naturally upon Bob Dylan, but let's pause for a moment to consider his sidemen, central to this story. Fifty years ago The Band's cultural significance, in helping remould rock 'n' roll at a moment of huge political, economic, and social disruption, was striking – even if, for all but the aficionado, this profound influence was soon forgotten. Timeless in its portrayal of an America fading fast in the collective memory, the group's eponymous second album, *The Band*, left a legacy – for Richard Thompson the album confirmed its creators as pioneers of the 'counter-counter culture.' Yet, for all the inflated claims of guitarist and songwriter Robbie Robertson, not least in *Testimony*, his 2016 memoirs, there is nothing to suggest he and his fellow musicians set out to do anything other than write and record songs rooted south of the Mason-Dixon Line, across a seventy-year time-line from the Civil War to the Depression.

There was no overarching vision – Arkansan drummer Levon Helm simply gave his Canadian bandmates a set of myths on which to work their magic. How their peers, especially in Britain, might respond to The Band's first two albums was no part of the equation – other than a simple desire for due recognition of densely-textured, well-crafted songs played impeccably by masters of their trade. It was Greil Marcus who as early as 1975 portrayed The Band as timeless music-makers, lodged deep 'in the very idea of America: complicated, dangerous, and alive.' Over thirty years after Marcus's best known book, *Mystery Train*, hailed the group's unique contribution to young – white – Americans' re-engagement with their country, he still saw their initial ability 'to lose themselves in the anonymity of their art, in music that seemed to predate them and was sure to outlast them' as a sign of greatness, however transient.

Yet, like Neil Young in the early 'seventies turning his back on popular acclaim, the five members of The Band recorded their first, and even their second, album with no clear idea of what would happen next. It's an elementary point with regard to contingency, but it needs repeating time and again: there may be a considerable degree of probability regarding future outcomes, but there can be no certainty. As a Nobel laureate once so famously said, 'something is happening here, but you don't know what it is, do you, Mr. Jones?'. In a long-forgotten TV interview promoting the execrable 1987 film *Hearts of Fire* Bob Dylan mused upon the unplanned and the unanticipated. Cynics will say nothing about Dylan's career is unplanned, but playing the part of a fading rock star, at a time when you are creatively bankrupt, is scarcely a calculated move.

Late in his musings on reflexivity Dylan unconsciously applied Heisenberg's uncertainty principle to himself: he had no direct knowledge of reality because other people's behaviour was unconsciously affected by his presence – he could only try and comprehend his immediate environment by forever standing outside and staring through the window. Back in March 1966 he had said something similar to the composer David Amram when they arrived for a party at a Greenwich Village town house: 'We walked in there, and sure enough everything changed.'

Dylan's immersion in domesticity and small-town life after his motorcycle accident in July 1966 was a short-lived attempt to see the world as it really is, without 'Bob Dylan' subverting the actuality. In such circumstances so many decisions regarding the future were short-term and pragmatic. There was no grand plan. Never was this truer than at the start of 1968 when neither Bob Dylan, nor his backing band, nor anyone else, had any notion of what would happen next. Equally, few at the time had a clear idea of what these six men had been up to in upstate New York across the previous eighteen months – the mythology surrounding 'The Basement Tapes' had yet to gain traction.

The proceeds of the two concerts held at Carnegie Hall on 20th January 1968 were donated to the Committee to Combat Huntingdon's Disease, a hereditary condition which Woody had died of four months before. His mind and body shredded by a ferocious neurodegenerative genetic disorder, Guthrie was largely confined to hospital for the last fifteen years of his life. Highlights of the two shows appeared on an early 'seventies album released by Columbia/CBS, *A Tribute To Woody Guthrie Part One*. The best of a second – technically a third – benefit concert, staged at the Hollywood Bowl on 12th September 1970, were showcased on *A Tribute To Woody Guthrie Part Two*, a simultaneous release from Warner Brothers (a truly rare occasion on which competing labels agreed to collaborate). Both albums were united on ever more comprehensive cassettes and CDs, culminating in a 2017 box set.

Accompanying the complementary LPs released in 1972 was a lavishly illustrated volume, *A Tribute to Woody Guthrie*, containing the music and complete lyrics for all twenty-three tracks – including a full version of 'Dear Mrs Roosevelt' – and a linking narrative in Guthrie's own words. *A Tribute to Woody Guthrie* fulfilled a dual purpose of raising money for a number of good causes, from medical research to funding a scholarship, and of consolidating the Guthrie family's copyright claims: Ludlow Music, a subsidiary of New York's Richmond Organization, already published 'This Land Is Your Land', and since the 1950s had secured a succession of best-selling folk songs by artists such as the Weavers: it made commercial sense for a major music publisher like TRO to support Guthrie's widow, Marjorie, in publishing what today we would label a coffee table book.

An introduction …

A Tribute to Woody Guthrie was edited by Millard Lampell. Prominent on the New York literary scene, he contributed a pen portrait, and an overview of Woody Guthrie's songs as seen in the context of the Depression. Millard eulogised Franklin Delano Roosevelt as essentially a man of the left, a people's president who died too soon. A harsher judgement is that FDR promoted progressive policies only when he deemed them pragmatic and desirable. He was never a radical, even if many of those appointed to direct and implement New Deal initiatives clearly were. Millard's nostalgia was a de facto rewrite of history, masking the belief of Communist sympathisers in the 'thirties and early 'forties that Roosevelt was at best a bourgeois reformist. This is an issue we'll need to return to later.

It's worth at this early stage establishing who Millard Lampell was, not least because he embodied the radical east coast intelligentsia which enthusiastically embraced folk music in the 1930s, and which features so prominently in this story. Radicalised in New Jersey during the depression, Lampell was a respected film and TV screenwriter who, like Pete Seeger, had been blacklisted in the 1950s for alleged 'un-American activities.' As we'll see, for two years at the start of the 'forties he had sung in the Almanac Singers with Seeger and another veteran leftie, Lee Hays; these three were joined by Woody Guthrie, and a variety of lesser luminaries on the fellow-travelling folk scene. Lampell had co-written 'Union Maid' with Guthrie, before creating the libretto for *The Lonesome Train*, Earl Robinson's wartime cantata on the death of Abraham Lincoln. Robinson is another key protagonist. He was a Communist composer, much admired by Eleanor Roosevelt. Blacklisted in the 'fifties like Lampell, Robinson fuelled McCarthyite indignation with labour anthems like 'Joe Hill', famous courtesy of Paul Robeson and Joan Baez.

Earl Robinson shared top billing with Pete Seeger and Lee Hays at a benefit concert for the Guthrie family in March 1956; an event marked by Pete Seeger's surprise announcement that a frail Woody had delayed entering hospital to come along and show his thanks. Millard Lampell wrote a script for the show using Guthrie's own words. Later that year Will Geer relied on Lampell's libretto when reading extracts from *Bound For Glory*, Guthrie's dustbowl memoir, on Folkways' album of the same name. Written in an Okie vernacular and published in 1943, *Bound For Glory* was compulsory reading for any left-leaning folkie from Greenwich Village to Berkeley. Lampell's 1956 script formed the basis of his concert commentaries in 1968 and in 1970, as well as the 1968 Newport Folk Festival's tribute to its fallen hero. If Arlo Guthrie had had his way there would have been no script in New York – he felt it undermined the spontaneity of the occasion, but his mother insisted on offering a narrative to anyone in the audience unfamiliar with Woody's life and times.

Let's go back to the LP released in 1972. Staring out from the front cover of the Carnegie Hall album's monochrome gatefold sleeve is the face of Woody Guthrie, as a backdrop to the concert's all-star cast together on stage for their climactic rendering of 'This Land Is Your Land'. Listening to that record it's Odetta and a pre-Woodstock Richie Havens who inject into the proceedings gravity, engagement, solemnity – and the voice of the African American. Woody Guthrie, class warrior and ornery bastard, would have approved (even more so had Sonny Terry and Brownie McGhee sung, as advertised). The sobriety of the two black singers contrasts with the cheeriness of Tom Paxton and Judy Collins, their performances illustrating the ease with which a sanitised Guthrie was assimilated into mainstream American folk. Predictably, Pete Seeger reminded the audience of Guthrie's alter ego as the purveyor of cheesy children's songs. This initial release was a small selection of the songs performed at successive concerts, and the same was true of Millard Lampell's libretto, read by Will Geer and Robert Ryan.

An introduction …

Unsurprisingly, Arlo Guthrie enjoys pride of place on the LP. Always his father's son, in January 1968 he was the unlikeliest of high profile celebrities. With its gently subversive title track on the play list of America's hippest DJs, the recently released *Alice's Restaurant* was riding high in the record charts. Guthrie sings three songs on the tribute album, including his Uncle Jack's 1946 surprise best-seller, 'Oklahoma Hills'. There's a pleasing authenticity about Arlo Guthrie's contribution, and you feel Woody would have cheered him on. More recently Arlo Guthrie has acknowledged how over-awed he was by the occasion, not least the 'scary' venue and the array of artists: Carnegie Hall saw an older generation still in control back stage. The same was true out front, with an audience visibly older than the average rock 'n' roll audience, and which dressed accordingly – judging by the official photographs taken at Carnegie Hall most men wore ties, and most women eschewed the prevailing hippie chic. For Arlo Guthrie, by the time of the second benefit, at the Hollywood Bowl in September 1970, the baton had been passed – Pete Seeger might bemoan the presence of a house band led by Ry Cooder, but he had to put up with it. New York was a concert, but LA was a gig.

The original LP only hinted at what it was like to be in the main auditorium of Carnegie Hall on 20th January 1968; and with a mono recording taped off the house sound system reproduction was poor. If the aforementioned selection of songs had been the album's sole content then hearing it for the first time would be a huge disappointment. Where is the excitement? Where is the passion? Why does the applause sound so laboured and polite? But there are of course three other songs, and even if they are perversely scattered across both sides of the record it's clear which set, both afternoon and evening, had seen the audience come alive.

Bob Dylan and his sidemen were suitably respectful, while at the same time putting on a show the staider devotees of Woody Guthrie would find hard to label 'folk'. To put it simply, Dylan and 'The Crackers' – as the former Hawks christened themselves for the day – rocked. For all the spontaneity of the occasion, they were tight and well-drilled, and they put on a show. Anyone familiar with *The Basement Tapes* can see how 'I Ain't Got No Home' and 'The Grand Coulee Dam' came straight out of the West Saugerties sessions the year before: Dylan sat in Big Pink singing countless covers and long-forgotten ballads, and when he and the Hawks revisited the Guthrie catalogue then this surely was how it sounded.

Hearing Robbie Robertson's highly distinctive guitar breaks your first thought is, 'This can only be The Band!'; but of course no-one on 20th January 1968 would have said that, as nobody in the audience could anticipate the musicians on stage going on to forge a fresh identity and a unique sound. 'I Ain't Got No Home' and 'The Grand Coulee Dam' were two of Woody Guthrie's best known songs, but 'Dear Mrs. Roosevelt' was new to almost everybody in the audience.

Release of the 1972 album, and its companion selection from the 1970 benefit, coincided with the Guthrie family establishing a foundation in Woody's name. In 1996 Norah, Guthrie's daughter by his second marriage and Arlo's sister, became the driving force in creating an open-access, now fully digitalised, archive of her father's papers. Norah Guthrie was – and is – hyper-active in promoting and organising projects and events related to Woody's work, whether musical, literary, or graphic. In consequence, the 2012 centenary celebrations attracted worldwide attention, and that momentum has been maintained ever since. One consequence was the complete archive moving from New York to Tulsa after a local trust bought the collection and established the Woody Guthrie Center, a museum, library, and concert hall located in the Brady Arts District of the city. In 2017 the Woody Guthrie Center and the German record label Bear Family released a box set containing all performances recorded at the 1968 and 1972 benefit concerts, as well as a wealth of related documentary material. Yet, for all the abundance of information, scant mention was made of 'Dear Mrs. Roosevelt', both the most obscure composition in the Woody Guthrie canon and the most obscure song in the Bob Dylan repertoire.

'Dear Mrs. Roosevelt is yet to re-appear on any of the Bootleg Series anthologies periodically released by the Columbia/CBS label, and its parent company Sony. Sanctioned by Bob Dylan, these archival compilations, usually thematic and accompanied by a suitably scholarly commentary, embrace countless out-takes, obscurities, and previously unknown compositions. Of the Carnegie Hall set only 'Grand Coulee Dam' has been rescued from oblivion: it appeared on a 2001 Japanese compilation of sixteen live performances from the previous forty years, and was, for Greil Marcus, the stand-out track. 'Dear Mrs. Roosevelt' is available as download or on CDs of the Guthrie tribute concerts – and streamed on Spotify, rendering it easy to access; but not as an individual Bob Dylan track or download. Furthermore, no recording exists from the late 1940s of Woody Guthrie singing the original pro-Soviet version. Every recording he ever made is in the public domain, and, however comprehensive the collection, 'Dear Mrs. Roosevelt' is conspicuous by its absence.

Today, thanks to forensic commentaries by the likes of Barney Hoskins and Greil Marcus, we have an encyclopaedic knowledge of what took place at West Saugerties in 1967-68, with a box set offering a definitive record of music made in and around the basement of Woodstock's most famous rented accommodation, Big Pink. The 2014 box set of *The Basement Tapes* highlights how much we now know about Dylan and The Band-to-be following his motorcycle accident in July 1966, but how little is known about their public appearances prior to the Isle of Wight Festival in August 1969. What *The Basement Tapes* in their entirety do confirm is that Dylan and his fellow music-makers ignored Guthrie's panegyric to Franklin Delano Roosevelt, thirty-second

President of the United States, and unique in being elected four times to the office.

Roosevelt died on 12 April 1945, at Warm Springs, his holiday home. *FDR's Funeral Train*, Robert Klara's 2010 account of the late President's last railroad journey, relies heavily on an unpublished memoir written by Henry Wallace, Roosevelt's second Vice President. As Commerce Secretary in FDR's final administration Wallace was a witness to the White House swearing-in of his successor as VP, Harry S. Truman, once news of the President's death reached Washington. No doubt reflecting upon what might have been, Wallace then joined Eleanor Roosevelt on the second half of her husband's final ride, from Washington to upstate New York. Robert Klara retraced Roosevelt's last ride, north from Georgia to the nation's capital, and then on to the family home at Hyde Park. With sombre crowds of mourners lining the route, the railroad catafalque made its way to Union Station, and a brief lying-in-state at the White House. The train then travelled from Washington to Philadelphia, and on to New York City; from where it steamed up the Hudson Valley to the President's final resting place. This was the apparent context in which Woody Guthrie composed his fond farewell. But appearances can be deceptive, and, as we'll see, the progressive platform of Henry Wallace helps explain why and when 'Dear Mrs Roosevelt' first saw the light of day.

'Dear Mrs. Roosevelt' is a song of immediate appeal and lasting significance, signalling as it does the distinctive sound of The Band, and Dylan's instinctive layering of rawness and profundity on to the simplest of melodies. This elegy to FDR has stood the test of time; yet by any objective standard it is not one of the great Bob Dylan songs. Nevertheless, this is a song which clearly boasts a history. At its simplest, it's a composition that is seemingly inspired by Private First Class Guthrie hearing Roosevelt was dead; and yet, it immediately prompts inquisition: how had Woody heard the news; when did he write the song; where was it performed; and why was it so little known? A myriad of other questions follow; above all, why had Bob Dylan and The Band-in-waiting chosen to perform this forgotten lament for the passing of the President that wintry Saturday in late 'sixties New York? Had they even known about the song, and if not then at what point did they become acquainted with it? Here was an exceptionally obscure composition, and, notwithstanding its brief airing fifty-two years ago, this has remained the case until now. What follows will focus first upon the context in which the last of several FDR-inspired songs was written, before exploring how and why a sanitised version regained the light of day in Carnegie Hall two decades later.

Bob and The Band – the road to Carnegie Hall, 20th January 1968

At Carnegie Hall in January 1968 The Band were still, in their own words, no more than Bob Dylan's 'scrounge road group.' They looked like a Talmudic study circle from Tombstone, their rabbi suitably besuited, bearded, and booted – in Lillian Roxon's concert review, 'so changed, serene, smiling, oddly respectable in his grey suit and open-checked blue shirt.' For Greil Marcus the frontier analogy conveyed a darker impression: only a few years earlier the Hawks had been snappy dressers, with hip haircuts and sharp suits, but now they looked and sounded like, 'the Earp brothers and Doc Holliday cleaning out the last pockets of resistance at the O.K. Corral.' Purist folk devotees backstage or out front doubtless viewed Dylan's sidemen with deep suspicion, but they were clearly in a minority – Bob and his band generated huge expectation and huge goodwill.

'The Crackers' was a ten-day soubriquet, lasting from the concerts to The Band-to-be's February signing by Capitol Records. With hindsight it is scarcely surprising that the five anonymous musicians on stage at Carnegie Hall sounded so similar to The Band. After all they were already recording tracks for their debut album at A & R Studios, just a few streets away. Their rural sojourn in upstate New York had bequeathed them a fresh focus and direction, enabling them to retain an association with Dylan while becoming artists in their own right: in a remarkable eighteen months period The Band would release two extraordinarily influential albums, and find themselves a headline act at 'The Woodstock Music and Art Fair'. In his memoir *This Wheel's On Fire*, drummer and de facto leader Levon Helm recalled how, when the group arrived at the concert hall, someone asked who they were. Helm answered with his home state's pejorative term for 'poor southern white folks' (renewed controversy in recent years over the term 'cracker'

101

means there is no way the moniker would be used today). The Crackers had attitude, and they had history. As Nik Cohn wrote at the height of their fame, 'The Band came from nowhere specific and their evocations were indistinct but they were the whole of the American past and all its space.'

The Hawks had been on the road in various incarnations since the late 'fifties. They started as veteran rocker Ronnie Hawkins' backing band, and numerous journeyman players passed through their ranks before natural selection created a union of five top-notch instrumentalists. Hawkins and Helm both hailed from Arkansas, but they hired mainly Canadian musicians: Hawkins was hugely popular in Ontario, especially after an under-age but highly talented Jaime – Robbie – Robertson was brought on board to play lead guitar. By 1963 the Hawks became fixed as four Canadians and one southerner, with Helm and Robertson joined by Rick Danko on bass, Garth Hudson on organ, and Richard Manuel on piano; each of them sang, and they all played more than one instrument. This was the beat combo which split from Hawkins, and which in succeeding years seemed scarcely aware of the British invasion.

Robertson recalled in *Testimony* how they jammed with Sonny Boy Williamson soon after he came back to Mississippi from touring with the Yardbirds. In Europe Williamson flattered his young admirers, but back home he assured the Hawks that they were in a different league from aspiring white bluesmen the far side of the Atlantic. By the time of *Rubber Soul* the Beatles seemed to have left behind early Motown artists, Chuck Berry, and the myriad of other black musical influences underpinning the original Mersey sound – an impression reinforced by the decision to stop touring. From Liverpool to LA, where the Beatles led, other groups followed. A mixture of commercial imperative and musical curiosity saw the likes of the Animals, the Yardbirds, and Paul Butterfield looking beyond Chicago blues and Detroit R and B. As Elijah

Wald points out in the aptly titled *How The Beatles Destroyed Rock 'n' Roll*, these were the earliest signs of what emerged post-*Sergeant Pepper* as a new album-focused form of popular music, soon familiar to one and all as 'Rock' with a capital R. The Hawks wanted success, and that meant writing a hit single; but at the same time they prided themselves on staying faithful to the music they had always played, whether on their own or with Ronnie Hawkins – this group was anything but a slave to fashion.

There is a double irony here in that by 1970 The Band's first two albums would be cited as evidence that rock music was something more than a transient phenomenon in a youth culture obsessed with the familiar and superficial; and yet that strong sense of permanence and solidity was rooted in the same fixation on continuity and musical tradition which had seen the Hawks refine but never compromise their delivery of high octane bar-room dance music rooted in both black and – via Memphis and New Orleans – white urban experiences. The Hawks ploughed their preferred furrow, and in a mid-sixties America fixated on the Beatles, the Beach Boys, and the Byrds 'Levon and the Hawks' looked and sounded old-fashioned. They were going nowhere, until the day Bob Dylan phoned Robertson to see if his band was free to tour. At that point everything changed, as from September 1965 to May 1966 they crossed three continents, dividing audiences with a requisite display of suitable aggression and a readiness to shock.

The Hawks scarcely featured in the studio, but each night on stage they effortlessly translated the 'thin…wild mercury music' of *Blonde On Blonde* and its immediate predecessors into a loud and powerful experience which fans either loved or loathed. The combination of Dylan's sneering, snarling, slurring voice and Robertson's piercing, penetrating, pin-point guitar work created something wholly unique: a transgressive sound intrinsically powerful, intense, and above all, disturbing. The Hawks were on a steep learning curve, but so too was

103

Dylan: Robertson urged him to park an obsession with lyrics, and in so doing to rediscover the exciting and elemental nature of stripped-down, supremely crafted rhythm and blues – a lot less Jack Kerouac, and a lot more Curtis Mayfield. Dylan served a fast track apprenticeship in playing live with seasoned musicians, four of whom relied as much on instinct as expertise. As confirmed once The Band went on the road, this was a collective endeavour rooted in both camaraderie and conviction, in other words, each member's supreme belief in the musical accomplishment of his fellow players. As Greil Marcus inelegantly pointed out in *Mystery Train*, 'The marriage of his [Dylan] linguistic instincts, his hipster savvy, and his unmatched feel for the mysteries of the American song to the Hawks' training and flair took them to places they never could have reached alone.'

Rooted in jazz Garth Hudson had eclectic musical tastes, but even he shared the other Hawks' preoccupation with the blues, R and B, rockabilly, and the rawest forms of country and rock 'n' roll. Before being hired by Bob Dylan they knew nothing about his songs, other than the hits heard on AM radio. After they met Dylan the band's circle of associates expanded dramatically, but they still felt most comfortable with like-minded musicians, whether white or black. Even after the retreat to upstate New York, and Dylan's crash course in the American tradition, it's hard to imagine the likes of Richard Manuel sipping beer in a Village folk club while listening respectfully to successive purveyors of 'wooden music.'

An exception was aspiring songwriter Robbie Robertson, whose session work and openness to new ideas brought him into contact with the east coast folk scene. When the other artists at Carnegie Hall introduced themselves to Dylan's accompanists Robertson was the one familiar face. The hostility experienced by the Hawks when they joined up with Dylan had seen Levon Helm soon leave, appalled by the confrontational nature of the early shows (his discomfort compounded by the immediate installation of Bobby Gregg, the drummer on both *Bringing It All Back Home* and *Highway 61 Revisited*; in turn making way for Mickey Jones, ex-cabaret accompanist and the unsung hero of the Dylan story). Helm reappeared only after his bandmates had settled in Woodstock, then still an obscure artists' colony, and urged him to join them there – he never left. On 20th January 1968 audience abuse and aggression was almost unthinkable, but backstage before the afternoon concert there was surely a degree of suspicion, especially among the older performers. No wonder Helm suggested a name synonymous with white trash.

The Crackers joined Dylan in subverting a sombre, worthy, and fitfully joyful occasion, playing, in the view of one observer, 'on a different plane' from their fellow performers. For thirteen minutes, matinee and evening, they worked their way through a raunchy, rackety, and raucous set, comprising 'Grand Coulee Dam', 'Dear Mrs Roosevelt', and 'I Ain't Got No Home' – a set list seen by veteran academic and journalist Sean Wilenz as rooting 'Guthrie's work historically in a particular time, the time of Dylan's early boyhood, and in an already bygone America, even as it channelled that work into a sound unlike anything anybody had ever heard before,' meaning the music laid down in Woodstock the previous year. Greil Marcus memorably described 'Grand Coulee Dam' as, 'a drunken rockabilly rave-up at the party thrown by the men who built the thing, on the night they opened the spillway for the first time.' One or two younger members of the audience even dared to dance in the aisles. Throughout the first set Sue C. Clark, from *Rolling Stone*, couldn't stop laughing – although no-one reading her dry, no-nonsense report could guess that she had such a great time (perhaps not so surprisingly given the audience, a much fuller and more exuberant review appeared in the *New Yorker*). Pete Seeger stared disapprovingly, but according to Robert Shelton he soon started drumming the back of a guitar.

Talking to Shelton at the Sheraton-Plaza Hotel between concerts, Robbie Robertson warned 'just wait for tonight'; and indeed the evening performance was even louder and livelier than the matinee, leaving fans at the end of the night demanding more Dylan. Levon Helm reckoned, 'our evening show brought down the house. Bob tore it up!' Barney Hoskyns labelled both sets, 'an explosion of lusty energy in the midst of the wholesome right-on-ness displayed by Dylan's old folk chums.' 'I Ain't Got No Home' and 'Grand Coulee Dam' were familiar Dustbowl/New Deal anthems, but lodged between them was a scarcely known lament for President Roosevelt. Roosevelt as in Franklin Delano, and not his turn-of-the-century predecessor Theodore (although, surprisingly, Eleanor Roosevelt's 'Uncle Teddy' is the president Dylan chooses to compliment in *Chronicles*: '[he] could have stepped out of a folk ballad.').

Arrangement and delivery of all three songs may have been mildly shocking to anyone seduced by the recently released *John Wesley Harding* into imagining measured, melodic, and respectful renderings of firm favourites; yet the lazy, loping – and undeniably loud – sound was consistent with the stripped back, disrespectful, earthy projection of 'people's music' which Guthrie had claimed came naturally to black bluesmen like Lead Belly; and which few white singers were capable of embracing. A now famous field trip to the Mississippi delta in the late 'fifties had seen the musicologist Alan Lomax arrive at a similar conclusion, albeit expressed in more elevated terms: the psychological make-up of white singers left them emotionally constrained by comparison with their 'negro' counterparts. Levon Helm and his boys had devoted their lives to disproving Lomax's theory.

The prevailing influence was rockabilly, with Richard Manuel's honky-tonk piano and Garth Hudson's growling organ an ever-present behind the clean guitar breaks and snappy fills which became Robbie Robertson's trademark once The Band began performing in their own right later that year. In their sound, if no longer their appearance, Dylan's gang still projected the rock 'n' roll persona that had proved so divisive two years earlier. Dylan hollered every verse as if addressing a Teamsters' meeting, and yet 'Dear Mrs Roosevelt' sounded surprisingly melodic, thanks largely to The Band-to-be's trademark harmonising on the chorus and the fade. Robertson felt sure Guthrie would have approved: interviewed years later for a history of The Band, he defended their approach, maintaining that, 'if a song is going to live it must live in its contemporary surrounding.' In January 1968 that meant a fusion of the folk tradition and electric instrumentation. The centrality of the electric guitar to popular music since the early 1950s was self-evident; but what constituted an American folk tradition remained highly contestable, witness the challenge laid down that day by Dylan and his sidemen.

Ever since the Byrds took flawless covers of Dylan and Seeger songs to the top of the charts in 1965, an assortment of artists had sought similar success. The resulting records were invariably sanitised and saccharine. The same could not be said for the music Dylan played at the Guthrie benefit concerts – this was folk music as raw, intense, and personal as the day it was written, and rendered even more so by the use of amplified instruments. The performance is seen by Sean Wilenz as 'a finale for the Basement Tapes,' but at the time no-one other than the six musicians on stage could see it that way. Tantalising insights into the music which Dylan and his one-time Hawks had played across the past year would soon start to emerge, helping to forge a fresh understanding of the relationship between amplified instruments and respective folk traditions: from Boulder to Brooklyn, and Belfast to Brest, a generation that had grown up with Dylan plugged in. 'Folk rock' was too crude a description of the myriad of different musical approaches emerging on both sides of the Atlantic at the end of the 1960s, but Bob Dylan and his band had already signalled something fundamentally new.

They knew this, as I suspect did the more insightful members of the audience; but, with plans for a documentary film soon shelved, this was a prelude to revolution witnessed by only a privileged few.

Concert reviews portrayed Dylan as the solitary king of cool, standing aloof and detached from the rest of the cast. Yet, as backstage shots confirm, the star performer was smiling and collegial. Unlike at Newport three years earlier he showed due respect to Seeger and the other veteran performers gathered to salute their lost comrade. After the second show Dylan joined the other artists at narrator Robert Ryan's apartment on the Upper West Side (in the Dakota building – five years later, following the film star's death, the flat was acquired by John Lennon and Yoko Ono). Ryan's party lasted until the early hours, with the cast joined by the likes of Paul Simon, Art Garfunkel, and Allen Ginsberg. Their star-studded hootenanny constituted a cross-generational gathering of east coast progressives. For all the big names present this was a very private affair. The irony of singing songs about poverty and protest in an apartment overlooking Central Park is obvious, and everyone there was an easy target. Yet this was nothing like Leonard Bernstein's Park Avenue reception for the Black Panthers; the notorious manifestation of 'radical chic' so ruthlessly skewered by Tom Wolfe in *New York* magazine thirty months later. Ryan's hard man image on the screen belied his work as a peace activist and educationalist. He and Dylan shared an invisible connection, as both men went on to star in Sam Peckinpah movies – within weeks of the tribute concerts Ryan would be on location in Mexico, playing William Holden's nemesis in *The Wild Bunch*.

Dylan defused the mystique surrounding someone scarcely seen in public for eighteen months (in reality he had spent almost as much time in Manhattan as Woodstock, but out on the street his privacy was respected or he was simply not recognised). When the time came for him to go out and perform Dylan was crippled by nerves, as would be the case on the Isle of Wight eighteen months later. Tom Paxton claims to have joked with Dylan, and relaxed him just enough that he could walk out and face an audience desperate to avoid disappointment. The relief was palpable, claimed Paxton: 'My God it was so exciting. The way he did it with The Band there, that was wonderful. This was certainly one of the best experiences I ever had in this whole mish mash.'

At the end of both performances Dylan and the Crackers enthusiastically joined Seeger and the rest of the cast in the inevitable finale – the audience joined in with ever increasing fervour on every chorus of 'This Land Is Your Land'. Pete Seeger, McCarthyite victim and honoured keeper of the Guthrie flame, had long since come to terms with Dylan's antipathy to being labelled a protest singer. As time passed Seeger ruefully recognised the irony of his tearful attempt to silence the fallen angel's debut performance playing electric at the 1965 Newport Folk Festival. The off-stage footage in *Festival!*, Murray Lerner's documentary record of Newport '65, shows Seeger's immediate sense of betrayal, and his thwarted attempt to stop the show. Paul Nelson's festival report for *Sing Out!* vividly conveyed Seeger's outrage over the divisive nature of Dylan's loud and iconoclastic scratch band. The next time Seeger saw Dylan perform was at Carnegie Hall. In his own begrudging way he was complimentary, recognising the intensity of the anointed one's performance, and acknowledging that, 'audience and press were keyed up not to mourn the death of Guthrie so much as to celebrate the return to life of Dylan.'

Most alarming for Seeger was when he found Mike Bloomfield backstage chatting with Dylan – here in the bowels of Carnegie Hall was the malcontent who had played lead guitar that fateful day in Newport three years earlier. Seeger's fears of another Fender-led assault upon the ears were in due course assuaged by the Crackers' respect for their visibly non-rock 'n' roll audience. If they played a lot louder than the other performers, only a handful found offence in a set which triumphantly defied expectations. Seeger was alone in resenting the presence of electric guitars (or at least acoustic guitars with pick-ups).

The same was true when the next fund-raising event was staged, at the Hollywood Bowl on 12th September 1970. The venue held eighteen thousand and the concert was sold out, so amplification via a reliable sound system was vital. Expectations were high, with an audience very different from the respectful mourners who had gathered to pay their respects at the two shows in New York. By the autumn of 1970 headliners Joan Baez and Richie Havens were playing far fewer solo gigs: their much vaunted performances at Woodstock, captured in the consequent movie, meant that they were earning more, and therefore could afford to hire seasoned musicians. Ironically, it was Seeger's protégé, Arlo Guthrie, who assembled a backing band of up-and-coming session men, which – unlike the Crackers – would be on stage for the whole show.

Psychedelic showman Country Joe McDonald had reinvented himself as an acoustic counter culture troubadour. This was courtesy of a well-received Guthrie covers album, and more especially, the anti-Vietnam 'Fish Cheer' in *Woodstock* (the presumption that an LA tribute concert would generate a younger and hipper audience saw the crowd-rousing hero of Yasgur's Farm suggest the show end with a suitably profane rendering of 'The Fixin' To Die Rag' – an idea immediately squashed by an image-conscious Baez). Ahead of his appearance at the Hollywood Bowl McDonald was given an obscure set of lyrics by Woody's widow and invited to write a song. Nearly thirty years before Billy Bragg and Jeff Tweedy took on a similar challenge and recorded *Mermaid Avenue*, Country Joe and Ry Cooder turned the erotic musing of 'Woman At Home' into a loud, louche blues number similar to the guitarist's soundtrack for *Performance*.

'Woman At Home' sounded like an out-take from the first Captain Beefheart album, confirming for Seeger – as he made clear to anyone in LA who would listen – that Dylan's presence at Carnegie Hall had opened the flood gates to amplified folk: the bastardisation of a people's music where artist and audience are presumed to be as one, with every performance a genuinely holistic experience. Both purist and polemicist, Pete Seeger always insisted that an audience best responded to a powerful song if those on stage were free from the trappings of ostensibly artificial instrumentation. The size of the venue was immaterial, witness a banjo-plucking Seeger on the steps of the Lincoln Memorial at Barack Obama's 2009 inauguration calling every verse as he and Bruce Springsteen led the vast crowd in a mass rendering of 'This Land Is Your Land': 'You sing it with us! We'll give you the words!'

Back on the afternoon and evening of 20th January 1968 fans and critics alike were struck by the strength and power of Bob Dylan's voice. Reviewing both sets in the *New York Times*, Robert Shelton applauded performances 'of disarming originality.' In the mid-fifties Shelton had seen his career as a political journalist shredded by Cold War manoeuvrings on Capitol Hill. In due course he had reinvented himself as a music critic, famously acclaiming Dylan's support act at Gerde's Folk City in September 1961 (on the strength of his *New York Times* review Shelton was invited to adopt a pen name and write the liner notes for Dylan's first album). Via the review columns of *Hootenanny* and the *New York Times*, Shelton chronicled and championed every step of the singer's career. Both men placed Woody Guthrie on a pedestal, and if anything, Shelton exceeded his protégé in lavishing praise on the sickly troubadour. Consequently, he became a close friend of Marjorie Guthrie. In 1965 Shelton accepted Marjorie's invitation to inspect the numerous boxes of unpublished material which Woody kept in the basement of the family home in Queens. The result was *Born To Win*, an anthology of prose and poetry. Title, design, and promotion all signalled Shelton's intention to sell the 'Father/Hero' of Dylan, Baez, et al to a generation for whom Woody Guthrie was little more than a name. The selected lyrics, verse, and trenchant observations on the state of the world ranged from the brilliant to the banal, with Shelton deaf to any suggestion that, for all his skills as an agent of agitprop, the man from Okemah was no literary giant.

Although seen on the east coast folk scene as a venerable father figure, at Newport in 1965 Shelton had responded to Dylan's set in a manner wholly at odds with that of Pete Seeger. In consequence, despite the difference in age, Robert Shelton remained on Dylan's radar even after he quit America for a new life in London at the end of the decade. Shelton's column in the *New York Times* confirmed just how eclectic his musical tastes were: at the time of the Carnegie Hall concerts his favourite band was the Jeff Beck Group. Dylan 'going electric' was a natural development, not a betrayal. In due course the veteran critic's lengthy interviews with Dylan – most notoriously on an amphetamine-fuelled midnight flight across the mid-West in March 1966 – formed the basis for a wordy if worthy biography, *No Direction Home*. Greil Marcus may have found Shelton's magnum opus 'bleeding with incomprehension,' but this didn't deter its most famous reader – in 2001 Bob Dylan informed a Spanish journalist that Shelton's was the last book he bought in order to discover Bob Dylan: 'It's difficult to read about yourself because in your own mind things never happen in that way. It all seems like fiction.'

Robert Shelton's closeness to Dylan gave him privileged access to the fourteen songs laid down in the Catskills and selected for circulation among various artists and record companies. In due course he would immerse himself in all the other original songs and cover versions, which together make up the Basement Tapes. Shelton later labelled them, 'Cellar compositions…flawed ensembles, rough-hewn singing, unkempt instrumentalism, disbalances, distortion [sic].' Here were a hundred or so songs, all displaying the 'sheer bravura, intimacy and excitement,' which would define Dylan and the Crackers' successive sets at Carnegie Hall.

The no-holds-barred creativity displayed by these six men across the year preceding the Guthrie concerts translated itself into what we now judge to be pivotal music. For The Band that music would soon be rooted in a particular historical perspective: that of poor whites generation on generation scraping a living off the land across a timeline from the Depression back to 'the war between the states.' Levon Helm lived forty-five years in Woodstock, but the drummer stayed a dyed in the wool son of Arkansas until the day he died. Reunited with his old bandmates Helm culturally relocated the four Canadians, and perhaps even the Minnesota-born Dylan, south of the Mason-Dixon Line. With Robertson his amanuensis and interpreter, Levon Helm initiated a myth-making process, which culminated two years later in The Band's eponymous – near perfect – second album.

Yet when Helm first arrived in Woodstock his erstwhile group remained a fledgling creative unit, still in search of a voice. Their earliest compositions contrasted starkly with Dylan's songs, each of which boasted a unique voice, while at the same time manifesting an obvious *joie de vivre*; here was the majesty, the maturity, and the spontaneity of a re-energised artist on a creative high. It was as if Dylan had a cultural agenda – nothing less than a reshaping of popular music – but was too busy having a good time to perceive exactly what that agenda was. Nor did his fellow music-makers; and yet the impact of *Music from Big Pink* in the second half of 1968 left The Band and not Dylan as the applauded agents of change. The first major outing for music from Big Pink was at Woodstock, where over half of The Band's set derived from the Basement Tapes; in contrast, at the Isle of Wight Dylan sang just three songs from his sojourn in West Saugerties.

Few in the audience at either of the Guthrie concerts were aware just how much music-making had taken place in rural upstate New York across the preceding summer and autumn; illumination would come courtesy of the first bootleg recordings, illicitly available on both sides of the Atlantic by the close of the decade. However laid back the atmosphere at Big Pink, on 20th January 1968 Dylan displayed the same self-discipline and application which three months earlier had impressed the studio musicians in Nashville hired to record a dozen songs written specifically for the next album. Gnomic and acoustic, *John Wesley Harding* had been generally well received on its release in late December. Some critics demurred, but in terms of record sales and popular appreciation Bob Dylan was still riding a tide of goodwill. A perceptive review by Robert Christgau in *Esquire* recognised the album's reductive qualities: Dylan, for too long a 'word crazy dramatist,' had finally learnt the value of understatement.

The stark contrast between *John Wesley Harding* and its immediate predecessors served only to heighten fans' expectations once it was known Dylan would appear at Carnegie Hall; songs such as 'Drifter's Escape' and 'I Pity The Poor Immigrant' were seen as a salute to Guthrie, who had died only a fortnight before the Nashville sessions began. It later transpired that Pete Seeger was a huge fan of *John Wesley Harding*, relishing the stark instrumentation and the biblical underpinning. He saw the album as evidence of Bob Dylan emerging from some dark night of the soul. Seeger stubbornly refused to change his mind when evidence emerged that life at Byrdcliffe, the Dylan family home in upstate New York, was nothing like the slough of despond.

Still inside Carnegie Hall,
20th January 1968

Producer Harold Leventhal later claimed that Bob Dylan approached him regarding a Guthrie commemorative concert: 'The day Woody died he called up and said, "Whatever you plan I'd like to be there," and he was...' $3.50 seats for the matinee and evening celebrations of someone whom many beyond the folk scene presumed long dead sold out within an hour. The announcement that Dylan had agreed to take part was an obvious incentive for younger ticket-holders. For this if no other reason, it's more likely the commercially savvy Leventhal approached Dylan, rather than the other way round.

Born and raised in New York's toughest boroughs, Harold Leventhal was a hard but thoroughly decent businessman, his progressive ideals earning him universal admiration and respect. He dedicated much of his life to defending and promoting Woody Guthrie, and the archives in Tulsa are a testimony to his passion, commitment, and organisational ability. Leventhal's well-established credentials as a left-leaning manager and concert promoter saw his appointment in the mid-fifties as the guardian of the Guthrie family's assets, not least Woody's literary and song rights. Encouraged by Marjorie Guthrie, Harold Leventhal was the inspiration and the driving force behind the Carnegie Hall concerts. He had helped organise the 1956 benefit, and nine years later had staged 'The Woody Guthrie Hootenanny' at Town Hall. Leventhal had screened film footage of Guthrie at the first concert. Now he had the idea to have repeat images of Guthrie's life and times projected on to a backcloth throughout each show (the same slides were later used in LA, but complemented by a purpose-built stage set based on Woody's drawings and cartoons).

For Leventhal, Carnegie Hall was the obvious location in which to celebrate the life of Woody Guthrie. In the 1930s and 1940s both

115

President Roosevelt and the First Lady, Eleanor Roosevelt, had travelled there to address various political gatherings. Notwithstanding its occasional use by opponents of the New Deal and advocates of isolationism, Carnegie Hall had acquired a symbolic importance for New York's liberals and radicals. Starting in 1938 with *From Spirituals to Swing*, a history of black music sponsored by the Communist magazine *New Masses*, the theatre management had actively encouraged integrated audiences. Unsurprisingly, right-wing parties and organisations, including the demonstrably fascist German Bund, preferred Madison Square Garden for their rallies. At the height of FDR's 1944 presidential campaign, New Jersey Democrats convinced the young Frank Sinatra to go on stage at the Carnegie and challenge Bing Crosby's endorsement of the Republican Party candidate, New York state governor and high profile mafia prosecutor Thomas Dewey. Meanwhile, up in New England Woody Guthrie was busy singing campaign songs in less grandiose settings.

Carnegie Hall looked very different in January 1968, as today a sixty-floor skyscraper towers over the original baroque-styled venue. Yet the large and imposing concert hall, built for symphony orchestras not rock bands or folk groups, still oozes gravitas. In the late 'sixties an especially raucous Rolling Stones gig had seen the Carnegie Hall's initial flirtation with pop music end abruptly. The idea of a Woody Guthrie benefit surely left Carnegie Hall's managers thinking long and hard before they agreed to seriously-minded if slightly scruffy lefties from the lower west side celebrate their late hero. Yet several of those scheduled to perform had previously played at the venue, most notably Pete Seeger, lead singer on the best-selling LP *The Weavers At Carnegie Hall*, recorded on Christmas Eve 1955. Bob Dylan had also sung at Carnegie Hall, in an upstairs concert room on 4 November 1961 and in the main auditorium in October 1965; the latter gig with the Hawks may have been a factor in the post-Stones ban on 'loud music.'

116

Late in life Harold Leventhal recalled 20ᵗʰ January 1968 as, 'a very emotional event. People cried throughout the evening [and presumably the afternoon]. Yes, Woody had passed away, but one thing was certain: we would never forget him.' At the end of both shows Leventhal brought Marjorie Guthrie, and her daughter Nora, out on stage to join the cast. Tom Paxton was stunned by the way in which 'the place went nuts' – not many accountants from the East Side could earn themselves a standing ovation, especially twice in one day.

At least one member of the audience at Carnegie Hall sat fixed in his seat. In the early 1960s Phil Ochs had been a protest singer mentioned in the same breath as Bob Dylan – beyond the folk cognoscenti he was best known as the writer of Joan Baez's Top Ten hit, 'There But For Fortune'. Unlike Dylan, Ochs had revelled in the notion that his politically-charged songs rendered him a 'spokesman for his generation.' 1964 saw the release of *Another Side of Bob Dylan* and of Ochs' debut album, *All The News That's Fit To Sing*: one record signalled a deliberate shift from the political to the personal, while the other was a witty if relentless social commentary on the woes of the nation. Civil rights, chronic inequality, and Cold War confrontation gave Ochs the material and the motivation to record three powerful and well received albums for Elektra. The political engagement remained as raw as ever, but in the mid-sixties Ochs switched labels, at which point he lost his way. By 1968 his career had stalled, ironically at the very moment when events at home and abroad cried out for 'protest songs' carrying the weight of anthems made famous via *All The News That's Fit To Sing* and its successor, *I Ain't Marchin' Anymore*.

Insistent that he alone of his generation had kept the faith, Phil Ochs was too intelligent not to know his moment had passed. Was it envy which fuelled hostility towards his one-time coffee house comrade? The two men shared a painful (for Ochs) and perplexing relationship until Ochs all but accused the chart-topping Dylan of having sold out to a spurious rock star lifestyle. The two men famously quarrelled in the back of a car: Ochs found himself dumped into a stream of Manhattan traffic; his dismissal accompanied by the charge, 'You're not a folk singer. You're just a journalist.' Ochs displayed an ambivalent attitude towards Dylan, performing a sneering parody of him on stage – 'Positively (Not) 4th Street' – while at the same time remaining fascinated by whatever his old sparring partner was up to. In 1966 Ochs pronounced publicly that Dylan was heading for a fall, and then curiously was proved right. Demoralised and depressed, Ochs had only a vague knowledge of Dylan's music-making after he fell off his motor-bike and withdrew from public life. Drawn by the chance to see Dylan's latest incarnation first-hand, Ochs acquired a ticket for one of the Carnegie Hall concerts. This was despite his undisguised fury over being ignored by Harold Leventhal.

Leventhal knew Phil Ochs well, and was familiar with his work, not least the plangent tribute to Guthrie, 'Bound For Glory'. Seen by many as the outstanding track on *All The News That's Fit To Sing*, 'Bound For Glory' was as familiar to folk fans as *Bob Dylan*'s 'Song To Woody'. It was certainly better known than 'Last Thoughts on Woody Guthrie', a torrent of *vers libre* which Dylan performed only once: if you weren't in New York at Town Hall on 13 April 1963 then you had to wait nearly thirty years before a recording of the recitation was finally released. Ochs probably was in the Town Hall audience that night, his literary antennae picking up the poem's indebtedness to the Beats, Baudelaire, and James Baldwin. Impressed but never in awe, Ochs matched the density of Dylan's *homage* in just five verses and a chorus: 'Bound For Glory' was in essence a ballad, a stripped down biography in the spirit of its subject. A companion song from Ochs's debut album, 'The Power and the Glory', was an unashamed attempt to match the vision and grandiosity of 'This Land Is Your Land' – and soon covered by Pete Seeger, who recognised the parallels with Guthrie's own alternative anthem. On the basis of these two songs alone, Ochs believed he should have been on stage at Carnegie Hall.

Instead he found himself having to watch Richie Havens, at that time a little-known artist, and with no obvious connection to Woody Guthrie. Ochs would have been even angrier had he known that his former manager Albert Grossman insisted Leventhal invite Havens to play: this was the price of having Bob Dylan close the first half of the show. Ironically, relations between Grossman and his biggest star had sunk so low that backstage at Carnegie Hall they ignored each other. A further irony was the setting: upstairs from the main auditorium was the Carnegie Chapter Hall, where back in November 1961 Grossman had spectacularly failed to orchestrate his young charge's breakout appearance. Levon Helm sensed bad blood between the two men, while at the same time welcoming Grossman's readiness to gamble on the Hawks' imminent regeneration: 'just as Bob was leaving Albert's stable, we were arriving.'

Leverage for Grossman was Leventhal's own manoeuvrings to secure his clients a place on the bill. Judy Collins was an obvious link between the older singers centred on Pete Seeger and the younger songwriters she showcased on her early albums for Elektra; and unlike Havens, Collins was a close friend of the Guthrie family. Recalling the occasion some years later, an embittered Phil Ochs insisted that, 'Woody Guthrie would not have been invited to the Woody Guthrie concert.' As evidence Ochs cited Leventhal reversing an initial decision to include Guthrie's most famous devotee: Ramblin' Jack Elliott learnt of his omission only the day before the event. Despite having driven thousands of miles to take part, Elliott's sole demand was two seats in the auditorium, his good humour ensuring an invitation to play at the California concert thirty months later.

Elliott had been born in Brooklyn, the son of a Jewish GP. From the early 'fifties Elliott reinvented himself as Ramblin' Jack, a singing cowboy devoted to Woody Guthrie. He purported to be his ailing hero's amanuensis but too often he wasn't taken seriously – his credentials as a folk singer were respected more in Europe than in his home country. Only in 2012, amid the flurry of books and articles generated by Guthrie's centenary, was Elliott properly recognised as the first true believer and a lifelong keeper of the flame.

Back in 1961 it was Ramblin' Jack who had offered the young Robert Zimmerman a direct link to his bed-bound hero, and the two men's paths frequently crossed until the day Elliott's one-time disciple dropped him from the Rolling Thunder Revue. By way of recompense, in *Chronicles* Dylan acknowledged how much he owed to Ramblin' Jack Elliott's tutelage at the start of his career. Dylan readily conceded that when in Minneapolis he first heard Elliott's impressive covers of Guthrie standards it was a shock. A couple of albums had been recorded live in England, and they made a deep impression upon the embryonic Bob Dylan. Here was an unlikely and unexpected role model. Until his Minnesota mentor Jon Pankake called him out, Dylan switched from imitating Guthrie to imitating Ramblin' Jack.

At the time, and in the years that followed, Ramblin' Jack empathised with Phil Ochs, embittered by his exclusion from the Guthrie concerts. Ochs was already a heavy drinker, and in 1976 he killed himself, almost certainly as a consequence of an undiagnosed bipolar condition. Drawing perhaps on his own experience with the Rolling Thunder Revue, Elliott saw Ochs as someone whose career had been blighted by Dylan's antipathy, 'cause Bob is a very competitive person. If anybody seems to be a threat to Bob, he's going to get rid of him, he's just that way.' Ochs waited forlornly for an invitation to join the Rolling Thunder Revue when it reconvened in January 1976. The call never came and within three months he was dead. Dylan was shattered by the news of

Ochs' suicide, presumably wracked with guilt over the contempt he too often displayed towards a flawed and fragile songwriter forced to acknowledge his lesser talent.

Tom Paxton shared Elliott's regret that Phil Ochs was not invited to perform, but his own relationship with Dylan was very different. The two men first met in 1961, and a year or so later Dylan asked Paxton to join him on a visit to Brooklyn State Hospital – the older man declined, on the grounds that both he and his hero would find the meeting stressful. Yet Paxton had more in common with Guthrie than Bob Dylan: he was himself an Okie, born at the height of the Depression less than thirty miles from Okemah. His CV included a college degree, a spell in the Army, an arrival in Greenwich Village as a fully-formed songwriter, and a raft of radio-friendly compositions. Paxton's frequently covered songs provided him with a comfortable lifestyle, while never compromising his reputation as a no-frills, politically engaged folk singer. Almost revelling in his unfashionable appearance – his only concession to the hippie zeitgeist a slightly drooping moustache – the polo-necked Paxton was the least likely person to be intimidated by Bob Dylan.

At the start of the 'sixties Tom Paxton had listened to and played alongside Dylan numerous times. In London a few years later he had witnessed Dylan's appalling, amphetamine-fuelled behaviour, as captured on the *Don't Look Back* documentary. After that Paxton kept his distance. Thus, he had never seen Bob Dylan perform with the Hawks, and in January 1968 had no idea what to expect.

Yet for anyone too young to have witnessed the self-styled 'Woody Guthrie juke box' aping his hero in Greenwich Village this was a wholly novel experience. Furthermore, no faithful cover of a Guthrie composition had ever appeared on a Dylan album. As it transpired, a further twenty years would pass before a solitary studio recording,

'Pretty Boy Floyd', quietly saw the light of day – perhaps, as Neil Corcoran has suggested, 'out of a combination of tact and self-preservation.'

There was a further novelty given the obscurity of Dylan and the Crackers' middle number, 'Dear Mrs Roosevelt'. Here was an unrecorded song familiar only to Marjorie Guthrie and old comrades like Pete Seeger and Will Geer. Judging by the set list for the only complete recording of Woody Guthrie in concert, the song enjoyed a short shelf life: one night in 1949 the audience at Fuld Hall, in Newark New Jersey, heard all the old favourites; but 'Dear Mrs Roosevelt' wasn't one of them.

This panegyric to a president only survived because the complete lyrics and musical notation could be found in Seeger's labour of love, the endearingly and honestly named *The Nearly Complete Collection of Woody Guthrie Folk Songs*. If the other two songs in the set were compatible with the frontier music emerging from the basement of Big Pink the previous summer, why should 'Dear Mrs Roosevelt' be any different? It wasn't, and yet there was one crucial difference: as will in due course become clear, the audience did not hear 'Dear Mrs Roosevelt' in its entirety; because Dylan chose to drop four verses. Did he do so because the song would have been too long, or because the lyrics were politically sensitive, or both? Presumably Dylan discovered the song in Seeger's 1963 compendium – what was it that attracted him to this particular song? There is always the possibility that Dylan already knew of its existence, but this is unlikely.

Dylan had paid his respects at the Guthrie home in Queens, but it was a brief visit: coffee and condolences offered scant opportunity for him to reacquaint himself with the vast array of writings and drawings which in due course would form today's archives in Tulsa. The family had recently moved from 85th Street on Howard Beach, the shabby Cape

Cod-style house which Dylan had visited in the early 'sixties. Not that an inspection of Guthrie's writings at that time had been anything but cursory. In *Chronicles* Dylan recalled the time he went to see Guthrie at Greystone Hospital in New Jersey asylum, and was urged to check out the papers stored in the basement of the family home: 'He told me that if I wanted any of them to go see Margie, his wife, explain why I was there. She'd unpack them for me.' He duly did so, but – unlike Robert Shelton's archive sampling in the basement some time later – visiting Marjorie proved a miserable experience, with no tangible outcome.

There seems a consensus among Guthrie's biographers that his widow and his daughter, Nora, were never especially fond of Dylan. However, the folk singer and author Daniel Mark Epstein gained a very different impression when he talked to Nora Guthrie: the family felt that the earnest young man from Minnesota was sincere in wanting to connect with his hero, but unconvincing to the point of offensive when he affected to look and sound like Woody on stage. There was, however, sufficient goodwill on both sides that, whatever the erstwhile folk singer got up to later in the decade, they kept in touch – when Dylan and The Band sold out Madison Square Garden in January 1974, front row tickets were reserved for Marjorie and Nora. If there had been any antipathy back in the day then it clearly didn't extend to Woody's son. Reconnecting with Dylan at Carnegie Hall in January 1968, Arlo Guthrie felt the same as he did when they first met in January 1961: 'I just liked the guy because I thought he wrote really cool songs, and he rode a motorcycle, and he had a good band…so I was an admirer, but it was not an idol worship kind of relationship, it wasn't intimidating.'

Anyone other than Bob Dylan would have taken one look at 'Dear Mrs Roosevelt', and deemed it wholly inappropriate for a gathering of the faithful, with every member of the audience keen to hear their fallen comrade's familiar anthems of solidarity and struggle. Perversely – yet characteristically – Dylan looked to rework Woody Guthrie's least known song. The result was a triumph, twice: on 20th January 1968 'Dear Mrs Roosevelt' sounded magnificent, and half a century later it still does.

The same might be said of all three songs, and, judging by the audience response on the box set CD, everyone out front at Carnegie Hall thought the same – including a disillusioned, quietly desperate Phil Ochs. Dylan and the Crackers constituted an alien presence, but also a welcome arrival (for all but a minority, namely Pete Seeger and a few other purists). There is a fine line between worthy and saccharine, and more than one artist veered perilously close to stepping over. Seeger certainly did; as was even more obvious at the Hollywood Bowl, where sadly he was joined by Joan Baez. The harshest critic would see the sincerity and eagerness to inform of a Pete Seeger, a Will Geer, or even a Robert Ryan as the equivalent of a well-intentioned uncle eager to educate mildly truculent teenagers; again, this was especially evident in LA. The most respectful performances sucked the soul out of Guthrie's songs…until, in New York, the final set before the interval. Woody Guthrie was not the nicest of individuals, and – as Ochs discovered, again and again – Bob Dylan doesn't take prisoners. One mean man inspired by another mean man, and doing so in the company of a hard rockin' bar band. It's no wonder Dylan and his sidemen were greeted with surprise, delight, *and* above all, relief.

Bob plays songs about the President!

Twenty years after its last outing Dylan and the Crackers had rescued 'Dear Mrs Roosevelt' from obscurity. Here was a song wreathed in mystery, and almost certainly Woody Guthrie's last complete competition. In 1968 no recording existed of Guthrie performing the song. Fifty years later we still hadn't heard Guthrie's farewell to the President in its entirety – finally, in the summer of 2019, the Dodge Brothers' Mike Hammond recorded the complete song for the podcast that preceded this book. In its subject matter 'Dear Mrs Roosevelt' was not unique: no president in the history of the United States has inspired so many songs to promote and celebrate his time in office. Courtesy of the First Lady, Roosevelt acquired a keen appreciation of America's folk tradition. This was not so surprising given that, despite his patrician background, FDR was no highbrow. His 'man of the people' musical preferences were never more obvious than at election time. As we'll see, Eleanor Roosevelt was remarkably knowledgeable about folk music, and she shared that knowledge with her husband. Woody Guthrie knew who FDR was, and the chances are that FDR knew who Woody Guthrie was.

Mrs Roosevelt certainly knew all about Woody Guthrie, and she could locate him within the explosion of American folk music that occurred in the 1930s, and which in no small way she helped bring about. Eleanor Roosevelt was a party to the first folk revival, and she was witness to the second. Here was someone who listened to Woody Guthrie's earliest recordings, and who lived long enough to hear Bob Dylan's first album. Like Guthrie, she immersed herself in the people's music, from California to the New York island. It's not too absurd to suggest that in the last year of her life Mrs Roosevelt found herself listening to Bob Dylan, recognising from the opening bars of 'You're

No Good' that here was someone of like mind, with the same hunger for the popular and the obscure, the venerable and the freshly composed.

Bob Dylan's lifelong immersion in American popular music is evident in his work, widely documented, and confirmed by those close to him. From Appalachian murder ballads to the Great American Songbook, it's all there. Dylan is fascinated by the archaeology of American music, but at the same time he's appalled by it: nomenclature, categorisation, and cultural/ethnic divides are an anathema (he surely hates the term 'Americana'). As he told the *New York Times* in 1997, 'My songs, what makes them different is that there's a foundation to them. That's why they're still around...They're standing on a strong foundation, and subliminally that's what people want to hear.'

Not always the easiest of reads, Greil Marcus's *Invisible Republic* located Dylan's place firmly within the American folk tradition, its touchstone the folklorist Harry Smith's early 'fifties vinyl box set of over eighty 'old time' songs from two decades before, *American Folk Music* (an 'unstable boil of surrealism and fatalism'). Dylan first heard this collection at the start of the 'sixties in Minneapolis, when briefly a student at the University of Minnesota. Marcus argued that among the various artists anthologised by Smith, a key influence upon the erstwhile undergraduate was the Virginia banjoist and songwriter Dock Boggs. Despite the formidable scholarship and persuasive argument, *Invisible Republic* makes scant mention of the author's liner notes for *The Basement Tapes* album, released by Columbia in 1975: Marcus implied the tracks were authentic recordings, despite their more recent 'enhancement' by The Band (for readers of Don Delillo's eerily prescient *Great Jones Street* a clear case of reality imitating art). For all the ammunition he gives his critics, Marcus is surely right to see Dylan's music-making in the Catskills, and his early 'nineties recording of *Good As I Been To You* and *World Gone Wrong*, the two 'back-tobasics' albums, as restorative and life-enhancing experiences, each in its own way vital to Dylan's survival as a creative force.

Indeed, Dylan said as much in *Chronicles*; and six years earlier in a *Mojo* interview to promote *Time Out Of Mind* ('I didn't have anything...I was concerned with how simple it was to make an album just with myself and nobody else. It was a challenge that I felt it was necessary for me to confront.'). Accompanying the interview was Marcus's album review: 'This is as bleak and blasted as any work a major artist in any field...has offered in ages...the reappearance of the forgotten past in an empty present is a talisman of *Time Out Of Mind...*' The CD's label design embodied Dylan's desire to retrieve and reinvent what he saw as the 'simplified music' of another age: Columbia revived its interwar 'race records' and country outlet, Viva-tonal/Electrical Process (a precursor to later, more ambitious adaptations of antique artwork, especially for the Bootleg Recording box sets).

In 1967 Robbie Robertson was astonished at how many songs, new and old, Dylan brought to Big Pink ('Bob was educating us a little. The whole folkie thing was still very questionable to us...but he remembered too much, remembered too many songs too well' – around ninety altogether). A more recent guitarist, Charlie Sexton, was similarly impressed by his boss's encyclopaedic knowledge: 'I'd keep asking him, "Is this one of yours?" and he'd just mumble in that gravelly voice, "Nah, it's from the Civil War".' The studio sessions for *"Love and Theft"* in 2001 were every bit as educational as the crash course in the nation's old-time songbook at West Saugerties over twenty years earlier.

Theme Time Radio Hour With Your Host Bob Dylan, broadcast between 2006 and 2010 on satellite radio in North America and on the BBC in Britain, offered both entertainment and education. The programme's host drew upon a half-forgotten yet all-inclusive musical heritage that transcended barriers of gender, class, and above all, race and ethnicity. The two-hour show 'President's Day – episode 68' was aired in America on 13th February 2008, during the presidential primaries, and again prior to the November election. Unsurprisingly, the playlist of its genial pro-Obama DJ was dominated by African American artists.

For his Oval Office special Dylan mined the rich load of Roosevelt songs. First off was 'FDR in Trinidad', still a well-known calypso courtesy of Ry Cooder's cover version. However, Dylan played the original recording, a hit in 1937 for Atilla the Hun, otherwise known as Raymond Quevodo. The song was written by fellow West Indian Fitz Maclean, who celebrated two visits to Trinidad by FDR in November and December 1936. Roosevelt was sailing to and from South America with his secretary of state, Cordell Hull: from Brazil they travelled via Uruguay to Argentina, where the President delivered the opening address to a long-forgotten body, the Inter-American Conference for the Maintenance of Peace. 'FDR in Trinidad' namechecked Hull, while outrageously flattering 'the democratic president of the great republic.' It would be tempting to see this as signalling at best indifference and at worst antipathy towards the King Emperor, but in practice songwriters like Maclean and the better known Quevodo regularly celebrated the Royal Family.

FDR's second visit coincided with the abdication of Edward VIII, who was himself the subject of a best-selling calypso. While the latter's knowledge of Caribbean music was presumably non-existent, the former was a fan. Roosevelt spent a lot of time in the West Indies, usually on fishing trips off the Bahamas. He and the First Lady saw Quevodo – 'The Atilla' – and his showband performing at a New York nightclub in 1934, and their enjoyment of calypso music soon became public knowledge. Recorded in a New York studio, 'FDR in Trinidad' became a hit thanks to the novelty of its popularity inside the White House. On the tenth anniversary of Roosevelt revisiting Port of Spain, 'FDR in

Trinidad' was sung by Gerald Clark and His Invaders at a celebration of Caribbean music at Town Hall. Roosevelt had been dead twenty months, but calypso in New York was very much alive, its presence on local radio akin to the BBC Light Programme's promotion of post-Windrush novelty songs at the start of the 'fifties.

Dylan followed 'FDR in Trinidad' with another highly complimentary song, released by the LA jazz label Aladdin Records in 1948: Willie Easton and the Soul-Stirrers' 'Why I like Roosevelt'. This was a gospel tribute to the late president written and recorded in April 1946 by a Philadelphia musician and concert promoter, Otis Jackson, and covered by several black artists in the early postwar era. A colourful character whose equally colourful career lasted into the 1960s, Willie Easton was a Florida huckster and musician who made as much money playing in the street as he did on stage. Easton's unique skills as a steel guitarist and arranger secured him regular work with 'race record' labels in the south, but he clashed with Jackson over copyright and royalty claims for reworked topical songs, and in particular 'Why I Like Roosevelt'.

A fabulous field song, deserving of a millennial hip-hop revival, Jackson's tribute acquired an afterlife courtesy of Jesse Winchester's 1974 album *Learn to Love It*. Winchester, who in 1967 had crossed into Canada to avoid the draft, switched halfway through the song from praising FDR to thanking the Liberal prime ministers who saved him from service in Vietnam, Lester B. Pearson and Pierre Trudeau. Well-intentioned but poorly executed, Winchester's song was a reflection of the album as a whole, intended to celebrate the singer's acquisition of Canadian citizenship. Devotees of presidential paens are better employed listening to Otis Jackson, or to Willie Easton's pirated revamp.

In the 1990s a Dutch musicologist, Guido van Rijn, compiled near definitive written and audio anthologies of blues and gospel singers telling the world what they thought of Franklin Delano Roosevelt. The message overall was one of goodwill. Yet the President's record in challenging segregation and promoting civil rights was poor. Black political activists deemed it abysmal, not least key figures in the 'Harlem Renaissance' such as Langston Hughes, a prolific writer and Communist sympathiser. Hughes's jaundiced view of a procrastinating president inspired the 'Ballad of Roosevelt', published by the left-leaning *New Republic* in late 1934 – after two years of failed promises, poor blacks had 'done stopped believin'/What they been told/By Roosevelt.' Although segregation of government employees was discontinued, Washington took no action to stop discrimination against impoverished African Americans on federal relief programmes. Notoriously, across the second half of the 1930s Roosevelt repeatedly refused to endorse an anti-lynching bill. The President defended his appeasement of the 'Dixiecrats' because he depended upon support from the Democratic Party machine across the southern states. His unholy alliance with southern power-brokers in Congress was vital for the enactment of New Deal legislation. Critically, re-election and control of Capitol Hill depended upon avoiding any issues that might alienate white southern voters.

Nevertheless, many African Americans did hold the President in high esteem. Admirers of Roosevelt in both rural and urban black communities saw him as a man of compassion who through personal affliction enjoyed some insight into their own suffering. Furthermore, he was married to a First Lady consistent in her condemnation of discrimination. Very much her own woman, Eleanor Roosevelt acted as a counterweight to southern-based aides and advisers inside the administration. Her actions in publicly refuting prejudice were of huge symbolic importance, most famously when she quit the Daughters of the American Revolution in protest at their ban on the contralto Marian Anderson performing at Washington's Constitution Hall: FDR authorised the Lincoln Memorial as an alternative venue, and then invited Anderson to sing at a state dinner for King George VI and Queen Elizabeth.

Roosevelt famously sought to minimise how much mid-life polio affected his capacity to operate as Commander-in-Chief, and yet songs in praise of the President invariably highlighted how bravely he had handled his health condition. 'Why I Like Roosevelt' saw Otis Jackson articulate black identification with a crippled yet resilient leader. Even the cantankerous delta bluesman Big Joe Williams was moved to mourn a white man so saintly, 'He helped the crippled boys and he almost healed the blind.' Williams wrote 'His Spirit Lives On' in April 1945. Perhaps it's the primitive percussion driving the song along, but Big Joe's studio recording has the spontaneity and immediacy of a man still in grief. Meanwhile, somewhere between Clarksdale and Chicago James 'Jack of All Trades' McCain recorded 'Good Mr Roosevelt' as a jumping-on-the-bandwagon 78. Poor sound quality means that in places McCain's sentiments are hard to comprehend, but the combination of voice and piano is curiously reminiscent of late period Randy Newman – this song would not sound out of place on the suitably named *Dark Matter*.

Despite the worst effects of the Depression on African Americans across the south no blues singers dared record songs hostile to the President in the way that JB Lenoir did once Eisenhower was in the White House. Born in 1929, Lenoir was too young to take on FDR. His patron in late 'forties Chicago, Big Bill Broonzy, did slip in an oblique reference to Roosevelt when, backed by boogie-woogie pianist Albert Ammons, he premiered 'Just A Dream' at Carnegie Hall in Christmas week 1938. On successive nights the producer, promoter, and anti-discrimination activist John Hammond staged *From Spiritual to Swing*, an all-star 'Evening of American Negro Music'. Broonzy was added to the bill after the news came north of Robert Johnson's death. The audience laughed so much when he sang, 'Dreamed I was in the White House, sittin' in the President's chair/I dreamed he's shakin' my hand, and he said "Bill, I'm so glad you're here"/But that was just a dream...', that Broonzy's label, Vocalion, released a studio version of 'Just A Dream' early in the New Year.

African Americans were by no means alone in singing FDR's praises, with each election marked by campaign and celebratory songs. In 1940 Irving Berlin raised no objection to the Democrats adopting 'God Bless America', the alternative anthem made famous by radio star Kate Smith. However, a more familiar theme tune was 'Happy Days Are Here Again', played first at the Democratic Party's 1932 convention, and resurrected every four years after. The song, first performed in the 1929 Hollywood musical *Chasing Rainbows*, was soon synonymous with the lifting of Prohibition.

Following 'The only thing we have to fear is fear itself...' inaugural speech, on 4 March 1933, W. Lee O'Daniel wrote the victory anthem 'On To Victory Mr Roosevelt'. It's a proto-Keynesian plea for action ('So cut expense tear down the fence between supply demand/Put folks to work don't let them shirk let farmers keep the land'), with a stirring upbeat chorus. Soon after Barack Obama's inauguration Loudon Wainwright III resurrected 'On To Victory Mr Roosevelt' for his scathing commentary on the post-2007 global financial crisis, *10 Songs for the New Depression* (the new President's inaugural address had pointedly drawn on New Deal rhetoric, urging the nation to 'dust ourselves off, and begin again the work of remaking America.') Wainwright added a further verse, and adapted the chorus, to mark the arrival of 'another president to help us find our way/A younger man with darker skin...' Such a prospect would have appalled 'Pappy' O'Daniel, famous in Texas for his songs serenading the Lone Star state, his promotion on the wireless of home-grown country artists like Bob Wills, and his ability to get elected as governor and then senator on a deeply conservative Democratic ticket – ten years after writing 'On To Victory Mr Roosevelt' Senator O'Daniel was loudly demanding that the leader of his party make way for a more cautious, less divisive figure.

Victory in November 1936 saw Kentucky's 'Dixie Songbird' Bill Cox write and record 'We've Got Franklin D. Roosevelt Back Again' for the Sears Roebuck label, Conqueror Records. This was a hillbilly singalong anticipating four more years of FDR 'putting money in our jeans' and keeping liquor legal – here was a President intent on giving everyone a good time. Over two decades later, on their album *Songs From the Depression*, folk revivalists the New Lost City Ramblers resurrected Cox's mail order 78 as a vehicle for virtuoso finger-picking; since then it's been a standard for bluegrass guitarists eager to impress. Bill Cox had a likeminded audience in poor southern whites, but the 1936 presidential election proved a pivotal moment in the black vote swinging solidly behind the Democratic Party: in July 1938 a *Fortune* magazine poll gave President Roosevelt an 84.7% approval rating within 'the Negro community.'

That autumn the topical revue *Sing Out The News* was staged in New York, spawning 'F.D.R. Jones', arguably the most famous song written about Roosevelt. The show was set in Harlem, and the lyrics gently satirised the President's popularity within African American families when naming their baby boys: 'He'll be famous, as famous as he can be/How can he be a dud or a stick in the mud/When he's Franklin D Roosevelt Jones?'. With Ella Fitzgerald on vocals, bandleader Chick Webb's cover of the song was a big hit on both sides of the Atlantic. Other black performers who recorded 'F.D.R. Jones' included Cab Calloway and the Mills Brothers; but the only interpretation on a par with Fitzgerald's was sung by a white artist, Judy Garland. However impressive her performance, the harsh reality is that Garland first sang the song when blacked up as a vaudeville minstrel, playing opposite Mickey Rooney in the 1941 film musical *Babes On Broadway*.

Chick Webb, ace percussionist and Harlem's 'King of Swing', refashioned the big band sound which had come out of Chicago, while still retaining its roots in New Orleans jazz. Webb was first and foremost an entertainer, with little time to reflect on his musical heritage. Yet by the mid-1930s a growing academic interest in 'Afro-American' folklore, including music, paralleled and cut across the eagerness of enthusiasts and serious scholars to record and revive folk songs from New England, Texas, and the Great Plains, as well as the Appalachians. The presumption of an indigenous folk tradition, but one marked by distinctive black/white identities, acquired academic respectability in 1937 when the musicologist Helen L. Kaufmann published her grand narrative of American popular music, *From Jehovah To Jazz*. This ivory-towered presumption of racial bifurcation flew in the face of reality, as anyone listening to say Lead Belly or Mississippi John Hurt would quickly discover. Eleanor Roosevelt was surely sceptical of any attempt to compartmentalise what today we would label roots music.

Franklin and Eleanor Roosevelt – White House folkies

During her husband's first term Eleanor Roosevelt was in correspondence with Virginia's folklorist and music scholar John Powell, accepting his invitation to attend the third White Top Folk Festival in the summer of 1933. The presence of the First Lady gave proletarian America's songs and ballads respectability, reinforced on 21 February 1934 when she broadcast nationwide from the White House to launch Powell's NBC series of 'Southern Folk-Music Programs'. The same year saw St Louis host the first National Folk Festival, an annual gathering of artists and field workers which today takes place under the auspices of the National Council for the Traditional Arts. Encouraged by FDR ('We have the best of man's past upon which to draw brought to us by our native folk and the folk from all parts of the world. In binding these elements into a national fabric of beauty and strength, let us see to it that the fineness of each shows in the completed handiwork.'), the Festival moved to Washington in 1938. Appointed as an Honorary Chair, Eleanor Roosevelt negotiated with the Daughters of the American Revolution to lease Constitution Hall, the Festival's principal venue until its wartime move to New York. She regularly attended concerts, and worked with Paul Green, the NFF's president, to ensure an inclusive agenda. Every race and ethnicity was represented, with Native Americans enjoying pride of place.

Both the First Lady and the President encouraged the New Deal's promotion of indigenous popular music. Various bodies sprung up under the umbrella of the Works Progress Administration, the federal government's flagship initiative. In 'My Day', the column syndicated six days a week to ninety newspapers across the nation, Eleanor Roosevelt regularly urged the American people to rediscover their history through traditional music. Her readers learnt how the presidential couple shared radiogram nights at Hyde Park or inside the White House.

These brief moments of domestic intimacy saw the First Lady and her husband listening to the latest releases from family friend Josh White, revered composer Earl Robinson, concert favourite Burl Ives, and the 'extraordinary' Paul Robeson.

Throughout the postwar years Eleanor Roosevelt would stoutly defend Robeson's right to sing and speak without fear of violent protest, while growing ever more critical of his praise for Stalin's Russia. By 1949 her patience was exhausted, although she did berate the racist and violent demonstrators who sought to silence Robeson's September concert in Peekskill, an outer suburb of New York City (where, as the riot unfolded, Woody Guthrie and Pete Seeger could be found among those literally fighting for free speech). Henceforth the once much loved Robeson was persona non grata in Mrs Roosevelt's 'My Day' column. A decade earlier Eleanor had used her journalism to promote federal funded music programmes; and it was through the WPA that she became directly acquainted with both the Lomax and the Seeger families, twin pillars of the east coast folk revival.

In 1935 musicologist Charles Seeger, the father of Pete (as well as Mike and Peggy), moved from New York to Washington. Seeger was a patrician figure, rooted in old money and Ivy League fraternity. Yet his years as a music professor at Berkeley before and during the First World War had seen him radicalised, to the point that he left his job and spent much of the 'twenties on a musical mission to enlighten poor southerners. Pacifist by inclination, he displayed a condescending if no doubt sincere concern for the well-being of his less privileged compatriots. A naive capacity to idealise the working class translated itself into a fascination with folk music as the purest manifestation of American popular culture. The classics made way for 'people's music' after Seeger met and married his second wife, the composer Ruth Porter Crawford. Seeger had joined the likes of Aaron Copeland and Earl Robinson in a 'Composers' Collective', the members of which wrote well-intentioned but instantly forgettable calls to action in the style of Weimar emigré and Brecht collaborator Hanns Eisler.

These were the sort of songs which Robinson wrote and arranged for various Communist cultural initiatives, notably the People's Chorus of the International Workers Order, a nationwide organisation providing cheap loans and life insurance. Up in the north-west fellow travellers and covert party members avoided these well-intentioned hymns of proletarian solidarity: Seattle Democrats' fund-raising concerts relied on genuine folk songs and, in a classic case of invented tradition, their organisers voted to call them 'hootenannies'. This obscure Appalachian word for a party reached New York in autumn 1941 courtesy of Seeger and Guthrie. Soon it was the default description of every Soho and Greenwich Village jam session or general get-together.

In due course Hanns Eisler would inspire both Woody Guthrie and Billy Bragg, but his music was best suited to Berlin, not Bakersfield or Brooklyn. Thankfully, Ruth Crawford and her collaborator, the veteran poet Carl Sandburg, opened Seeger's eyes to the riches – and radicalising potential – of the American folk tradition. In 1927 Sandburg had published a pioneering collection, *The American Songbag*. On stage he was twenty years ahead of his time, combining folk song with performance poetry. Nine years later Sandburg's book-length poem *The People, Yes* was hugely influential within liberal and leftist circles through its inclusive definition of what constitutes 'the people.' Charles Seeger admired Sandburg greatly, while Pete Seeger enthusiastically adopted *The American Songbag*, and embraced its editor's populist projection of national identity.

Charles Seeger's lingering loyalty to the Composers' Collective died after the tough-talking balladeer Aunt Molly Jackson found herself in New York, entertaining and enlightening east coast leftists with her hard-hitting songs of the Kentucky coalfield. As one might expect of an

Appalachian coal-miner's wife, she told Seeger and his comrades exactly what they could do with their experimental music. Recalling this fiery encounter, Seeger acknowledged: 'We were all on the wrong track – it was professionals trying to write music for the people and not in the people's idiom.'

By the mid-thirties a re-educated Charles Seeger felt suitably qualified to take a job with the Music Unit, a very minor body within the vast relief operation which operated under the auspices of the Resettlement Administration, later renamed the Farm Security Administration. Film and photography flourished within a federal agency keen to record its success in fighting poverty; but music achieved little other than enthnographer Sidney Robertson Cowell's field recordings in the Ozarks and the Appalachians. Cowell was Seeger's assistant, and, while she was out in the wild preserving timeless tunes on shellac, he was busy cultivating Eleanor Roosevelt's affection for home-grown American music.

Seeger's reward was appointment in 1937 as assistant director of the Federal Music Project (from 1939 the WPA Music Program). The Project had energetically promoted music at every level, from high school tuition to concert stage performance, but the emphasis was very much upon the European classical tradition. Seeger sought to widen the scope of the FMP, encouraging those directors eager to embrace music unique to their home state. The second Mrs Seeger – Ruth Crawford – was similarly evangelical after she joined the Project. With Congress eager to cut the agency's budget, there was keen debate inside and outside the Project over what its focus should now be. One sign of shifting priorities was the resignation in May 1939 of the director, Nikolai Sokoloff. Creator and conductor of the Cleveland Orchestra prior to taking on the FMP, Sokoloff resented a repositioning of his original programme at the expense of classical music.

Unsurprisingly, Charles Seeger was invited to organise the White House concert for King George VI and Queen Elizabeth on 8 June 1939: Marian Anderson's arias were juxtaposed with a five-minute medley of mountain music by the Appalachian string band, the Coon Creek Girls (later replicated for a concert recording, and available today on YouTube). No evidence exists to suggest the royal couple shared the Roosevelts' enthusiasm for rocket speed Kentucky bluegrass. Nor was this the only folk music on show. Did the King and Queen politely applaud Library of Congress archivist Alan Lomax's worthy efforts to reinvent himself as a performer; and did FDR's next-day note of appreciation advise he stick to his day job? Keen to orchestrate every aspect of the state occasion, Roosevelt had personally approved the evening's entertainment. Despite the oppressive heat and discomfort, he clearly enjoyed himself, discarding the State Department's much reworked speech to propose a more heartfelt toast to the 'Great Gentleman' and his 'Gallant and Gracious Lady' – the Coon Creek Girls' southern charm had surely worked its magic.

By the time of the royal visit three years of civil war in Spain was at an end. Back in December 1936, when the Duke of York to his deep dismay had found himself head of the British Empire, the fight for Madrid was into its fifth month, with the Nationalist insurgents thwarted in their initial attempt to capture the capital. Open-minded and instinctively progressive, Eleanor Roosevelt was already seen by American war correspondents in Spain as sympathetic to the Republican cause, and therefore willing to persuade her husband that the administration lift its arms embargo. The journalist Martha Gelhorn was both a lobbyist and a friend, sending the First Lady detailed accounts of appalling conditions in Madrid and Barcelona. Eleanor Roosevelt failed to convince FDR that the United States should abandon its non-interventionist position, primarily because the Democratic Party feared losing the Catholic vote. Her only solace was in due course to enjoy music inspired by the bravery of the International Brigades.

Mrs Roosevelt was said to take solace from Ernst Busch's *Six Songs for Democracy*, an album released by Keynote Recordings in 1940, a year after Madrid surrendered to Franco's forces. Exiled from Nazi Germany, Busch was a Communist composer who, when not serving on the front line with the Thaelmann Battalion, had written songs to boost civilian morale. Busch adapted for his comrades Alex McDade's famous rewrite of 'The Red River Valley', 'Jarama Valley'; but he played down the English song's emphasis on sacrifice and loss: the combat experience of veteran street-fighters from Berlin was very different from the British and American baptism of fire at Jarama in February 1937. Pete Seeger and Woody Guthrie tailored their version to the memory of the Lincoln Battalion's virgin soldiers, nearly half of whom were killed the first time the American volunteers went into battle. Together and separately, the two men played benefits for Spanish exiles, with Eleanor Roosevelt courting controversy within Washington by adding her support for Republican refugees entering the United States via Mexico.

Closer to home the First Lady was deeply conscious of indigenous American music's capacity to survive, and to renew itself in the face of economic adversity and social deprivation: migration and the wireless gave rural popular music – black and white – an added urban dimension, not least in the extent to which 'working' songs of the Depression embraced social commentary and a radical political agenda. These were the fledgling years of Chicago blues, with renewed migration north once the economy saw genuine signs of recovery. Blues and gospel inspired quintessentially 'modern' musicians, notably George Gershwin, whose so-called 'folk opera' *Porgy and Bess* was first staged in September 1935 (a parallel for folk and country music were the settings of Ruth Crawford Seeger, Aaron Copland, and even Elliott Carter, unmistakably

American composers seeking a synergy of the nation's classical and folk traditions).

At the same time African American music gained a wider audience and a more progressive patina through the growing appeal of Paul Robeson – black music became increasingly mainstream, recognised by white listeners as underpinning and complementing New Orleans and big band jazz. Eleanor Roosevelt's admiration of Marian Anderson, and her qualified respect for Paul Robeson, reflected the political and aesthetic sensibility of someone sensitive to profound changes in African American popular culture. She applauded the National Folk Festival's desegregated concerts, and the [white] founders' enthusiastic embrace of country blues and Memphis or New Orleans jazz. When the Daughters of the American Revolution vetoed Marian Anderson's performance at Constitution Hall they had no idea that W.C. Handy had played there a year earlier: in 1938 Mrs Roosevelt had been insistent that if the NFF moved to Washington there could be no colour bar on stage.

Left-leaning musicologists like Charles Seeger and the youthful Alan Lomax actively promoted the politicisation of American folk in all its myriad forms. Ace banjo player turned academic Dick Weissman felt either man deserved the title 'Cultural Commissar of American Folk Music'. Their endeavours were endorsed by the American Communist Party, which after 1933 mistakenly perceived 'people's music' as a populist tool for promoting the Popular Front. As in Europe, the Party followed Moscow's edict to abandon its isolated vanguard role, and to propagandise for a broad progressive alliance committed to countering fascist aggression, both open and covert. Singers such as Woody Guthrie gave this alliance an authentic proletarian voice; unlike the well-educated, well-provided for, but nevertheless well-meaning liberals who saw folk music as an agent of change, and who grabbed a guitar – or in Pete Seeger's case a five-string banjo. UCLA sociologist William G.

Roy memorably labelled successive generations of Lomaxes and Seegers as 'movement entrepreneurs and activists.'

Alan Lomax may have entertained a king and queen inside the White House, but his forte was finding artists, not trying to be one. A polymath, a philosopher, a performer, a record producer, a programme maker, and above all an avid field collector, this most unlikely of Texans was the Library of Congress's folk song archivist for five years from 1937. Lomax's qualifications for the job rested on interviews and performances previously lodged with the Library, his contagious enthusiasm, and his precocity – by the age of 24 he had already edited two encyclopaedic volumes of white and 'negro' songs and ballads. His appointment in Washington (held until Congress killed off funding after Pearl Harbor) left Lomax plenty of time to travel the back roads of the nation, socialise and organise with fellow-travelling intellectuals in New York, fulfil his educational remit courtesy of CBS radio and the RCA record label, and introduce the likes of Guthrie and Lead Belly to an audience of white liberals and leftists the length of the eastern sea board.

Inside the Library of Congress Alan Lomax worked closely with a celebrated if controversial man of letters, the modernist writer and New Deal defender Archibald MacLeish. The enduring nature of both men's commitment to 'the people's music' became clear as late as 1968 when a bemused Bob Dylan learnt that the Pulitzer Prize-winning poet was an admirer eager to meet him –a lengthy passage in *Chronicles* is dedicated to the author's meeting with MacLeish at his Massachusetts home, the sexagenarian's words of wisdom amply compensating for time wasted on a foredoomed collaborative project (a joint Broadway production, mapped out while at the same time writing and recording *John Wesley Harding, and* bringing the sessions at Big Pink to a satisfactory conclusion).

Franklin and Eleanor Roosevelt – White House folkies

Like John Hammond, Alan Lomax's early achievements were impressive; and like John Hammond, his finest moments were still to come, starting in the summers of 1941 and 1942 with field trips to Stovell plantation, outside Clarksdale, Mississippi, and the first recordings of McKinley Morganfield – a year later Muddy Waters was on stage in Chicago warming up the audience for Big Bill Broonzy.

Alan Lomax's lifelong passion for folk music and the blues owed much to his father, the Austin autodidact and author, John Lomax. The older Lomax's list of credentials included college administrator, amateur anthropologist, and exhaustive anthologist. Lomax collected cowboy songs; unfortunately, he wasn't averse to sanitising them, or indeed adding a verse or two when deemed appropriate. Lomax junior was more of a purist when it came to song collecting, and thus a reverse role model when the Library of Congress gave its approval to John's most ambitious expedition. The Depression having ended his brief incursion into banking, Lomax made it his mission to establish the fledgling Archive of American Folk Song as a vital element within the Library of Congress. He and Alan set out in the summer of 1933 to record African American work songs: father and son bonded on an exhausting tour of southern prisons, famously discovering Huddie Ledbetter and his twelve-string guitar at Angola State Prison Farm in Louisiana. It was John Lomax who secured Lead Belly a pardon, took him to New York, and put him on stage in convict clothes. The likes of Charles Seeger applauded when the well-dressed Lead Belly told the white honky what he could do with his prison stripes and his condescending paternalism. Nevertheless, Seeger saw John Lomax and his son as natural allies when it came to consolidating folk music within the national psyche.

Criss-crossing the Deep South, hauling a heavy recording machine from one hell hole to the next, John and Alan Lomax were united in a mission of discovery. Yet Marybeth Hamilton's *In Search of the Blues* suggests a working and personal relationship repeatedly tested by

143

clashing egos and conflicting politics. According to fellow folklorist John Henry Faulk, who shared the younger Lomax's radical agenda, Alan's father 'hated old Roosevelt, hated the whole damn New Deal, he was very conservative in his politics.' Yet ironically, it was John Lomax who had fired the Roosevelt family's enthusiasm for folk music: before the First World War he persuaded Teddy to write a characteristically idiosyncratic introduction to *Cowboy Songs and Other Frontier Ballads*, a unique collection of 'wild west' music-making. A further irony was that he loved listening to Woody Guthrie. Having said that, John Lomax hated everything Guthrie represented – rootlessness, mischief making, and a rarely qualified disrespect for authority. All these character traits were what made Woody so attractive to Alan, the junior Lomax.

Woody takes on Washington –
with some help from Pete Seeger

In a 1941 collection co-edited with his son, Alan, song collector John Lomax declared Woody Guthrie to be one of America's finest singers: a hallmark of the 'dust-bowl ballad-maker' was his authenticity. In private Lomax looked down his nose at someone so disrespectful of his elders and betters. The same was certainly not the case for Charles Seeger and his extended family. In the early 'forties they all shared Alan Lomax's readiness to tolerate his protégé's erratic behaviour. Each Seeger saw the need to promote a unique talent and a potent political force; none more so than the idealistic ingénue Lomax hired to help edit a Library of Congress anthology of Guthrie's songwriting. Time and again over the next ten years the 'Dustbowl refugee' tested Pete Seeger's patience, sometimes to breaking point, but in 1940 the younger man embarked on a lifelong mission to make all the world aware of Woodrow Wilson Guthrie and the songs he sang.

The East Coast liberal intelligentsia was tolerant, even supportive, of Guthrie's homespun collectivism, fashioned by direct experience and a readiness to translate ideas into action. By the time Guthrie met Alan Lomax and Pete Seeger, he – and they – endorsed the Communist Party's hardening line towards the New Deal: government intervention was nothing more than the convenient tool of a foredoomed capitalism. Thus, Roosevelt's ostensibly humane reforms were again seen by card-carrying members, and a good many fellow travellers, as serving solely to preserve a free market status quo. With the adoption of a Popular Front strategy in 1935 the Party had revised its initial indictment of the National Recovery Administration as the pathetic face of 'social-fascism': a dramatic improvement in workers' rights courtesy of union-friendly legislation was scarcely compatible with an insistence on FDR as a capitalist wolf in sheep's clothing. The Communist Party chairman, Earl Browder, ran for president in 1936, but – unlike when he stood again in 1940 – the campaign was low key, with Roosevelt's victory seen as progressive forces across America uniting to defend democratic-reformism in the face of incipient fascism. As the New Deal lost energy and momentum, recovery stalled in 1937-38, and defence expenditure rose, so the Communists' disdain for the Administration deepened.

Guthrie's early months in California, where he stayed for two years from 1937, had marked a blessed escape from the horrors of the Dustbowl. However, his initial gratitude and goodwill towards all forms of federal relief ebbed away. Ironically, modest reward on the West Coast as a performer and newspaper columnist generated a growing disenchantment with the New Deal. Woody's intimacy with fellow travellers and Communist Party members fuelled a firm belief that, for all the grand projects in the Tennessee Valley and elsewhere, FDR had failed to match the soaring ambitions of his first inaugural address.

Guthrie had neither the intellect nor the inclination to immerse himself in Marxian dialectics, but he soaked up the Communist critique of global finance, not least Wall Street's capacity to thrive in the face of economic crisis through remorseless exploitation of 'ordinary working men and women.' While in the late 1940s he claimed to have been a member, Guthrie's biographers have found no evidence to suggest that he ever joined the Communist Party. According to Will Geer, there was no way the CPUSA would recruit someone the executive saw as incorrigible, ill-disciplined, and invariably indifferent to the prevailing party line. In practice Guthrie was rarely at odds with whatever policy Moscow imposed on its Californian comrades; but he was open to a whole host of other ideas, many of which were deemed incompatible with Communist orthodoxy.

Woody takes on Washington – with some help from Pete Seeger

In the 1938 mid-term elections Guthrie had still sung his support for local Democratic candidates: 'Lookin' for the New Deal Now' advised 'The Workin' Folks...to stick with Mr. F.D.R./And Mr Olson your gover-nor.' Yet twelve months later a hardened attitude towards Roosevelt and an unashamed affinity with the local Communist Party had cost him his show on the Los Angeles radio station KFVD. Guthrie complemented his 'old-time' and original songs with a typically quirky, often charming, but always unsophisticated, commentary on the state of the nation and the state of the world. This was a level of analysis long on polemic and short on nuance. Not surprisingly, KFVD's owner brusquely dismissed Guthrie's claim that the Soviet Union's non-aggression pact with Germany, and its subsequent occupation of eastern Poland, was crucial to the survival of the world's first socialist state. Such thinking was equally unwelcome when Guthrie and his family settled back in Oklahoma, prompting the restless and unrepentant militant's departure for a more congenial New York City.

From February 1940 Guthrie was based on the eastern seaboard. Unlikely as it may seem, he became a New Yorker; and for a while his family came over from LA. While the journey north was decidedly uncomfortable, not least when hitchhiking out of Pittsburgh in the middle of a snowstorm, Guthrie found Will Geer's apartment a comfortable berth when he arrived in Manhattan. Woody's leisurely experience in his first lodging – days spent reading newspapers in New York Public Library, or fashioning an early version of 'This Land Is Your Land' in a Bowery bar – constituted a leisurely, even stress-free experience, wholly at odds with that mythologised by Bob Dylan in '11 Outlined Epitaphs', the liner notes to *The Times They Are A-Changin'* (here we have a bleak if romanticised picture of gnawing hunger and ceaseless busking in subway cars, mid-town bars, and union halls; a mythical state of affairs which the writer wishes he had either replicated or, ideally, shared).

Alan Lomax famously heard Woody Guthrie's New York debut at the Forrest Theatre in February 1940. Will Geer was staging a 'Grapes of Wrath' benefit for farm workers, and the lowly billed Guthrie caught Lomax's attention by playing up his Okie persona. He was quickly whisked off to Washington for a marathon studio session of songs and stories – only in 1965 did the Library of Congress release a box set of these recordings. Lomax went on to secure Guthrie extensive radio exposure and a contract with Victor to record a package of records, *Dust Bowl Ballads*. In effect the younger Lomax launched his discovery's East Coast career; while receiving scant gratitude for all the time and effort taken to make Guthrie feel at home in an environment very different from his native Oklahoma or his adopted California.

Guthrie collaborated with Lomax and Seeger on the unequivocally anti-capitalist and aptly titled compilation, *Hard Hitting Songs for Hard-hit People*: out of an astonishing 243 songs, 28 were self-penned. In addition, Guthrie drafted a highly personal introduction and an angry, uncompromising commentary. In a militant collection unpublished for over a quarter of a century, Lomax served as the anthologiser and Seeger acted as the arranger. Both men in their different ways hardened Guthrie's antipathy towards the Roosevelt administration, as the White House responded to events in Europe with further increases in defence expenditure.

Not that Guthrie, however disillusioned, ever wholly reneged on the New Deal. In the spring of 1941 he reasserted the state's potential for rescuing Roosevelt's 'forgotten man' when recording his Columbia River songs, commissioned by the Bonneville Power Administration in Washington state. He was employed for a month, on the assumption that after four weeks the Department of the Interior would find out about his Communist sympathies and sack him. In that short space of time Guthrie wrote an astonishing twenty-six songs for the soundtrack of a feature film which in its original form never saw the light of day. Seeger's favourite, which he sang at the 1970 concert, was the majestic, and suitably panoramic 'Roll On, Columbia'. A more obvious choice for Dylan and the Crackers was 'Grand Coulee Dam', and with it an oblique reference to FDR: 'Uncle Sam took up the challenge in the year of thirty-three/For the farmer and the factory and all of you and me.' Guthrie later linked construction of the publicly-funded dams to the war effort, but his involvement in the BPA project preceded Operation Barbarossa let alone Pearl Harbor.

Guthrie's seventeen-verse ballad 'Tom Joad', written in the spring of 1940 for *Dust Bowl Ballads* and set to the tune of the Carter Family's 'John Hardy', was wholly supportive of federal efforts to alleviate the horrendous conditions in which so many migrant families were forced to live. The song echoed its fictional protagonist's praise for the Farm Security Administration settlements set up in California as a secure and genuinely communitarian alternative to the 'jungle camps' hastily erected by the orchard owners or their migrant workers. The FSA as a force for good is further highlighted by the contrast between the well-run 'Weedpatch Camp' in *The Grapes of Wrath* and the shockingly poor 'Hooversville' Guthrie stumbles across in *Bound For Glory*. 'Weedpatch' was based on the FSA's Arvin Sanitary Camp, run by Tom Collins. Steinbeck drew heavily on Collins' encyclopaedic knowledge of Okie songs and stories, and he dedicated his novel 'To Tom who lived it.' In 1942 Eleanor Roosevelt provided the text for *This Is America*, a morale-boosting album of photographs by the sociologist Frances Cooke Macgregor. The First Lady wrote approvingly of the fifteen FSA camps, quoting two verses of 'Tom Joad', and implicitly endorsing Woody Guthrie's radical sentiments.

By the time Mrs Roosevelt's *This Is America* was published, the nation was at war and Woody Guthrie was a member of the Almanac Singers; but very much the square peg in a round hole. The Almanac Singers can best be described as a folk group of middle-class, generally well-educated, serious-minded agit-propagandists who enjoyed mixed fortunes before and after Pearl Harbor. The group's driving force was Pete Seeger, collaborator, travelling companion, and faithful acolyte of Guthrie from the moment Alan Lomax brought the two men together in the spring of 1940. Guthrie singing with the Almanac Singers gave the group an empathy and authenticity they demonstrably lacked, so it's unsurprising that members shared Seeger's excitement when the man from Okemah started playing with them in the early summer of 1941. Over succeeding months Seeger's principal partners, Lee Hays and Millard Lampell, saw their tolerance of Guthrie's wayward lifestyle tested to the limit. Lampell had been writing freelance for the *Nation* when he struck up a friendship with Hays, a southern poet and lyricist with a background in 'people's theatre.' Both men found Woody unreliable, unpredictable, and unruly, and yet at the same time they could see that here was a songwriter in full creative flow, with a stage presence they could never emulate. The reality is that, while Guthrie's friendship with the saintly Seeger defied differences of class, age and education, there was little to connect him with Hays, Lampell, and the other earnest young leftists who at various times made up the Almanac Singers.

Unusually, these were musicians whose name was known in the White House, not least because their leader was a Seeger and their mentor a Lomax. If Eleanor Roosevelt's engagement with folk music ebbed and flowed across the course of the 1930s, the arrival of the Almanac Singers had revived her interest. This was a group led by a young man who she greatly admired: on 19 February 1941, in her syndicated daily column, she praised Alan Lomax for his energetic promotion of folk music, not least within the armed forces. Yet this was also a group which on record and in performance sang ceaselessly about her husband's supposed failings, not least his refusal to adopt a pacifist stance towards the war in Europe.

Woody takes on Washington – with some help from Pete Seeger

Once the Soviet Union and the United States were at war then old quarrels could be forgotten, but before June 1941 the situation was very different. With far left and far right forming an unholy alliance in advocating isolationism, both First Lady and President were outraged by the Almanac Singers' debut album. *Songs For John Doe* was recorded while Guthrie was back on the West Coast and yet to join the group full-time. Small and vulnerable, the Keynote record company released its package of six songs on 'Almanac', an anonymous label. Pete Seeger took the lead on five of the six songs (the traditional ballad 'Billy Boy' had bluesman and occasional Almanac Josh White on guest vocals). Four numbers were self-penned, each of which was unflinchingly hostile towards Roosevelt, all but labelling him a war monger. Seeger could sing songs, but he couldn't write them. His lyrics constituted little more than name-calling and sloganizing. They contrasted sharply with those of the stand-out composition, 'Ballad of October 16'. On this song Millard Lampell, eager to replicate the trenchancy of Guthrie's 'telling-it-like-it-is' lyrics, excoriated FDR for forcing conscription through Congress: 'He said, "I hate war, and so does Eleanor/But we won't be safe 'till everybody's dead."' On stage, this was the anthem which generated the biggest response from the Almanacs' predominantly pacifist audiences.

The Almanac Singers and their 'incendiary' album were in many respects the creation of Alan Lomax. It was Lomax who, on its release in May 1941, ensured *Songs For John Doe*'s unusually high profile; and it was Lomax who secured the album's speedy withdrawal once the Soviet Union found itself under attack. The launch of the German offensive on 22 June 1941 saw the Communist Party quickly abandon its non-interventionist stance: how soon could the United States come to the aid of Stalin's Russia? Lomax duly convinced Eric Bernay, the owner of Keynote Records, to cease distribution of his politically embarrassing record, and to destroy any remaining stock. Bernay happily acquiesced, but the Almanac Singers' popularity saw him promptly release *Talking Union*, an uncontentious album of labour songs.

Lomax's influence on Woody Guthrie in 1940-41 was equally potent, not least in encouraging a succession of anti-war and/or anti-capitalist songs that conveyed a real sense of anger. From August 1940 Guthrie featured prominently on Lomax's thrice-weekly radio programme for CBS, *Back Where I Come From*, his songs echoing the show's pacifist, socially conscious message. The 'authenticity' of Guthrie, contrasting so sharply with the comfortable upbringing of Seeger and his fellow Almanacs, manifested itself in a harsher tone of delivery, even when singing as part of the group.

Yet Seeger himself urged Guthrie to play predominantly political songs when on stage. Trade unionists instinctively acknowledged Woody as genuine and as one of their own, whereas the other Almanacs never wholly convinced audiences of their adopted proletarian credentials: why, smartly suited workers asked, did Seeger et al dress down when putting on a show, and urge grown men and women to sing songs last heard in junior high. Union-organised rallies and concerts which featured the Almanac Singers were overwhelmingly white. It was the make-up of the audiences, William G. Roy points out in *Reds, Whites, and Blues*, which explains why Lead Belly, Sonny Terry, and Josh White rarely if ever played alongside Seeger, Guthrie, and the other comrades.

Like Seeger, Hays, and Lampell – and Alan Lomax – Guthrie had been insistent throughout 1940 and into the spring of 1941 that Stalin was right to denounce Europe's 'imperialist war', and that Roosevelt should do the same. He believed the French and British governments had sought to avoid war by pointing Hitler eastwards, but had then paid the price of their folly. This conclusion was consistent with the view of many left-leaning intellectuals, some of whom displayed undisguised pleasure when witnessing Chamberlain's demise and Churchill's desperation. In his 'Woody Sez' columns for LA's *People's World* and later the *Daily Worker* he defended the Molotov-Ribbentrop Pact. The *Daily Worker*'s circulation had grown to around 30,000 in the late 1930s after it started to cover sport and the arts; lively baseball reports and concert reviews were a welcome relief from the grim Stalinism of its editorial and news pages. A 'Woody Sez' commentary such as 'Adolph and Nevilline', published in the Communist Party newspaper on 12 March 1941, exemplified Guthrie's readiness to reduce complex international affairs to a succession of homespun aperçus, articulated in a cheesy fake dialect, the charm and attraction of which soon faded.

Guthrie's earliest performances in New York saw him convey an uncompromising anti-war stance courtesy of his well-honed everyman persona: "If someone simple like me can see that war is a way for the rich and powerful to control and destroy the poor and powerless, then why can't you educated folks?". Although still unknown he was acclaimed at a benefit for Spanish Republican refugees on 25 February 1940 after singing 'Why do you stand there in the rain?'. This was a caustic commentary upon FDR's fiercely anti-Soviet speech to the six thousand delegates of the American Youth Congress gathered on the White House lawn a fortnight earlier. The drenched delegation had been invited at the behest of Eleanor Roosevelt, despite clear evidence that the previously broad-based coalition was now a front for the Young Communist League; among whose members was Pete Seeger. On stage at Manhattan's Mecca Temple was a singer named after the last president to lead the United States into war criticising the current president for covertly seeking to do the same – *any* support for the Allies was unacceptable ('And the war lords play the same old game again/They butcher and they kill, Uncle Sam foots the bill' – immediately one thinks of Dylan, particularly 'God On Our Side' and 'Masters of War', but the brutal directness of the lyrics signal a less subtle polemicist, Phil Ochs).

Guthrie was preaching to the converted, and overnight he became a hero of New York's progressive intelligentsia: what Alan Lomax saw from the wings at the Forrest Theatre benefit was an authentic 'voice of the people' whose star was already in the ascendancy.

From the spring of 1940 Woody Guthrie made it acceptable for left-leaning musicians to berate the President. He complemented his on-stage attacks with a running commentary on FDR's alleged militarism in his 'Woody Sez' column for *People's World*, and his intermittent contributions to the *Daily Worker*. The only time Guthrie tempered his pro-Soviet, anti-intervention message was when he appeared on the radio, a handy income source in the summer of 1940.

The Almanac Singers were similarly disrespectful, covering 'Why do you stand there in the rain?' on stage, and recording *Songs for John Doe* – where Guthrie led, Millard Lampell followed. The sardonic, disrespectful sentiments of 'Ballad of October 16' set a new high – or a new low – in satirising the White House. Roosevelt supposedly dismissed these songs on the basis that no-one would hear them. Yet just occasionally they would be sung in front of a large audience, as in May 1941 when the Almanacs performed before thousands of striking transport workers at a rally in Madison Square Garden. It was the group's last performance of any significance before Hitler's invasion of the Soviet Union, and Guthrie's arrival back in New York.

Woody and Pete go to war – and mourn the President

Just as the Communist Party after June 1941 viewed the war in Europe as a heroic anti-fascist struggle, so Woody Guthrie, now back in New York, exhorted Pete Seeger, Lee Hays, and whoever else currently constituted the Almanac Singers, to adopt a wholly different stance towards their president: henceforth Roosevelt must be exhorted to maximise American support for the Allies. In the little known song 'On Account of This New Situation' Guthrie recognised the irony of so many political contortions in so short a space of time. Bess Lomax, the sister of Alan, recalled how, 'Woody was also continually frustrated by the curves of history which were wiping out our repertoire. He really wanted to write songs that would last...' Meanwhile Seeger, in the words of his biographer, 'faced the occupational hazard of political singers: song obsolescence.' Interviewed by Tim Robbins in 2006 for a Pacifica Radio tribute programme, Pete Seeger portrayed Guthrie as the Almanacs' de facto commissar. Political sophisticates like Lampell and Hays didn't need their semi-detached comrade to point out what every party member and fellow traveller were all too conscious of: FDR remained a legitimate target, but only if the United States failed to give Stalin all he needed to stem the Nazi tide. Meanwhile Lomax airbrushed *Songs For John Doe* out of the Almanacs' already chequered history.

With his family back in California, an unencumbered Guthrie joined the Almanac Singers as a permanent member. Before embarking on a tour of the West Coast, followed by concerts across the north-east, the group spent a day in the studio with Lomax. Guthrie sang lead vocals on three of the songs recorded for *Deep Sea Chanteys and Whaling Ballads* and for *Sod-Buster Ballads*. These antique albums were released in the late summer of 1941 by General Records, a New York label only marginally better known than Keynote. Not surprisingly the Almanacs enjoyed only modest record sales, but they were now attracting more newspaper and radio coverage. However, long hours together on tour led to sharp differences of opinion within the group. Lampell grew increasingly unhappy with Seeger's reductionist view of global politics, shared in his own idiosyncratic way by Guthrie; but in the end it was Lee Hays who left in a huff. From then on group membership became even more fluid than it had been before.

The contortions in the Communist Party ended only after America entered the war in December 1941. Throughout this period Guthrie generated a steady stream of anti-fascist compositions, of varying quality. Between Barbarossa and Pearl Harbor isolationism remained a potent force in domestic politics; for the Almanacs its right-wing advocates were now objects of scorn and no longer uncomfortable allies. Although written sometime after the Japanese attack on Hawaii, Guthrie's 'Mister Charlie Lindbergh' epitomised the tone adopted by his group towards Washington's most vocal isolationists, the America First Committee. Roosevelt's predecessor, Herbert Hoover, joined a long list of malcontents, but the song's principal target was the Atlantic-crossing Charles Lindbergh, accused of encouraging Axis aggression as a means of advancing his presidential ambition – an ambition Philip Roth famously returned to in his counterfactual novel, *The Plot Against America*.

As in the mid-thirties Roosevelt could now look to support from organised labour and the left, in this instance advancing his pro-British and now presumably pro-Soviet agenda – but only so long as the transition to a quasi-war economy was not at the expense of jobs, wages, and workers' rights. Essentially, this was the revived Popular Front message of Almanac songs written and performed in the summer and autumn of 1941, and it remained so in material composed after the onset of war brought the group into the political and cultural mainstream.

Woody and Pete go to war – and mourn the President

In the immediate aftermath of Pearl Harbor the Almanac Singers were hot property, signed to a major New York agency and, courtesy of CBS's Saturday night showcase, broadcasting to an audience of over thirty million listeners. Respectability was short lived as an FBI investigation and hostile newspaper coverage saw Seeger's group become the focus of unwanted attention. Network broadcasts and a record contract with Decca brought only brief success once charges of double standards and Communist Party membership accelerated the Almanacs' demise. Dropped by their agent and their record label, the group's bookings dried up. Long drives to solitary gigs, and fierce quarrelling over money and lifestyle (Seeger's puritanism verses Guthrie's and Hays's hedonism), saw old friendships tested to the limit.

By the summer of 1942 the Almanac Singers scarcely existed as a group, its members absorbed into the armed forces and the war economy. Their break-up followed a fifth and final album: *Dear Mr. President* was recorded by Alan Lomax in February 1942 and released by Keynote two months later. As signalled in the title song – a Seeger talking blues – the album sought reconciliation with Roosevelt, in order to 'lick Mr Hitler' and together secure 'a better America.' Almost every song stressed inclusivity and a common effort, *and* a newly acquired respect for FDR. Lomax ensured that a copy of his protégés' olive branch be heard in the White House, boasting later that the album had earned presidential approval.

Like the Almanac Singers' earlier albums, *Dear Mr. President* was a worthy effort, but singularly lacking in excitement. This was an act better seen than heard. However, one song stood out, famously standing the test of time. Woody Guthrie let Pete Seeger sing 'The Sinking of the Reuben James', his memorable lament for the sailors drowned when their destroyer was torpedoed six weeks prior to Germany declaring war on the United States. The ship's loss was a key moment in Roosevelt's increasingly belligerent response to submarine attacks on American shipping. At the Hollywood Bowl in September 1970 Seeger chose 'The Sinking of the Reuben James' as his contribution to the evening's entertainment. This was an appropriate selection given Seeger's heroic role in convincing Guthrie that an interrogative chorus ('Tell me what were their names?') meant 115 verses – one for every sailor killed – might be shrunk to four.

'The Sinking of the Reuben James' presaged Woody Guthrie's principal contribution to the war effort: from June 1943 to August 1944 he served as a merchant seaman in the Atlantic and the Mediterranean. With Cisco Houston a shipmate – unsurprisingly both men brought their guitars on board – Guthrie twice saw his ships torpedoed, with another crippled by a mine. Before and during his service at sea he wrote, ranted, and sometimes even recorded, a remarkable number of propagandist anthems. Most were rooted in a simple narrative of how unionised workers in every Allied nation were bound by a common goal of fascism's inevitable downfall. The song 'All You Fascists Bound to Lose' dates from this time; as does 'This Machine Kills Fascists', the legendary slogan on Guthrie's Gibson. The working men and women in these songs were united also in a shared belief that Stalin's soldiers had suffered disproportionately given the absence of a Second Front.

Woody Guthrie wrote prolifically from the moment America entered the war. Yet these deeply political, emotionally charged, deliberately morale-boosting compositions constituted a fraction of his overall output. Prose and poetry, much of it unpublished, articulated a simple polemical message: American workers must be uncompromising, both in their commitment to winning the war overseas *and* to protecting their hard won rights and liberties at home. This was an anti-fascist crusade rooted in proletarian solidarity, where even the staunchest blue collar patriot had to acknowledge the Soviet Union's unique contribution.

Guthrie was by no means unique in expressing such sentiments. In 1943 the acapella gospel group, the Golden Gate Jubilee Quartet, secured extensive air time on the radio after recording Willie Johnson's 'Stalin Wasn't Stallin''. Josh White's tribute to Soviet endeavour, 'Little Man', was especially notable given the close relationship he and his wife enjoyed with the Roosevelts. Although White had sung at FDR's second re-inaugural, regular trips to the White House only started after his anti-segregation album *Southern Exposure* became Keynote's biggest seller to date, prompting an invitation from Eleanor to play at an official reception, and to then meet the President. White's work with the Almanac Singers was conveniently forgotten, but so too was *Southern Exposure*'s demand for desegregation on the shop floor and on the front line. A genuine voice of protest, hailed in Harlem by the likes of Langston Hughes, Josh White's credibility within the African American community collapsed once newspapers named him the 'Presidential Minstrel'.

Churchill's presence within the 'Big Three' could scarcely be ignored, but Woody Guthrie dismissed his rapprochement with Stalin as a short-lived marriage of convenience. Visiting Britain in mid-1944, on his last tour of duty as a merchant seaman, did nothing to change Guthrie's mind. Roosevelt had no comparable history of Bolshevik-baiting, hence the belief shown in songs such as 'Ballad of Teheran' that only the Kremlin and the White House could forge 'our new union world.' The Teheran conference of 28-30 November 1943 had marked a high water mark in ostensibly harmonious relations between the Big Three, or to be more precise, in dealings between the Soviet and American delegations (the British delegation let it be known that FDR had treated Churchill shoddily, and that his second son, Elliott, had behaved appallingly). This was the conference at which Stalin notoriously proposed a toast to the victorious Allies shooting fifty thousand prominent Germans, generating silent agreement from

Roosevelt and a vehement protest from Churchill. For the American left a historic meeting in Iran between the Soviet leader and the President signalled the clear potential for postwar harmony. Yet such a goal could only be achieved if Roosevelt secured a fourth term – who else in Washington had the authority and experience to retain the Russians' healthy respect?

Viewing Stalin's closure of the Comintern as a statement of intent, in May 1944 American Communists demonstrated their faith in the strength and efficacy of the grand coalition by voluntarily dissolving the party. Former party members rallied round a 'Roosevelt Bandwagon', intended to complement the official campaign of the Democratic party machine. Their enthusiasm was scarcely dented when the idealistic New Dealer Henry A. Wallace returned from a vice presidential tour of Russia to discover Roosevelt aides now deemed the anonymous senator from Missouri Harry Truman a safer running mate: states were persuaded to choose a candidate as unfamiliar to the President as he was to most of the delegates on the convention floor.

Singing at events organised by the ostensibly non-party Communist Political Association, Woody Guthrie's involvement in the 1944 re-election campaign was a largely unhappy experience. Long and tedious train journeys on the 'Roosevelt Bandwagon' took him far from his new home on Coney Island, shared with future wife Marjorie Mazia and their daughter Cathy. At large union-backed rallies Guthrie, Cisco Houston, Will Geer, and other left-leaning artists out on the campaign trail were invariably well received. Each rally ended with performers and politicians all on stage singing 'The Girl with the Roosevelt Button'; Guthrie loathed the song, which fittingly has disappeared without trace (the campaign song can't be found in the archives of the presidential library and museum at Hyde Park, the Roosevelts' home beside the Hudson River in up-state New York). Those meetings not staged by organised labour were often miserable affairs. Radicals with no obvious track record of backing the President were labelled opportunists by their critics. Outside of New York artists like Guthrie and Geer encountered fierce hostility. Partisan newspaper coverage of virulent pro-Republican, anti-Communist protests resulted in half-empty halls, with a consequent effect on morale. On-stage quarrels were commonplace. Nevertheless, the final result brought satisfaction with a job well done, and Guthrie returned to writing, a weekly radio show, concerts, and any other means of making money to pay the rent and fund the food bill; he had no intention of going back to sea, assuming the war would be over before he heard again from the draft board.

Whatever money Woody Guthrie made in the winter of 1944-45 it wasn't from record sales. In March 1945 Asch Records released *Folksay*, a sixteen-song selection on three discs. The songs derived from Guthrie's most comprehensive recording session, almost a year earlier. Ironically, that session came about courtesy of John Lomax, a man who, as we've seen, admired Guthrie's singing as much as he loathed his politics. Somewhat surprisingly, Lomax's *Cowboy Songs and Other Frontier Ballads* was a book beloved of New York record producer Moe Asch. Asch and his family had escaped persecution in prewar Poland, but in the 1920s he returned briefly to central Europe: in Weimar Germany he discovered a talent for repairing radios, a love of minority music, from kletzmer to cowboys, and a readiness to embrace radical politics. By April 1944, when Guthrie wandered into the mid-Manhattan studio of Asch Records, its proprietor was a veteran promoter of progressive causes, Yiddish culture, home-grown folk, and cutting-edge electronics.

Moses Asch was the only man who could talk on equal terms with both Alan Lomax and Albert Einstein. Strangely, for someone who seemed to know everyone left of Mayor La Guardia, Asch had never heard of Woody Guthrie. Yet by the spring of 1944, in New York if not the nation at large, the writer of *Bound For Glory* had become a minor celebrity – and a master of self-mythologising. The success of Guthrie's memoir rested on the timing of its publication, its author reinventing himself as a seer of the Depression, urging friends and neighbours in mid-thirties Texas to prepare for the day America would find itself fighting Hitler and Mussolini. With Guthrie and Houston due to ship out in mid-May, Moe Asch brought both men into the studio to record a jaw-dropping 125 songs and tunes. A shortage of shellac meant a twelve-month delay before *Folksay* was released. The collection's mixed reviews and meagre sales reflected Asch's uninspiring choice of takes, with the earliest version of 'This Land Is Your Land' left languishing in the stacks.

In the spring of 1945 Guthrie retained his belief in Franklin Delano Roosevelt as fundamentally a force for good. Reporting of the Yalta conference suggested continuing good relations with Russia, and red baiting remained muted. Politically energised, Guthrie remained positive about the future even as his widely assumed Communist affiliation again came to limit his creative freedom and his ability to make a living: in February 1945 Naval Intelligence revoked his seaman's papers, rendering him liable for the draft. Never was a man less suited to life in a uniform, but from May to December he served as a signaller in the US Army. The title was a misnomer as in reality Woody was a painter. He maintained the depot notice-board, with its predictable leftist bias, while doing all he could to secure an early discharge. On leave in November 1945 Guthrie married Marjorie, his new wife noting early signs of incipient Huntington's disease.

Woody Guthrie had been blacklisted well before Roosevelt's death on 12 April 1945. Yet the Guthrie family was in no way immune to the deep sense of grief that engulfed all but Roosevelt's fiercest critics in the immediate aftermath of his death, on 12 April 1945. Robert Klara, in *FDR's Funeral Train*, a fascinating account of the dead President's final train journey, from Georgia to Hyde Park, described the dramatic scenes when his body was brought back to Washington: 'As the cortege crossed 9th Street…an elderly black woman broke across the police line and ran out onto Pennsylvania Avenue. "Lord God," she wailed, "take care of us now."' In 'Dear Mrs Roosevelt' Woody captured the moment when he learnt that FDR was dead: 'I was a GI in my army camp that day he passed away/And over my shoulder talkin' I could hear some soldier say/"This world was lucky to see him born."' Guthrie was in fact still a civilian when news broke of the President's passing. Nevertheless, the verse echoes a grieving soldier's remark to Frances Perkins, Roosevelt's Labor Secretary, outside the White House: '"I felt as if I knew him. I felt as if he knew me – and I felt as if he liked me."' Another soldier, Bill Livingstone, was in a POW camp when he and the other prisoners heard of the President's death: 'Tears ran down my face, as they did on the faces of the rest of the group.'

Woody Guthrie's misfortunes, and those of his comrades similarly blacklisted – as well as the Communist Party's reversion from coalitionist inclusivity to its former sectarian status – were all seen as direct consequences of Truman's arrival in the White House. The deterioration in east-west relations, evident in Greece even prior to the Yalta conference, was attributable in the eyes of the left to a change of administration. In his behaviour towards the Soviet Union Truman was portrayed as manifesting inexperience, nuclear triumphalism, and a deep-rooted antipathy towards Communism at home and abroad.

Stuck in an Illinois barracks Guthrie railed over the absence of the Communist Party at such a critical time, asking himself why the nation went to war given that the right again appeared in the ascendant. However, the re-establishment of a staunchly pro-Moscow Party in the late spring of 1945, and the rapid spread of industrial action in the weeks following VJ Day, gave Guthrie cause for optimism – as did news of his imminent discharge. Guthrie's version of events immediately following the German surrender, and his insistence that FDR would have avoided Truman's perceived miscalculations, resembles a view of the period popular on the left at the time of the singer's death.

As postwar politics became more polarised, and state harassment of Communists became harsher, so Woody's rough-hewn political analysis became increasingly moulded by a distorted nostalgia. Thus in his mind the Roosevelts became more radical than had ever been the case, certainly as far as the late President was concerned. In one of his many letters to Moe Asch, written on 15 July 1946, Guthrie claimed both Eleanor and FDR were as much victims of a mass smear campaign as the millions of Americans currently 'branded by the capitalist machine as "communistic".' Once more a civilian Guthrie worked with Asch on several projects, notably the song cycle *Ballads of Sacco and Vanzetti*, commemorating the anarchists executed in 1927 on trumped-up charges of murder. The album only appeared in 1964, reflecting the difficulty Asch Records experienced in releasing politically contentious material. The harsh reality was that a collection of Woody Guthrie recordings was unlikely to generate a decent return for either the company or its artist.

People's Songs – the rise and rise of Henry Wallace

Guthrie saw Roosevelt's legacy in the array of Popular Front-style bodies set up to challenge the Truman administration's increasingly interventionist response to perceived Soviet threats across the world and in America's own back yard. Americans for Democratic Action was a late entry into the field. Boasting the former First Lady as a member and retaining close links to the Democratic Party, the ADA was a powerful counterweight to the much more left-wing Progressive Citizens of America. The PCA's criticism of Truman was uninhibited by any residual party allegiance or refusal to countenance the Communist point of view. It was formed in 1947 from a merger of the National Citizens Political Action Committee and the better known Independent Citizens' Committee for the Arts, Sciences and Professions. The ICCASP's high profile supporters in New York and Hollywood swiftly disassociated themselves from their new home in the Progressive Citizens of America once allegations of Communist infiltration became more vociferous.

In the immediate postwar years Woody Guthrie's warm regard for the Roosevelts owed much to Eleanor's continued immersion in public life, not least her chairmanship of the United Nations Commission on Human Rights and her prominence in Americans for Democratic Action. Americans for Democratic Action was established in January 1947 to help realise the ideals of the UN and, in its own words, 'To keep the New Deal dream – its vision and its values of an America that works fairly for all – alive for generations to come.' Woody, like most acolytes of Progressive Citizens for America, failed to note the new body's formal denunciation of Communism, and its status as a progressive force firmly rooted within the broad coalition that constituted FDR's political legacy: Eleanor Roosevelt's presence in the ADA ensured its unequivocal allegiance to the Democratic Party.

Henry Wallace had served throughout Roosevelt's first two administrations as Secretary of Agriculture, a post held by his father ten years before. His term in office was marked by controversy, albeit largely confined to the corridors of power. Never having stood for office, there was a certain naivety and innocence when confronted with the harsh reality of party politics. Wallace was a charming, good-looking, and intelligent mid-westerner liked by both Franklin and Eleanor; they indulged and even encouraged his interest in eastern mysticism. This unique claim to expertise in both agronomy and the occult was derided by Wallace's critics in the Republican and the Democratic parties, all of whom considered him dangerously liberal in his thinking. Republicans deemed him a traitor, while Democrats asked why he had served in the Administration for three years before finally switching sides. Wallace was therefore deeply unpopular within the Democratic party machine, and his nomination as vice president in 1940 was solely because FDR over-rode all objections.

An experienced administrator, Wallace enjoyed a significant range of responsibilities for the nascent war economy before and after Pearl Harbor. Turf wars with the Commerce Department saw the VP's dealings with conservative Democrats deteriorate to the point where Roosevelt felt it expedient to redefine Wallace's role within the Administration. No longer exercising executive power, Wallace henceforth fulfilled the Vice President's traditional role as an ambassador. To his credit, a tour of South America saw several governments declare war on the Axis. Later, however, he participated without protest in a strictly orchestrated tour of the Gulag Archipelago, returning home to restate the shared values of the United States and the Soviet Union: Kolyma's labour camps were compared with those of the New Deal; and it would be another ten years before Wallace finally admitted that the well-fed 'prisoners' he met were in fact disguised guards. While finding favour with Stalin, Wallace had previously enraged Winston Churchill: in May 1942, with the Japanese at the gates of India, a much-publicised address to New York's Free World Association had welcomed 'the century of the common man,' free from domestic exploitation and colonial oppression.

By 1944 the Vice President was deemed an electoral liability, and he was dropped from the ticket in favour of Harry Truman. To his opponents' chagrin, Wallace was nominated as Secretary of Commerce in the new Administration. In the Senate conservatives on both sides of the aisle sought to prevent his confirmation, or at the very least curb his powers. Wallace was confirmed, and his department left intact, but many in Congress were appalled by his call for a generous minimum wage, and for aggressive interventionism should the return of peace trigger a slump in the economy. As far as Wallace was concerned the war was merely an interruption in the Federal Government's pursuit of economic prosperity *and* a fairer and more equitable society: if the war effort had actually aided the pursuit of these admirable goals then the argument for top-down control and direction in peacetime was that much greater.

In the year after Roosevelt died Henry Wallace became closely associated with those left-leaning organisations insistent that Truman had turned his back on New Deal values. Increasingly remote from White House thinking the Commerce Secretary was forced to resign in early autumn 1946 after publicly urging an emollient policy of peaceful co-existence with the Soviet Union. On 12 September Wallace addressed a mass meeting of the Independent Citizens' Committee for the Arts, Sciences and Professions in Madison Square Garden. Unwisely he revealed the content of a letter written to Truman on 23 July in which Wallace questioned the Administration's response to the 'long telegram' sent five months earlier by George Kennan, chargé d'affaires in Moscow. The diplomat's five thousand words despatch to Secretary of State James Byrnes is now seen as a key moment in America recognising the reality of a Soviet threat. Kennan portrayed that threat as rooted in a potent combination of revolutionary ideology and Stalin's keen sense of insecurity. Returning to Washington Kennan urged the USA to take the lead in forging a global network of security arrangements intended to contain Soviet ambitions, most especially in central and western Europe; his influential article for the July 1947 issue of *Foreign Affairs*, written under the pseudonym 'X', projected a new world order which Wallace found an anathema.

Wallace's indiscreet speech to the ICCASP in September 1946 had made public a fundamental belief that Kennan and his admirers in and around the White House, notably the veteran Navy Secretary James Forrestal, had completely misread Soviet intentions. Yes, Stalin felt insecure, but, given the regime's experience after 1917 and June 1941, this was wholly understandable. Thus the United States and its allies should be accommodating not threatening. Wallace's analysis ran counter to strategic thinking and policy development as they unfolded across the winter and spring of 1946-47, particularly after the former chief of staff General George C. Marshall succeeded James Byrnes at the State Department in April 1947. The former Commerce Secretary had minimal influence inside both government and party, but for a long time refused to recognise his greatly diminished position.

Throughout 1946 Eleanor Roosevelt remained an admirer of Henry Wallace, defending his actions and ideas at length in 'My Day', her daily column. She was insistent that Wallace did not constitute the continuance of FDR's foreign policy, and maintained her belief that he didn't think so either. Even when her old friend criticised the offer of Marshall Aid while visiting Paris and London, Eleanor took a sharp intake of breath but refused to write him off. Writing in the *New Republic*, of which he became editor in October 1946, Wallace courted Eleanor Roosevelt, insisting that her world-view and his were compatible, and that their differences could easily be resolved. Yet by the spring of 1947 editorial content increasingly signalled a parting of the waves. Not that Wallace was ready to break with the Democratic Party, however fierce his criticism of the State Department and the White House.

Henry Wallace's admirers often failed to appreciate that he was quietly ambitious. Refusing to acknowledge just how unpopular he was on Capitol Hill, Wallace remained loyal to the Democratic Party for a further fifteen months after his dismissal as Commerce Secretary. He therefore dismissed ever louder calls on the left for a third presidential candidate, and he insisted that a reassertion of Roosevelt liberalism would reverse the Republicans' success in the 1946 mid-term elections. In Wallace's opinion only a progressive Democratic Party could regain control of Congress. Reviving the best of the New Deal would see the party reclaim its lost leader's moral compass. Had he still been alive FDR would no doubt have asked 'What moral compass?'. Here, however, was a powerful myth for disillusioned progressives to cling to. If anything, the myth was strengthened by the Democrats' disastrous showing in November 1946, when they lost control of both the Senate and the House of Representatives – the Republicans' landslide victory was seen by Wallace and his allies as vindicating their pre-election call for a more radical agenda. The onset of the Cold War strained the party loyalty of leftist Democrats to near breaking point.

On 12 March 1947, at the height of the Greek civil war, President Truman famously informed Congress that, 'it must be the policy of the United States to support free people who are resisting attempted subjugation by armed minorities or outside pressures.' That pledge was swiftly turned into material and military support. The 'Truman Doctrine', followed soon after by the Marshall Plan, signalled a new Atlantic alliance, formalised two years later in the establishment of NATO. Truman's commitment to Greece and Turkey, and America's readiness to join west European allies in countering a perceived Soviet threat, strengthened his standing in the country. A more hard-line foreign policy helped Truman secure a surprise victory in the 1948 presidential election; as did a reorientation of the Administration's domestic agenda to head off Republican claims that the Democratic Party was soft on Communism.

Woody Guthrie was not alone in lamenting the President's readiness to distance himself from his party's liberal wing, still committed to keeping the New Deal flame alive: 'Truman has proved to me that he don't like organised labor, don't like the Communist Party, don't like the human race.' Like Henry Wallace, Guthrie was appalled by the Truman Doctrine, championing the Communists in the Greek civil war and blaming Churchill for the Allies siding with the monarchists after German forces abandoned Athens in autumn 1944. Although Winston Churchill was no longer in power, in Guthrie's eyes he remained the embodiment of British imperialism, witness his efforts to delay Indian independence. Truman's presumed endorsement of Churchill's 'Iron Curtain' speech in Fulton, Missouri, on 5 March 1946 was seen to illustrate how far the President had drifted from his predecessor's fundamentally anti-colonial posture.

An incipient 'red scare' saw members of the House Committee Un-American Activities, both Republican and Democrat, compete to prove who was the most patriotic. Even Henry Wallace was threatened with a subpoena. In 1947 HUAC's aggressive pursuit of alleged Communists in Hollywood fuelled a climate of fear among artists active in left-wing politics on both sides of the country. The covert and increasingly open harassment of Communists real or imagined, the courting of a disgruntled but loyal labour movement, and a crude but effective appeal to patriotism, together served to divide progressive opinion across the United States. A climate of fear and suspicion threatened the already threadbare relationship between leftist artists and intellectuals and the Congress of Industrial Organizations, the more militant of America's two trade union federations (the CIO's affiliates had broken away from the Federation of American Labor at the height of the Depression).

Ironically, the more remote the resurrection of whatever mythical values FDR was seen to embody, the deeper the sense of loss – as articulated by People's Songs Inc., founded in Greenwich Village on New Year's Eve 1945, 'to create, promote, and distribute songs of labor and the American people.' Here was a realisation of Pete Seeger's ambition to build on the experience of the Almanac Singers, and to create a coalition of artists and activists eager to establish American folk music as a vibrant and vital element within the life of the nation. By establishing a close-knit network of performers, organisers, agents, writers, and promoters, starting in New York and then spreading out from state to state, folk music could gain in credibility and be commercially viable; a weekly newsletter, a quarterly bulletin, and an annual convention meant friends and fans far from the eastern seaboard could feel part of a nationwide movement intended to promote the people's music *and* the people's politics. Evidence of this was the early establishment of a People's Songs satellite on the West Coast, its founders as intent on cultivating trade union connections as Seeger and his allies back east.

In promoting an unashamedly political agenda People's Songs' elected president was supported by Lee Hays, Alan Lomax, and an army of fellow-travelling folkies (all white, other than Josh White and an already ailing Lead Belly). They all signed up to an agency, People's Artists, and for the first year enjoyed multiple bookings on the back of a sharp deterioration in industrial relations as the war economy wound down. People's Songs was a regular presence at trade union rallies until relations soured, and shop floor suspicion of 'Commie sympathisers' deepened. Committed to the cause, but increasingly erratic in his behaviour, was Woody Guthrie, delighted by a hard-line takeover of the

Communist leadership but dismayed by the CIO's purge of party activists.

Guthrie labelled People's Songs 'the best sounding Democracy I've heard so far,' but more and more he resented Seeger's efforts to generate audience participation, especially when the song being sung was his own: 'This Land Is Your Land' was now welcomed by every audience as, in Dorian Lynskey's words, 'a bona fide people's song.' Woody wasn't alone in questioning a policy of encouraging all-comers to play, however primitive their skills. Alan Lomax was similarly sceptical, but inclusivity prevailed. A combination of undiagnosed illness and hard drinking affected Guthrie's performances, which on a good night were self-indulgent and on a bad night downright offensive. Given his reputation, knowledgeable audiences were forgiving, but too often his combination of rambling anecdote, casual insult, and reworked favourites proved damaging to People's Songs' image and reputation.

Seeger, Lee Hays, and Lomax were appalled by the death of four year old Cathy Guthrie in a fire at 3520 Mermaid Avenue. Yet at the same time they were quietly relieved when a grieving Marjorie agreed her husband should accept an invitation to play in Spokane and then head west, before making his way home in time for the birth of their second child. The People's Songs organisers in Los Angeles had no idea what to expect when Woody rolled in to town, his arrival coinciding with that of HUAC's private investigators, digging the dirt on Hollywood 'reds'. Guthrie dismissed their significance given that as far back as 1941 the House Committee had named him a seditious Communist. Most left-wing movie makers in LA were less gung-ho, while quietly confident that the planned hearings in Washington would not be taken seriously by the big studio bosses. This of course was a huge miscalculation. By the time those hearings commenced in October 1947 Guthrie was back in Brooklyn once more flying the (red) flag for People's Songs.

Had Seeger and Hays attended a HUAC sitting four months earlier they would have been bemused to learn that People's Songs' success in subverting the nation's youth was largely attributable to its least reliable director. Woody Guthrie's influence extended to his intermittent musings in the *People's World*, and his presence on supposedly pro-Communist albums released by Keynote Records. In *Woody Guthrie American Radical* Will Kaufman identified the real victim of the House Committee's July hearings as Hanns Eisler, by now a Hollywood composer. Back in 1940 Eisler had contributed to *Six Songs for Democracy*, the Keynote album so admired by Eleanor Roosevelt. Despite a high profile campaign organised by fellow composers Aaron Copland and Leonard Bernstein, Eisler found himself on a Hollywood blacklist. He was deported in March 1948. Although an Austrian Eisler settled in East Germany, where, despite composing the anthem of the German Democratic Republic, he soon fell foul of the fledgling regime. His treatment in the GDR scarcely differed from that meted out to him by the American authorities once HUAC had declared him an agent of Communist subversion. As Kaufman pointed out, the words of 'Eisler On The Go', to which Wilco and Billy Bragg added music fifty years later, signal how much Guthrie feared a subpoena to appear before the House Committee. This was a body capable of shredding a simple musician's reputation, while ignoring the real danger to national security, namely the President: 'Eisler him write music/Eisler him teach school./Truman him don't play so good and/I don't know what I'll do.'

From James Madison to Sinclair Lewis writers had warned that an America under threat might one day embrace tyranny by dismissing the fundamental principles of liberty on which the nation was founded (as in the adage favoured by Trump's critics that fascism will come to the USA 'wrapped in the flag and waving a cross.'). Guthrie saw this scenario as a very real prospect unless those presently in power made way for a new and genuinely progressive leadership. The 1948 presidential election was a final opportunity for the people to reassert those values synonymous with the idealised – if not the real – Franklin Delano Roosevelt.

People's Songs as a flawed movement for mobilising the American working class was attributable in part to chaotic organisation outside of California, scant sustained enthusiasm among the unionised labour it eulogised, and close association with Communist front organisations at a time when fears of domestic subversion invariably trumped good intentions. In its first year the network went a long way to realising the aims of the ambitious manifesto drafted by Seeger for the first issue of the quarterly bulletin. Directors and staff, working out of a tiny office in Time Square, were to some extent overwhelmed by the range of activities taking place under the People's Song umbrella. Yet because no symbiotic and lasting relationship was established with the trade unions, or with the Communist Party, the long-term survival of People's Songs became ever more uncertain. The attacks on its principal personalities, all assumed to be card-carrying Communists, were relentless, and bound to inflict psychological damage on even the strongest personality. The most visible legacy of People's Songs was its publications, principally *Sing Out!* magazine, and its booking agency. Guthrie's general disillusion with the condition of America was inseparable from his disillusion with People's Songs; one major grievance was the way in which artists like Josh White and Burl Ives had sold out and secured commercial success on the back of People's Artists' success in finding them work.

However, People's Songs' unhappy experience in the late 1940s should not obscure a high point in its history: the movement's enthusiastic and wholehearted support for Henry Wallace's challenge to the President and his Republican opponent in the 1948 election. Throughout the summer and autumn of 1947 Wallace addressed numerous well-attended rallies on the eastern seaboard, carried his de facto campaign deep into the South. For all the cheering crowds, a lingering delusion – that, faced with prospect of defeat, the Democrats might dump Truman and seek a more radical alternative – finally died. Despite the reality check, Wallace now came to believe that a third candidate just might triumph in the electoral college. He would contest the 1948 presidential election.

Woody Guthrie, Pete Seeger, the Weavers, and Un-American Activities

On 29th December 1947 Henry Wallace burnt his bridges with the Democratic Party and accepted an invitation from the leftist alliance that constituted a Progressive Party to run as its presidential candidate the following fall. Eleanor Roosevelt was damning in her condemnation: it was incumbent on liberals to win over one of the two main parties, not leave themselves open to Communist manipulation. Henceforth the former First Lady's column took every opportunity to attack Wallace as a naive dupe. In February 1948 she was appalled by his explanation of the Communist coup in Prague: this was a regrettable but necessary means of thwarting American plans to engineer a right-wing coup.

Worse was to come that May, when Wallace delivered a speech in the form of an open letter to Stalin. Most of Wallace's proposals were by no means outrageous, but they seemed so in the fevered atmosphere of the time. What really hurt him was the serious but enthusiastic response from the Kremlin less than a week later. Furthermore, questions arose about the means by which he communicated with the Soviet leadership, and his readiness to visit Moscow without State Department approval. If Wallace lacked political nous he was never short of self-confidence, even courage. The same month he wooed Stalin, Wallace lectured HUAC on the Progressive Party's moral entitlement to defy any congressional control on free and unfettered speech. His idealism fuelled his naivety: Wallace's most recent biographers suggest he never suspected close surveillance by the FBI, on the direct orders of J. Edgar Hoover. That surveillance extended to deep penetration of the Progressive Party.

A populist 'Progressive Party' had enjoyed some success in taking on the two dominant parties before and after the First World War, but other than the name it had nothing in common with the liberal and leftist coalition created to promote a raft of ambitious social policies, an extension of civil liberties, and a readiness to recognise Russia's genuine concerns. The latest incarnation of the Progressive Party was a revival of the Popular Front, reinforced by the wartime revelation of just how much state intervention could achieve when executive and legislature shared a common political will. The Progressive Citizens of America, along with the American Labor Party, formed the backbone of a party which only became a reality in late July 1948. A national convention in Philadelphia endorsed a radical, unequivocally anti-Truman manifesto, and nominated Henry Wallace as its presidential candidate (with a one-term junior senator from Idaho as his running mate – the commendably anti-segregationist Glenn Turner boasted a remarkable CV, which included a spell as a country and western singer; in 1950 'The Singing Cowboy' of Capitol Hill left office a pauper, but in later life his re-invention of the toupée made him a millionaire).

Historians continue to debate the degree of control exercised by the Communist Party behind the scenes. Wallace always sought to distance himself from his Communist supporters, and his espousal of 'people's capitalism' demonstrated an ideological gulf. Yet it was clearly in the interest of the Progressive Party's opponents before and after the 1948 election to portray this coalition of the left as no more than a Communist puppet. Undoubtedly the CPUSA did have a major presence, exercising considerable influence over the party; but was this tantamount to manipulation, as suggested by intimidated or disillusioned ex-party members in later evidence to HUAC? The extent to which Communists were or were not in key positions within the new organisation seems scarcely to have bothered Wallace, who focused largely upon the issues, leaving organisation to others. Because the principal issue was a need to negotiate not remonstrate with the Russians, the candidate was unlikely to clash with those orchestrating the campaign.

Recriminations came later, culminating in Wallace's break with the remnants of the Progressive Party over his support for American involvement, under the auspices of the United Nations, in the Korean War. In succeeding years Henry Wallace further distanced himself from the views he had expressed so forcefully after 1945, most notably his criticism of the Marshall Plan and his over-hasty defence of the Communist takeover in Czechoslovakia. He and his party made a disastrous strategic error by seeming to parrot Moscow's dismissal of the European Recovery Program. This was at a time when bipartisan support for Marshall Aid was overwhelming, with the requisite legislative bills securing near unanimous support when submitted to Congress in the spring of 1948.

People's Songs invested all its resources and political capital in supporting Wallace's campaign (but presumably drew the line at signing Glenn C. Turner to People's Artists). Pete Seeger and Alan Lomax saw a victory for Henry Wallace as, in the words of William G. Roy, 'the best hope to return to the enlightened commitments of the New Deal and a retreat from the chilling politics of the cold war.' Following the July convention Lomax urged campaign organisers to ensure that every rally included a healthy injection of music, led by the best known voices on the People's Artists roster. Seeger followed Wallace around the country, acting as a de facto warm-up act before the candidate spoke, invariably preaching to the converted. Venturing down south, the two men never addressed segregated audiences, or stayed in segregated hotels. Meetings in Virginia proved surprising peaceful, but the atmosphere proved very different in North Carolina, where the Ku Klux Klan was intent on silencing anyone tolerant of God-less Communists. Shouted off stage in Hickory, Wallace drew on Christ's advice to his disciples: 'shake the dust of that town from your feet and go elsewhere.' In Burlington, when faced with a violent counter-demonstration, Seeger was aghast to witness Wallace caught up in a fist fight. Before they joined forces for the campaign Henry Wallace was scarcely aware of Pete Seeger, and it's unlikely he had any idea who Woody Guthrie was.

Given his deep loathing of the President, Guthrie was enthused and energised by the chance to oust Truman; like so many enthusiasts for a third party candidate in a tight election he refused to consider the possibility of a split vote enabling the Republicans to win. Ironically, Wallace himself saw this scenario as a further reason for standing: four years of harsh Republican rule would create a wave of popular discontent such as to guarantee the Democrats victory in 1952. The presidential campaign brought Guthrie back into the People's Songs orbit after an extended period in which he had distanced himself from Seeger et al. In the first half of 1948 he had played gigs of his own choosing, usually to local union branches, wrestled with writing a novel (published in 1976 under the title *Seeds of Man*), and struggled with the demands of domesticity. In the summer and the autumn of 1948 he was out on the campaign trail, entertaining supporters with a variety of new or reworked songs in support of Henry Agard Wallace, man of the people.

Most of these songs boasted simplistic, often outrageous, lyrics, their impact lying in the use of familiar tunes like 'The Wabash Cannonball'. A common theme was the depiction of Wallace not Truman as Roosevelt's heir, witness the candidate's readiness to talk with Stalin. The more Guthrie and others sang of Wallace the peacemaker the more his political enemies portrayed him as a Soviet dupe, and the Progressive Party as a Communist front: for a full eighteen months leading up to polling day Truman's speeches made obligatory references to 'Henry Wallace and his Communists.' All major announcements on foreign policy now emanated from the White House not the State Department, with Wallace's approval of the Czech coup and dismissal of the Truman Doctrine providing critics either end of Pennsylvania Avenue with ample opportunity to dismiss his ostensibly naïve pleas for peace. At the same time Wallace's dabbling in mystical and eastern religions gave hostile journalists every opportunity to warn the electorate they risked voting in to the highest office a man who displayed poor judgement and lacked firm Christian beliefs.

In private Guthrie was sceptical of Wallace's credentials as a 'union man' (he had after all made his money in agri-business), but on stage the message was very different. Ironically, the price People's Songs paid for campaigning so enthusiastically on Wallace's behalf was the deepening distrust of most trade unionists. Other than a handful of unions under Communist influence, almost all CIO and AFL affiliates remained loyal to the Democrats. Truman had kept organised labour on side by vetoing – unsuccessfully – the previous year's Taft-Hartley Act, an undisguised attack on the unions. Equally unforgiving was the liberal wing of the Democratic Party. Nostalgic New Dealers such as American Democrats for Action, despite their sympathy for Wallace's views in the first year of peace, soon came to see him as only ever a token member of their party. Throughout the course of 1948 the ADA attacked Wallace and his supporters, remaining silent whenever the Democratic party machine besmirched his name. Truman's campaign team, and its allies in the press and on radio, had ample ammunition given the extent to which the Progressive Party's campaign so clearly depended upon Communist organisation. Senior Democrats orchestrated a successful campaign strategy of demonising Henry Wallace and neutralising Republican claims that the administration was 'soft on Communism.'

Wallace stayed out on the campaign trail day after day. The same was true of Thomas Dewey, the Republican candidate, and of the President himself. The young Robert Zimmermann was unlikely to witness Pete Seeger let alone Woody Guthrie urging the crowd to sing along in support of the workers' champion, but on 13 October 1948 he was taken to hear Harry Truman address the staunchly Democrat citizens of Duluth. In *Chronicles* he recalled the deep and lasting impression that Truman – a serious and slow-speaking Midwesterner, just like his parents' friends and neighbours – made upon him. Twelve years later, on 2 October 1960, the Kennedy bandwagon rolled in to Hibbing, with Dylan's mother among those gathered to greet their man: 'He gave a heroic speech, my mom said, and brought people a lot of hope.' That speech placed a heavy emphasis upon continuity, and the legacy of previous Democratic administrations. Even without Eleanor Roosevelt beside him on the podium, Kennedy placed his domestic agenda in a direct line back to FDR. Notably, he located his foreign policy in a direct line back to Harry S. Truman.

On 2 November 1948, when nearly 49 million Americans voted to choose their president, Truman, against the odds, secured a notable victory. Henry Wallace came fourth behind the southern segregationist Strom Thurmond. The ostensible third candidate attracted a mere 2.37 per cent of the popular vote, and in consequence no votes were cast for him in the electoral college. On 6 November 1948 in her daily column Eleanor Roosevelt wrote, 'I was sure the American people would express themselves in no uncertain terms on policies which he [Wallace] stood for, and my faith in their common sense proved correct.' The 1,157,328 who did vote for Wallace tended to be free-thinking members of an educated middle class, nearly half of whom were registered in New York state; with the remaining fifty per cent largely concentrated along the eastern seaboard and in California. Wallace later claimed that he would have been happy had he secured three million votes, as such a visible expression of dissent would no doubt influence foreign policy-making, prioritising compromise over confrontation.

If every crisis really is an opportunity, then Alan Lomax and Pete Seeger found solace in the social composition of those who had turned out to support Wallace, and on 2nd November 1948 had voted for him. If a bankrupt People's Songs had lost the trust of organised labour, leading to its closure in March 1949, then its founders could look to a fresh audience for folk music. Out on Coney Island Guthrie saw the situation as desperate, but back in the city his old comrades looked to more savvy ways of maintaining the struggle.

In the ensuing months Alan Lomax, thanks to his sister and campaign activist, Bess, identified a younger generation of folk fans. These were well-educated, idealistic third party supporters who had attended rallies or hootenannies and relished the entertainment. People's Songs might not be around to fuel their enthusiasm but a despondent Seeger could capitalise upon this newly established audience base, as soon proved the case with the Weavers. The original line-up of the group he founded with Lee Hays in late 1948 would last six years, at which point the Weavers' chart-orientated formula of sanitised folk finally fell foul of McCarthyism – to the extent that Decca deleted all their records from its catalogue (astonishingly, the label had just signed Woody Guthrie, who almost immediately was released from his contract).

Despite the group's resurrection on Vanguard, and their triumphant reunion concert at Carnegie Hall in December 1955, Pete Seeger was blacklisted throughout the three years of the Weavers' second incarnation: he had been indicted on a charge of contempt earlier in the year after quoting the First Amendment when ordered to give evidence at a HUAC hearing. Seeger was still deemed a threat to national security when a teenage Bob Dylan saw him singing Almanac songs at a campus concert in Madison, Wisconsin. When Dylan sat down to write 'Talking John Birch Paranoid Blues' presumably he had in mind the American Legion members picketing Seeger's performance eighteen months before.

When summoned to Washington in 1955 Pete Seeger displayed remarkable courage in not answering all of the HUAC chairman's questions. Two years later he was indicted for contempt, but the eventual conviction was in due course reversed, on the basis that the Committee's authority to pose questions unanswered by Seeger was unproven.

Similarly courageous, albeit to a lesser degree, was Lee Hays, who pleaded the Fifth Amendment. The dignity of Hays and Seeger – and of Earl Robinson, who also defended his right to remain silent – contrasted with other comrades from the heyday of the Almanac Singers: Josh White unconvincingly claimed he was a Communist dupe, and Burl Ives saved his skin by naming names. Despite the many times he was mentioned – rarely by friend but often by foe – Woody Guthrie somehow escaped a subpoena. Perhaps word had reached Washington that this notorious Communist was already incarcerated, in Brooklyn State Hospital.

From their inception in late 1948 Woody Guthrie had provided the Weavers with tried and tested material. He made so much money on the back of the group's success that he contemplated his own less clean-cut version. The Weavers' wholesome image, and their readiness to record with an orchestra, constituted an uncomfortable fit with what Guthrie considered 'real' folk music. Ironically, Wallace's Communist advisers had been wary of Alan Lomax's performers deviating too far from the musical mainstream. Nevertheless, in his seven-page election inquest Guthrie insisted that industrial workers would have ditched the Democratic Party had the songs sung at campaign rallies been more rousing and less respectful: performers should have eschewed any acknowledgement of popular music, adhered to a radical American folk tradition rooted in class war, and not been afraid to ask 'which side are you on?' Naturally excluding himself, Guthrie blamed his fellow performers and their songs for failing 'to touch the 'heartstrings and conscience of the hard hit masses.'

Thus, the lesson of Wallace's doomed campaign, and the subsequent collapse of People's Songs, was not to follow the path Seeger and Lomax planned for the Weavers and to seek – short term – respectability. Instead, Guthrie promised, 'to get a good deal louder from now on, because I am slowly commencing to think that I've forgotten more about writing progressive songs of social protest than the rest of our entire staff combined.' Whether or not Alan Lomax read Guthrie's lengthy charge sheet, to identify him as the person directly responsible for the Wallace campaign's failure was neither fair nor accurate. With friends like these, it's no wonder that within two years Lomax had left for England, followed soon after by a flood of fellow victims, all subject to an unashamedly anti-intellectual political witch-hunt.

As already suggested, Guthrie's behaviour – especially towards women – was more and more affected by the early stages of Huntington's disease, as yet unsuspected. His condition continued to deteriorate throughout the late 'forties and into the 'fifties, but it was after 1951 that, in Will Kaufman's words, a 'neurological disintegration' led to a lengthy spell in hospital and a clear diagnosis. The preceding years had seen Guthrie's political judgement – never subtle or sophisticated, but always well-intentioned – become ever more clouded. His almost obsessional loathing of Truman extended to every individual or organisation associated with American foreign policy and national security. Relying heavily on Notebook 64 in the Woody Guthrie archives, Kaufman quoted ever more bloodthirsty lyrics and letters, thankfully often unsung and unsent, chronicling Guthrie's descent into defending the indefensible. Thus early disaffection with the United Nations, and a justified unease over the scale of American military force in Korea, tipped over into unreserved praise for Kim Il-Sung and his regime.

When a beleaguered Communist Party, and veteran fellow travellers still brave or reckless enough to put their heads above the parapet, opposed or queried the defence of South Korea, Henry Wallace cut any lingering ties with the Progressive Party. His antipathy towards the party contrasted starkly with the spirit of optimism and solidarity on display in Philadelphia two years before. Addressing delegates, the newly adopted presidential candidate had articulated the disillusion he and other alienated liberals shared when lamenting lost opportunities and a lost leader. Wallace solemnly informed the convention that, 'In Hyde Park they buried our president – and in Washington they buried our dreams.' The White House had witnessed an 'exodus of the torchbearers of the New Deal,' and a consequent subversion of 'the course Franklin Roosevelt had charted for the nation in peace.'

Wallace was of course echoing what Woody Guthrie had been saying, albeit more trenchantly, from the moment Truman took office. As the eponymous song said, FDR's death signalled 'another man's done gone.' His successor lacked the dignity of someone whose disability had brought with it a keener sense of empathy towards those less fortunate than himself: 'Maybe if I hadn't of seen so much hard feelings/I might not could have felt other people's.'

'To F.D.R.', an elegiac poem from the summer of 1947, found Guthrie recalling President's 'fireside chats'. The distant voice on the wireless was that of a family man. In some strange way that same man's fecundity, and his zest for competition, paralleled Woody's fiddle-playing 'blacksmith uncle John': 'I say you and my uncle/John's anvil and fiddle are/two things I could go on/and listen to for twenty/more elections.' Was this the same writer who, back in the winter of 1940-41, had seen FDR as nothing better than the warmongering tool of the capitalist elite? The notion of a wealthy New Yorker like Roosevelt bearing comparison with a hammer-wielding son of the Dustbowl was perhaps best confined to Guthrie's crowded note book.

More enduring of course is 'Dear Mrs Roosevelt', a song which, if its lyrics are to be believed, was a speedy response to the President's death in April 1945. In actual fact the song was written on 18 January 1948, three weeks after Wallace had crossed the Rubicon and agreed to run against Truman (and almost twenty years to the day in advance of Dylan and the Crackers performing it at Guthrie's benefit concerts). The date of the composition was discovered by Jorge Arévalo Mateus, the Brooklyn ethnomusicologist who first took on the task of archiving Woody Guthrie's voluminous pictures and writings; and who won a Grammy in 2008 for producing *Live Wire*, the enhanced recording of a 1949 New Jersey concert, at which 'Dear Mrs Roosevelt' was conspicuously absent.

'Dear Mrs Roosevelt' – the real [new] deal

'Dear Mrs Roosevelt' is an epistolary song, employing a mode of address familiar to Americans ever since the then untested First Lady gained national recognition in the spring of 1933. The size of Eleanor Roosevelt's postbag was common knowledge, with literally millions of Americans during the Depression and the war years eager for her to intercede on their behalf. Children were known to be her keenest correspondents, but as an exhibition at the Hyde Park presidential museum and library makes clear, in 1945 the newly widowed Mrs Roosevelt received condolences from a broad cross-section of the population, young and old, rich and poor, Democrats and Republicans. Again, this was widely known, and Guthrie was adding his voice to a rich and resilient narrative of bereavement.

Like all Guthrie's compositions, 'Dear Mrs Roosevelt' is firmly rooted in the American folk tradition, in this instance drawing heavily upon the ubiquitous African American murder ballad, 'Frankie and Johnny'. Every folk and blues singer worth her or his salt has sung 'Frankie and Johnny' – it's almost a rite of passage. Even Elvis recorded it, as the title song of an execrable movie made at the lowest point in his career, round about the time Bob Dylan was recording *Highway 61 Revisited*. Dylan was singing 'Frankie and Johnny' in Duluth, Greenwich Village, and Soho at the start of the 'sixties; and he was still seeking solace from it thirty years later. On the painfully honest *Good As I Been To You*, he sang the more concise 'Frankie and Albert', first performed as far back as Hibbing in 1959. Over thirty years later Dylan used an arrangement by Mississippi John Hurt of the version which Lead Belly had sung to John Lomax at Angola State Penitentiary in the summer of 1933.

Champion Jack Dupree relocated the revenge story of good love gone bad to New Orleans for his rewrite ballad 'Rampart and Dumaine'. A more authentic son of the Delta, Charley Patton, enjoyed what, by the standards of the day, constituted a hit single when Paramount released his take on 'Frankie and Albert' in 1929 – the booze he bought on the back of this momentary success led to a lengthy spell in jail. Completing the circle, a creatively reborn Dylan included 'High Water (for Charley Patton)' on the 2001 album *"Love and Theft"*, and in *Chronicles* named the Mississippi master of murder ballads as a lifelong influence. That same year, at a press conference in Rome, Dylan floated the idea of recording a whole album of Charley Patton covers. Back in January 1968 he stayed with 'Frankie and Johnny/Albert' when rearranging 'Dear Mrs Roosevelt', but added chord changes which some Dylan scholars consider a compositional approach unique to his work at end of the 'sixties, as evident on *Nashville Skyline*, and in particular 'Lay Lady Lay'.

As we've seen, Guthrie gave himself the voice of a mournful GI urging FDR's widow to temper her grief by appreciating that, as emphasised in the one-line chorus and the final verse, 'This world was lucky to see him born.' In succeeding verses Roosevelt is a child of privilege but doesn't take this for granted, being studious at school and Harvard *and* a born athlete: 'Outrun every kid a-growin' up 'round Hyde Park just for fun.' Hence the cruel irony that, 'He got struck down by fever and it settled in his leg'; and then the double irony that the polio generated goodwill from the stricken patrician to all 'that wished him well,' leaving him peculiarly well equipped to challenge the racketeers and profiteers ('"You money changin' boys have sure 'nuff got to fall;"'), and corrupt politicians ('...he used his gift of tongue/To get you thieves and liars told and put you on the run;'). Here was a president who deserved re-election because he fulfilled his promises, and '...tried to find an honest job for every idle man.' There then follows the key verse, differentiating the assumed anti-labour Truman from his predecessor: 'He helped to build my union hall, he learned me how to talk;/I could see he was a cripple but he learned my soul to walk;/This world was lucky to see him born.' While during his presidency Roosevelt's disability was the unspoken secret shared by all, with cameramen endeavouring to disguise the Commander-in-Chief's incapacity, in Guthrie's song it provides a focus – and an explanation of the empathetic power that made this lost leader a true man of the people.

At this point in Dylan's recorded performance the song cuts to the penultimate verse ('I was a GI in my army camp...') before the backing musicians are left to up the tempo, led by Richard Manuel on honky-tonk piano. This allows a hollering Dylan due emphasis on the final and repeated assertion of how lucky this world was 'just to see him born.' The song's rousing climax appears an unforced and natural conclusion to a simply-structured well-balanced composition; and yet the reality is that four verses have been omitted.

The first verse seems innocuous, even when read as an assertion that unionised labour defeated a fascist threat at home as well as abroad – were America's working men and women really fighting a war on two fronts? More contentious are the next two verses, portraying as they do a president prescient as to which allies share his respect for the ordinary Joe. At Yalta and Teheran Roosevelt is seen as a sound judge of character, dismissing De Gaulle, Chiang Kai Shek, and Guthrie's favourite bogeyman, Winston Churchill – an Allied leader who, as a letter to Moe Asch from February 1945 made clear, he considered no different from the fascist dictators. In Guthrie's song FDR has the guts to criticise the British prime minister 'man to man', and the good sense to recognise the grand alliance's most dominant force: 'Shook hands with Joseph Stalin, says "There's a man I like!"' If we dismiss the Yalta conference, when an ailing Roosevelt had only two months to live, it's true to say the meeting in Teheran fifteen months earlier saw Stalin and Roosevelt express mutual admiration, at the expense of Churchill. As for De Gaulle and Chiang Kai Shek, Roosevelt saw the one as a dictator-in-waiting and the other as an expendable war lord.

The final verse missing from Dylan's version of 'Dear Mrs Roosevelt' sees Guthrie recall being torpedoed 'the day he took command,' which, if he meant the occasion of FDR's inauguration in either 1941 or 1945, was an obvious display of poetic licence. More to the point is that his captain 'hated' a president 'loved by all ship's hands,' not least because they were members of Guthrie's much loved but much maligned National Maritime Union. Before and during the war the NMU was closely aligned with the Communist Party, even sharing officials. At the union's Cleveland convention in 1941 the Almanac Singers' rousing version of 'Which Side Are You On?' had generated a level of audience participation beyond even Pete Seeger's wildest dreams. Over the next two years Guthrie had been encouraged by the NMU to write numerous pro-union/pro-Soviet songs, of varying quality, and to share his unique take on the war via the members' magazine, the *Pilot*. Joining the Merchant Marine meant that at last he could acquire a union card – in New York it was the NMU not the shipping lines who controlled the hiring of crew. Once at sea he got himself elected as a union rep, and soon he was demanding better conditions for his shipmates. Throughout his time in the merchant navy he gained immense pleasure from antagonising the officers, celebrating his successes in ships' newsletters and songs like 'Talking Sailor Blues'. Yet by the time Guthrie came to write 'Dear Mrs Roosevelt', four years later, even the National Maritime Union had been neutralised. A leadership intent on purging the union of any lingering connection with the CPUSA boycotted People's Songs and worked hard to keep Woody at a distance.

The irony of the January 1968 concerts is that, while no less than four verses were missing from 'Dear Mrs Roosevelt', Dylan found himself singing the full version of 'This Land Is Your Land' when Pete Seeger and Arlo Guthrie brought all the performers back on stage for rousing renditions of Woody's most famous song. As became increasingly common across the ensuing decades, culminating in Seeger and Springsteen's pre-inauguration performance on 19th January 2009, the 'lost' verses of the Depression were included: verse four on the 'big high wall there that tried to stop me/A sign was painted said Private Property,' and the deliberately shocking and unsentimental verse six: 'One bright sunny morning in the shadow of the steeple/By the relief office I saw my people/As they stood hungry, I stood there wondering if/This land was made for you and me.' Seeger, increasingly uncomfortable with how 'America's alternative national anthem' had become an innocuous feel-good song that anyone – of left or right – could embrace, reinstated the anti-capitalist verses in the mid 1960s, before adding a few of his own.

Arlo Guthrie had been taught the full version by his father a decade earlier when an already ailing Woody feared his songs might disappear or be emasculated once he was dead. The sanitised version was the one for which Richmond Ltd., the publishing company of Guthrie admirer Howie Richmond, held the copyright. Richmond licenced *Sing Out!* to publish the words and music in 1954, and he published the sheet music two years later: the 1956 version of the song was subsequently authorised for replication in assorted anthologies and textbooks. As Robert Santelli explained in his excellent history of 'This Land Is Your Land', Howie Richmond and his son Jonathan were keen to promote the song as an anodyne 'popular patriotic chant.' This was the version which American children grew up with in the 1950s, and then heard in television commercials for airline travel a decade later.

Bob Dylan's astonishing interpretation, sung before just fifty-three people at Carnegie Chapter Hall on 4 November 1961, was still not the definitive version; but it scarcely mattered. In a reflexive essay for the *Times Literary Supplement* in 2012 Neil Corcoran described Dylan's haunting delivery as, 'something close to threnody…one of the most melancholy things he has ever done, and one of his most exquisitely heartfelt performances.' In other words, here is a lament on the state of the nation, both shocking and sad, by a prescient twenty-year old far wiser than his years, and as such stubbornly resistant to the prevailing zeitgeist. If Dylan ever sang his strikingly downbeat version of 'This Land Is Your Land' to Guthrie, the stricken hero must surely have approved. Nearly seven years later, on stage with Woody's old comrades for the grand finale, Dylan came into line. By 1968 this was as much Pete Seeger's song as Woody Guthrie's – only with the soundtrack of Scorsese's *No Direction Home* in 2005 did Bob Dylan's early seizure of the song become apparent to all.

Howie Richmond could scarcely stop Seeger and Arlo Guthrie, along with the other performers, from singing all six verses of 'This Land Is Your Land'; or veto the song appearing on Columbia's commemorative album when it finally appeared in 1972. By then public performance – if not necessarily official recording – of the original song, with or without ad hoc further verses, was a fait accompli.

It's notable, however, that – unlike the 2017 box set – Columbia's first 'Bootleg' highlights of the Rolling Thunder Revue did not include the ensemble's nightly grand finale. At the time of the album's release – early in the new century – did Jonathan Richmond withhold permission (or were the royalties and licencing issues too complex)? Today, Bob Dylan's official website does replicate in full Guthrie's original riposte to 'God Bless America' (in 1940 its working title was 'God Blessed America', challenging directly Berlin's 'patriotic prayer', updated two years before). In his history of the song Robert Santelli implied that, had Ramblin' Jack Elliott not been present, Dylan's entitlement to sing 'The Land Is Your Land' would somehow have ceased: 'By the mid '70s Dylan had moved so far away from his Guthrie roots as to be hardly recognizable.' Nothing could be further from the truth, as Dylan has demonstrated time and again over succeeding decades. Santelli saw the baton as having passed from Guthrie to Seeger to Springsteen, citing *Nebraska and The Ghost of Tom Joad* as evidence. There is no place for Dylan in Santelli's narrative, which didn't make sense when his book first appeared (in 2012), just as it didn't make sense at the time of the Rolling Thunder Revue; and it certainly made no sense at the time of Guthrie's death.

As far as 'Dear Mrs Roosevelt' is concerned, Richmond's rebranded successor, TRO Essex, remain sensitive regarding the full set of lyrics. Ten years into a new century the manuscript of Will Kaufman's *Woody Guthrie, American Radical* was generally well received when read by members of the Guthrie family. However, the music publisher refused Kaufman permission to quote 'Dear Mrs Roosevelt' unless he removed the verse that claimed FDR had spurned De Gaulle and Chiang Kai Shek but then, 'Shook hands with Joseph Stalin, says: "There's a man I like!".' In his preface Kaufman commented on the irony that, 'in the year 2010, a petty exercise in airbrushing – one of Stalin's own pet practices – should be demanded in order to prevent engagement with some of Guthrie's more inconvenient opinions.'

Why, back in January 1968, had this and the other contentious verses remained unsung? Had something similar occurred, with word reaching Howie Richmond that the forthcoming concerts' most high profile performer was, albeit unintentionally, about to besmirch Guthrie's reputation? Did Richmond feel the need to intervene? Did a still mentally fragile Bob Dylan engage in self–censorship, concluding that Cold War sentiment negated his singing a song in which the sainted Roosevelt was said to like Stalin as much as he disliked Churchill? At the height of the Tet offensive in Vietnam any such suggestion was ammunition for conservative critics of anti-war liberalism, of presumed Communists like Seeger and the late Woody, and above all, of the protest singer turned rock star still considered a symbol of purposeless generational discontent. Dylan was surely aware of this, and he was not the only one

– alarm bells would have rung for Pete Seeger, Moe Asch, and any other veteran of the Wallace campaign helping organise the concerts.

In the absence of authoritative advice from Bob Dylan one can only speculate – needless to say, all attempts to approach him (and Robbie Robertson) have proved fruitless. When censoring the song Dylan knew what he was doing: the 1963 compendium introduced by Pete Seeger contained the music for 'Dear Mrs Roosevelt' and a full set of lyrics. This was, however, the only published source, as a collection edited and published by Howie Richmond two years earlier, at the height of the Berlin crisis, had omitted the song altogether. Presumably co-editor Pete Seeger preferred no 'Dear Mrs Roosevelt' to a sanitised version. This was after all a very different song, in both quality and profile, from 'This Land Is Your Land', and pragmatism prevailed. Perhaps the same was true seven years later, with Dylan asking how a fifteen minutes, three song set could – or should – accommodate the faithful rendering of a song which hardly anyone in the audience was aware of. Dumping four verses with dated references enhanced the intensity of the performance, enabling the Crackers to drive the song along to its six voice crescendo; the intention was to excite the audience, not to test its patience. Was this, therefore, a case, not of deliberate censorship, but of simple common sense; in other words, a combination of Dylan's natural caution and his sidemen's fear that taking too long to deliver a near-anonymous song would subvert the urgency and immediacy of a set deliberately intended to shock and surprise?

No mystery or suspicion surrounds the better known of only two other recordings of the song (the lesser known being by Bob Collum, an Oklahoma musician now resident in south Essex). Dylan's performance was the template for San Diego folk singer Joel Rafael when recording 'Dear Mrs Roosevelt'. Rafael's version appeared on the album *Woodeye*, released in 2003 by Jackson Browne's independent label Inside Recordings (which describes itself as 'a haven for music that might not find a home in the mainstream'). *Woodeye* was a collection of Guthrie songs, most of which were well-known, plus Rafael's setting for the lyric 'Dance A Little Longer'. Four more unpublished lyrics were set to music on *Woodyboye*, a second Guthrie covers album released two years after the first. Both recordings boast an impressive roster of southern Californian musicians, including the likes of Van Dyke Parks, Jennifer Warnes, and not surprisingly, Jackson Browne.

Joel Rafael is a veteran civil liberties campaigner, with famous friends. He's an ever-present at the Woody Guthrie Folk Festival, held in Okemah every year since 1998 on the nearest weekend to 14 July, birthday of the town's most famous son. The festival, free for the first seventeen years, attracts as headliners the likes of Steve Earle, Billy Bragg, and Graham Nash, as well as Arlo Guthrie; with music complemented by plays, poetry readings, and opportunities for radicals old and young to bemoan the state of the nation and recharge their political batteries. Whether on stage alone, or alongside the cream of home-grown Americana, Joel Rafael is a mainstay of the festival.

Woodeye was released the year Rafael toured with the ensemble show *Ribbon of Highway, Endless Skyway*, staged by Guthrie evangelist Jimmy LaFave, veteran Texan songwriter and co-organiser of the Okemah festival until his death in 2017. Rafael's set list may have changed many times since he recorded 'Dear Mrs Roosevelt', but the song has rarely if ever formed part of his repertoire. He has confirmed that when compiling his first tribute album he simply copied the Dylan version. Only later did Rafael acquire *The Nearly Complete Collection* of Woody Guthrie Songs, at which point it became apparent that unintentionally he had broken his own strict rule of always singing every lyric, however contentious.

A conclusion

From early on in his career Dylan generated referential, often reverential, songs, with David Bowie and Joan Baez competing for the best known if not the best. Every decade deserves – and invariably gets – one or more songs inspired by and about Bob Dylan. Woody Guthrie was late to the sub-genre of salute songs, with the notable exception of the first and the most famous. 'Song to Woody' was recorded in November 1961, only six months after Cisco Houston died. 'Here's to the hearts and the hands of the men/That come with the dust and are gone with the wind'; and of course that includes Houston, whose death triggered a succession of tribute songs from Greenwich Village veterans like Peter La Farge and Tom Paxton. Given that Bowie's 'Song for Bob Dylan' echoes 'Song to Woody', what we have here is a Venn diagram of folk revival references. Is it any wonder that Dylan's first composition is still subject to serial deconstruction?

Fast forward to the 1990s and into the present century, and successive Guthrie-themed anthems can be clearly located in time and political context. In the mid-nineties Steve Earle's early promise as a singer-songwriter and political activist was a distant memory. Turning his back on alcohol and drugs, he again garnered critical acclaim with albums like *El Corazón*. The much covered opening track, 'Christmas in Washington', is Woody Guthrie for Generation X. Although written and recorded before Bill Clinton's relationship with Monica Lewinsky became public knowledge, the irony of the song's opening stanza was evident by the time *El Corazón* was released in 1997: Republicans crowing, '"They'll be no more FDRs"'. Greil Marcus brutally dismissed 'Steve Earle's putrid where-have-all-the-lefties-gone lament' – and that was before he heard Joan Baez's cover. Marcus is way too hard on Earle, but the song does give the impression, if unintentionally, that its writer is not merely following in the footsteps of Cisco and Woody – one day he'll be up on the podium alongside them.

'Woody Guthrie' was the late Jimmy LaFave's heartfelt but frankly turgid tribute to a man he was all but obsessed with in the last twenty years of his life – it appeared on the adopted Okie's 2001 album *Texoma*, 'Woodrow' was a 2005 elegy recorded by Tom Russell (a double eulogist, his Dylan *homage* – 'Mesabi' – standing out in a crowded field). The Guthrie tribute is a rare play-again track on Russell's over-ambitious concept album, *Hotwalker*: a Waits-style, Beat-inspired lament for an alternative and artistically vibrant Los Angeles, a city exciting to grow up in but sadly long gone. The song pulls no punches re the later life of a one-time LA hero, broken in body but not in spirit ('Oh Mrs Guthrie, look what they've done, to your brown-eyed baby now'). It's a post-9/11 warning of what lies ahead in a 'land of dread and fear,' where the sons and daughters of Woodrow Wilson Guthrie are quickly silenced when they challenge the abuse of state power and they speak out in defence of civil liberties.

With 'The words of Woody Guthrie ringing in my head,' Jay Farrar anticipated imminent environmental disaster on 'Bandages and Scars', the opening track of another album from 2005, Son Volt's suitably titled *Okemah and the Melody of Riot*. However inspiring, Guthrie was clearly no role model, as Farrar's lyrics were no less dense and demanding than usual (channelling several other songwriters, from Lead Belly to Gil Scott Heron – Farrar's obsession with Guthrie, first signalled on Uncle Tupelo's acoustic album, *March 16-20, 1992*, extends to a custom guitar built from pieces of wood he picked up in Okemah, to which he returned in 2018 to record half of *Union*, Son Volt's most explicitly political album).

Not even in their worst nightmares could Tom Russell and Jay Farrar anticipate the dysfunctional, demoralised state of the Union a dozen years down the track. On Ry Cooder's *The Prodigal Son*, 'Jesus and Woody' voices the plea of a world-weary Saviour that Guthrie should, 'drag out your Oklahoma poetry, 'cause it looks like the war is on.' Donald Trump is never mentioned by name, but when Jesus sees, 'they're starting up their engine of hate,' it's clear who the Son of Man has in mind. In Cooder's song Jesus looks up to Guthrie, not the other way round: deity and man are fellow dreamers, and both 'like sinners better than fascists.' This, it suggests, leaves the latter beyond forgiveness and redemption, and thus fair game – here, in its own quiet way, is a call to arms. It's also an echo of Earle twenty years earlier, with 'Christmas in Washington' similarly assuming that Woody Guthrie sits at the Lord's right hand – why can't the two of them come back down and purge the nation of its malcontents?

On *The Prodigal Son*'s inner sleeve the lyrics of 'Jesus and Woody', with their seamless incorporation of Guthrie song titles, are superimposed over an image of the Asch Recordings 78 of 'Jesus Christ'. Guthrie's 1940 Jesus robs the rich to feed the poor, just like Jesse James (with whom he shares the same tune) and Pretty Boy Floyd – this is an outlaw mythology where god and gunman share moral equivalence. As D.A. Carpenter points out, Guthrie was happy to call himself a 'prophet singer' and be compared with Jesus, 'A hard-working man, and brave.' Bob Dylan on the other hand shunned the 'collectivist outlaw tradition' mythologised in the Dustbowl Ballads. In 1970 Dylan told Robert Shelton that one reason he kept a low profile was that, 'Being noticed can be a burden. Jesus got himself crucified because he got himself noticed.'

When, as the evening performance ended on 20th January 1968, younger members of the audience chanted 'We want Dylan,' did they seriously believe he would step out from behind the curtain to provide a solitary encore? What did they expect him to sing – 'Song to Woody'? Such a scenario was inconceivable. Seeger, Leventhal, and the Guthrie family would have quickly stamped on any subversion of a genuinely collective enterprise. Dylan himself would have been appalled at the notion that he should place himself above all the other artists. The old guard, disenchanted and disappointed since Newport '65, if not before, had welcomed their renegade messiah back into the fold. All were guided by Pete Seeger's response, presumably unaware that he had already been won over by *John Wesley Harding*. Ever the purist, Seeger hated all the trappings of rock 'n' roll, and the Crackers made only modest concessions to the unspoken assumption that everyone would play acoustic. Yet anecdotal evidence suggests Seeger was quickly won round once Dylan and his sidemen launched into their afternoon set; and in the evening he knew what to expect.

Unlike several other artists Dylan and his band didn't spend time on stage rehearsing ahead of the first show, which prompts the question as to whether Seeger, Leventhal, Geer, and their fellow organisers saw the set list in advance. When did they realise that Dylan had selected a song that was toxic in 1948, and was even more so twenty years later? It's unlikely that they only found out at the moment that he launched into 'Dear Mrs Roosevelt', but if they did have advance notice then the obvious question is whether at any stage Dylan was asked what precisely he intended to sing. For over twenty years Pete Seeger had time and again demonstrated the strength of his beliefs. Few doubted his courage, yet even Seeger must have baulked at Dylan's choice of 'Dear Mrs Roosevelt', with its derogatory remark about Churchill and flattering reference to a dictator most Americans twinned with Hitler as an embodiment of evil. Hardly any organisers and performers backstage at Carnegie Hall would have known of Woody's campaign song from almost twenty years earlier. Perhaps only Howie Richmond and Will Geer could have shared Seeger's alarm that a convivial celebration of their old comrade might be adversely affected by an unanticipated echo of Popular Front politics: was this Woody loudly proclaiming an unrepentant message about Stalin from beyond the grave?

Harold Leventhal had known Bob Dylan since he was a kid fresh off the bus, and he would have had no hesitation in telling him what was and was not unacceptable. Yet almost certainly he had no need. Dylan knew full well which verses were contentious and therefore redundant. In any case he wanted a song that was short, punchy, and rocked – Leven Helm wasn't going to tolerate a fourteen verse panegyric, especially one which halfway through declared Joe Stalin to be a regular guy. Nevertheless, the matinee performance must have seen the organisers unsure as to how Dylan would cover a composition so fixed in the politics of its time. Backstage the relief must have been palpable as both singer and band rushed towards their joyous climax, in non-partisan fashion eulogising the nation's greatest war leader since Lincoln. Anyone hearing the song for the first time, and that constituted almost everyone present at each of the concerts, naturally assumed the lyrics were complete. The presumption would be that Guthrie had written 'Dear Mrs Roosevelt' while in the Army as an early mark of respect for the passing of a fine man. Why would anyone not in the know conceive of any alternative scenario? When the concert recording appeared in 1972 a wider audience would have heard Guthrie's farewell to the recently deceased FDR, and assumed that Bob Dylan was singing every verse.

Dylan's self-censorship wasn't duplicitous. He had no idea that, having resurrected one of Woody Guthrie's most obscure songs, almost everyone who heard it would assume that this was a definitive interpretation. The song was in the public domain, and no-one was stopping any other artist from performing the complete version. It never occurred to the California singer Joel Rafael, or anyone else interested in 'Dear Mrs Roosevelt', to check to see if there were any other verses. No one knew better than Bob Dylan that folk songs are shape-shifters, with no definitive version. Dylan, like Guthrie, has always worked within a timeless tradition of reworking old songs, mapping fresh lyrics on to well-established tunes or simply reshaping an established narrative. Performers do this all the time, not least when singing Woody Guthrie compositions.

Guthrie repeatedly reshaped his own songs, rewording, omitting, or adding lyrics. There are, for example, multiple versions of 'Pretty Boy Floyd', its hero mythologised by Guthrie as a much maligned Robin Hood of the Dustbowl, not a suspiciously psychotic bank robber with a penchant for shooting G-Men. The same of course is true for Dylan. His relentless reinterpretation far exceeds Guthrie's readiness to rework the old favourites. At the same time Dylan has always had his own unique take on Woody Guthrie: *his* studio version of 'Pretty Boy Floyd' is typical in the way that it respects the original while at the same time reinventing itself as 'a Bob Dylan song.' In January 1968 Dylan was suitably respectful of 'Dear Mrs Roosevelt', but the lyrics were as open to radical rearrangement as the music. Thus, it's hard to imagine Dylan agonising over the verses cut from Guthrie's pro-Soviet take on a fast-descending Iron Curtain. There was no emotional investment, unlike his near obsession with the lifetime incarceration of the black middle-weight boxer Rubin 'Hurricane' Carter.

In the mid-seventies Dylan was convinced Carter had been framed for murder, and at the heart of the Rolling Thunder Revue was a high-profile campaign to secure the boxer's retrial and release. Outside the United States scarcely anyone would have known about Carter's supposed plight had Dylan and New York polymath Jacques Levy not written 'Hurricane', the opening track of the December 1975 album *Desire*. Played at every gig on the first half of the Rolling Thunder tour, the song was then dropped from Dylan's set list: in Mobile on 26th April 1976 he informed disappointed fans that, 'Hurricane's out now. We don't have to sing that no more.' The song has never again featured in a Bob Dylan concert. Yet 'Hurricane' remains *Desire*'s stand-out track, thanks mainly to Scarlet Rivera's scorching violin breaks – as Lester Bangs pointed out in a searing indictment of Dylan's periodic attempts to revive his persona as a 'protest singer', 'the performance is so drivingly persuasive' because the music is so good. For all the pleading and the passion, this was a story that never rang true; even before it emerged that Dylan's version of events, from Carter's world championship potential through to his movements in Paterson, New Jersey, on the night of a triple killing in June 1966, was deeply flawed.

'Hurricane' highlights Dylan's readiness to reshape a song if expedient, just as he did with 'Dear Mrs Roosevelt' seven years earlier. He and Levy wrote and recorded 'Hurricane' in July 1975. Two months later the planned single was premiered at a TV recording in Chicago of a Public Service Broadcasting tribute to John Hammond, Columbia's legendary producer of Dylan, Aretha Franklin, Bruce Springsteen, et al. By that time the original lyrics had already been changed as a consequence of the record label fearing libel suits from lawyers representing the petty criminals named by Dylan and Levy as having falsely testified that Carter was seen at the murder scene. The finer points of the Carter case are not pertinent here. The pertinence lies in Dylan's willingness to rewrite his saga on the insistence of Columbia's in-house attorneys, after which he re-recorded the song ahead of the Rolling Thunder Revue's New England debut. He had done something similar twelve years earlier when tweaking the lyrics of 'The Lonesome Death of Hattie Carroll' for his third album, albeit with the original version still sung live.

Words can of course be deceptive, especially when incomplete, and, as we've seen, a straight reading of 'Dear Mrs Roosevelt' obscures the real date of its composition, nearly three years later. Equally false is the impression conveyed by the lyrics, whether whole or in part, that Woody Guthrie's admiration for FDR was unqualified. His feelings towards

Roosevelt ebbed and flowed, in a relationship best described as complex and contradictory. Woodrow Wilson Guthrie never met Franklin Delano Roosevelt, but if he had then the President would have revealed a disarming familiarity with his work, courtesy of the FBI but also thanks to a First Lady supportive of America's folk revival first time around. Another fifteen years would pass before that revival truly blossomed, by which time Guthrie was a chronic invalid – a tragedy, and a cruel irony.

Although Huntington's disease was as yet unsuspected, Guthrie was already ill when he composed 'Dear Mrs Roosevelt'. It's one of his final songs, complete with lyrics and melody. Indeed it may well be Woody's last complete song. Byrds and Baez favourite 'Deportee (Plane Wreck at Los Gatos)', also written in January 1948, is often cited as the last Woody Guthrie composition. It was in fact written as verse, to ensure the anonymous fruit pickers killed in a southern Californian air crash would never be forgotten – Guthrie gave the anonymous Mexicans imaginary names. On stage Woody would chant the poem, with his guitar providing a percussive accompaniment. Thus, the tune by which 'Deportee' is known today dates from a decade later, courtesy of a schoolteacher called Martin Hoffman. 'Dear Mrs Roosevelt', on the other hand, was always meant to be sung; ideally in front of a large audience, many of whom would join in on the chorus. There was no place for poetry when out on the campaign trail in the fall of 1948.

'Dear Mrs Roosevelt' has to be seen in the context of disillusion with the path being pursued by the Democratic Party, and Wallace's consequent decision to run in November 1948 as a genuinely radical alternative; but its composition was not solely a consequence of anti-Truman myth-making. Woody Guthrie had many faults, but hypocrisy and cynical manipulation of popular sentiment are never going to rank high on the charge sheet. On the one hand his roughly-hewn Marxisant world view, proletarian and populist, saw him dismiss FDR as the acceptable face of liberal capitalism, blanching at the prospect of systemically transforming depression-wracked America. Here was a harsh, hostile view of the President, articulated via a crude homespun philosophy reflective of the Communist Party's late 'thirties disenchantment with the New Deal, and its isolationist opposition to rearmament pre-Pearl Harbor.

Yet at the same time Guthrie refused to dismiss tangible evidence of New Deal initiatives creating jobs, raising living standards, and enhancing working men and women's quality of life. The twenty-six songs written for the Bonneville Power Administration in May 1941 together constitute a powerful, poetic, and in their own way deeply moving, testimony to the transformative effects of the New Deal's most ambitious initiatives. 'Dear Mrs Roosevelt' – Guthrie's last great political anthem – was rooted in an acknowledgement, however begrudging, that here was a president who by dint of his executive authority had facilitated the federal state's positive impact upon individual lives. The provision of work, whether that be painting murals or building dams, restored pride and dignity to millions of men and woman brought to their knees by an economic whirlwind.

In the months and years following Roosevelt's death Guthrie was not alone in refashioning the late president as a more liberal, left-leaning and interventionist statesman than had in fact been the case. FDR became in effect the lost leader, whose progressive legacy was being betrayed by someone accidentally placed in the White House as a consequence of Wallace's ill-treatment at the Democrats' 1944 National Convention. Eleanor Roosevelt, opposed to Truman's vice-presidential nomination, encouraged New Deal nostalgists in 1946-47, but never at the expense of party loyalty. Like many Communist fellow travellers observing the Democratic Party from outside, Guthrie failed to appreciate the power of the party machine that FDR himself had forged across the interwar period.

Written in January 1948 to mark Henry Wallace's final break from the Democrats, 'Dear Mrs Roosevelt' hailed a late president implicitly betrayed by his own party. For many radicals it was the Truman Administration's betrayal of FDR's progressive legacy which now forced former loyalists like Wallace to throw down the gauntlet, however reluctantly – here was a now former Democrat still faithful to his dead leader's vision of a prosperous, peace-loving nation. This heroic narrative ignored the inconvenient fact that Wallace had for much of his life been a registered Republican, switching allegiance only after Roosevelt appointed him Secretary for Agriculture. It also disguised the fact that the quasi-Communist Guthrie had no illusions about Wallace, campaigning for him in 1948 only because no one else seemed capable of mounting a serious challenge to the anti-Soviet posturing of both main parties.

Guthrie's qualified endorsement of Wallace was an obvious political miscalculation, but it didn't necessarily appear so at the time. Woody Guthrie was by no means alone in believing the United States was ripe for change. The 1948 presidential election proved a harsh reality check, and yet in terms of popular culture this marked a key moment for folk music as it lodged itself in the national psyche. Guthrie may have viewed campaigning for Wallace as a bitter experience, but the Lomax siblings and Pete Seeger had the prescience to see the rallies and hootenannies as a springboard for establishing a fresh audience among liberal America's young educated middle class. It was that same generation, and more especially their offspring, who would come to see Guthrie as a powerful presence in the nation's musical heritage, and who enthusiastically embraced Bob Dylan's pretensions to be his natural successor.

When Dylan tore into 'Maggie's Farm' at Newport on 25th July 1965 the older generation were appalled, and yet across the 'sixties their presence on the east coast folk scene remained as powerful as ever.

A conclusion

Ironically, one reason why Dylan decided to play an amplified set was his anger over Alan Lomax's condescending attitude towards the Paul Butterfield Blues Band – three of them would be on stage a day later when Dylan strapped on his Strat. Popular mythology sees the old guard swept away as Bob Dylan 'goes electric,' silencing his arran-sweatered critics with a succession of brilliant albums and a stage show which defined the raw, elemental nature of a fresh cultural phenomenon, 'rock music'. Except that the likes of Lomax and Seeger didn't disappear, if only because, contrary to the distorted perception of arrogant youth, they weren't old. Indeed, freed finally from the bonds of McCarthyism, Pete Seeger's best days were still to come. Like the slightly older Lomax, Seeger was middle-aged, which – given the volume at which Dylan and his sidemen played their three song set – goes a long way to explaining why he was so appalled by a perceived betrayal of all that ageing folkies held dear: arguably 'Like A Rolling Stone' did in due course change the world, but not in the way a banjo-playing east coast liberal aged 45 might imagine on first hearing – assuming in the first instance that he could make out what young Bobbie was singing.

A lot of water had flowed under the bridge by the time Seeger, Lomax, and their comrades again stood backstage listening to a Bob Dylan three song set. The world in January 1968 was a far more dangerous place, and – as events at home would swiftly confirm – nowhere more so than on the streets and campuses of the United States. Those events had already conspired to reinforce the New York/New England intelligentsia's individual and collective world view, not least re the radicalisation of youth culture. The 1968 Woody Guthrie memorial concerts constituted the final rallying of a generation born into the Depression, if not before, whose political thinking was moulded by the New Deal, the fight against fascism, and a Cold War realisation that social equality and shared prosperity demanded a uniquely American brand of social democracy far removed from Soviet-style Communism.

Mostly, but not entirely, white, they welcomed civil rights legislation and Johnson's 'Great Society' initiatives; but they were increasingly appalled by a Democratic administration's military intervention in south-east Asia.

Opposition to the Vietnam war united the smartly dressed, lifelong liberals seated up front at Carnegie Hall and the denim-clad children of the counterculture dancing in the aisles throughout Dylan's second, no-holds-barred set: this was a passing of the political baton, to the sound of Woodrow Wilson Guthrie refashioned for a generation who had come of age to the sound of the Beatles and the Byrds, not the Weavers and the Kingston Trio. Seeger and Lomax could have reacted in the same way that they did three years before, but, even if both men either could not articulate the changes in their emotional response to contemporary folk music, or were simply unaware of how much more enlightened and tolerant they had become, they did appreciate why Dylan and his band generated such an enthusiastic response from every part of the audience, young and old.

Chronicles ignores the Guthrie benefits, and – with the exception of Robert Shelton's *magnum opus* – Dylan biographies invariably display little or no interest. In their memoirs Robbie Robertson and Levon Helm devote only a page or so to the Crackers' solitary gig. Articles and books about The Band, not least the writings of Barney Hoskyns, record the group's presence on 20th January 1968, and then quickly hurry on. After all, the following six months would see the recording and release of *Music from Big Pink*; and 'The Band' re-establish themselves as musicians in their own right. Carnegie Hall was the last occasion on which the Hawks-as-were/The Band-to-be performed as Bob Dylan's sidemen. Henceforth, their presence on stage with Dylan would reflect a more equal relationship. At the close of the 1960s it was The Band, not their mentor, making the weather: Clapton closed down Cream and camped out in the Catskills because he wanted to absorb the honesty, authenticity, craftsmanship, musicianship, and keen sense of tradition that rendered The Band's first two albums so remarkable, and so influential. Had Eric been in the audience at Carnegie Hall for the last fifteen minutes prior to the interval he would surely have found what he was looking for – a concentrated outburst of energy and excitement more potent than a joyless, self-indulgent guitar solo testing the patience of both audience and fellow musicians.

What's striking from the recordings and the photographs is that Robertson, Helm, Manuel, Danko, Hudson, and above all, Dylan, were having the time of their lives, rediscovering that moment in the past when stepping on stage signalled an explosion of exuberance and ego-massaging pleasure. In the privacy of West Saugerties they fostered a fresh spirit of creativity and camaraderie, and then, on a chilly New York weekend in early 1968, they shared that same good-time feeling with the wider world. This was no deliberate fulfilment of a master plan; but that doesn't diminish the significance of the Carnegie Hall sets as an event. The significance of that event has for too long been overlooked, as has the added import of Bob Dylan singing a song as obscure – and as potent – as 'Dear Mrs Roosevelt'.

This is not a great Bob Dylan song, and in any case he didn't write it. Nor is it a great Woody Guthrie song, inexplicably absent from the canon. But it is a great Bob Dylan performance, not least because The Band-to-be play with that same precision, instinctiveness, engagement, and vivacity which is the hallmark of consummate musicians forged into a single entity. The Band were lucky with their live albums, not least *Rock of Ages* (the star-studded *The Last Waltz* is by definition an artificial representation). Here was a group that always rose to the occasion, as on their solitary excursion as the Crackers. Yet, once the first flush of fame had passed, excess and ennui generated too many box ticking sets – fans with long memories should forget an underwhelming appearance at Wembley Stadium in September 1974, and focus upon the revelatory performance that prefaced Dylan's Isle of Wight performance five years before.

All this was still to come when the Hawks-that-were stepped onstage at Carnegie Hall on the afternoon and evening of Saturday 20ᵗʰ January 1968. None of the audience were there to see the sidemen, and it's safe to assume that most if not all of Dylan's fans had anticipated he would play solo.

Neither the audience, nor the organisers, nor the other artists, nor even the players themselves, had any idea what lay ahead. For the Crackers it was global recognition, in a collective persona not that different from what was on display at Carnegie Hall. For Dylan the immediate future lay in the studio; but it would be decades before his admirers appreciated just how much music he recorded in the ostensibly fallow years at the turn of the decade: the 2014 compilation *Another Self Portrait (1969-1971)* signalled a continuity from the Basement Tapes when alone in the studio, confirming Dylan's attraction to long forgotten songs like 'Dear Mrs Roosevelt'. That attraction is lifelong, but it doesn't stop songs being rediscovered, and then discarded. 'Dear Mrs Roosevelt' served its purpose perfectly on the day, but then was of no further use: in Dylan's mind sentiment can't dictate a set list, and so the song has never been sung again. When it has been resurrected, notably on an album of Guthrie covers by Joel Rafael, then it's Bob Dylan's and not Woody Guthrie's version which serves as a template for reinterpretation. Why search out the original lyrics when Dylan's version provides such an easily accessible model? Any conscientious artist who does delve into the Woody Guthrie archives has little incentive to sing a fourteen verse song certain to provoke a sharp intake of breath the moment listeners learn of Roosevelt looking up to Joe Stalin.

Yet, at a time when, thanks to the efforts of family, folklorists, and archivists, so much of Woody Guthrie's less familiar work is finally resurfacing, we need to know what the uncensored version of 'Dear Mrs Roosevelt' sounded like. Seventy-two years ago a sceptical Wallace supporter was out on the campaign trail regaling the crowd with probably his last complete composition. It might be fourteen verses but that would not have stopped Woodrow Wilson Guthrie delivering his New Deal panegyric with characteristic humour, vitality, and empathy. Guthrie was already a sick man, but he still knew how to put on a show and woo a crowd. These days Bob Dylan is more likely to be rifling the Great American Songbook than consulting the Woody Guthrie Archives to recall what he left out of 'Dear Mrs Roosevelt' back in the day. Even if he can't remember every verse which did survive the cut, he won't have forgotten the song. Five decades have passed since the day he performed 'Dear Mrs Roosevelt', and throughout that time he's never sung it again. Yet Dylan is notorious for suddenly on stage recalling a song from way back when, and expecting his band to join in with scarcely a beat missed – it was said to infuriate the Heartbreakers when he toured with Tom Petty. Is it too fantastical to anticipate that somewhere, some time, on some future leg of the Never Ending Tour, after yet another iconic song has been tested to destruction, the bemused successors to Robbie, Levon, et al will hear their master launch into, 'Dear Mrs Roosevelt, don't hang your head and cry...'?

Postscript: 'If you want to keep your memories, you first have to live them'

This is a strange story, which, as with any story that involves Bob Dylan, raises more questions than it does answers. In its own weird way it seems a fitting coda to the history of 'Dear Mrs Roosevelt'.

In early 1978 the music press carried details of dates, venues, and ticket availability for the European leg of Dylan's forthcoming world tour. Nine eventful years had passed since his appearance at the Isle of Wight, and naturally I was eager to see him in concert. As I didn't have much money at the time, I gave careful thought as to how I could secure a decent seat. Although living in east Kent, my idea was to see Bob in the Midlands rather than the most obvious location, London. Tickets for Leicester's De Montfort Hall would be available from a Sunday morning some weeks prior to the June gigs Dylan would be playing in England.

On the weekend in question I was back in Coventry. At first light on the Sunday I drove my dad's car over to Leicester and joined the short queue outside the De Montfort box office. Others soon lined up behind me, and everyone present shared a smugness and self-satisfaction, secure in the knowledge that we would enjoy a front row view of Bob and his band. Around breakfast time hubris arrived in the form of a milkman. He asked why we were there, our answer prompting the news that several hundred Bob Dylan fans were presently queuing outside the council box office in the city centre. Appalled by the news, and suitably deflated, I drove into the middle of Leicester, and on seeing the size of the crowd didn't bother to stop. I resolved to apply by post for a ticket to see Dylan at Earls Court, and in due course was pleasantly surprised to find myself seated within a reasonable distance of the stage.

For well over thirty years this is how I remember my abortive trip to Leicester, and several times I have told this story against myself. Yet evidence now available on the internet renders my anecdote pure fiction. Bob Dylan did not play at the De Montfort Hall in 1978, the last time he was there being thirteen years earlier (also, milkmen don't usually deliver on a Sunday). My parents can no longer confirm or deny my borrowing the family car on a day when it would normally be needed to get them to church. Yet I have clear visual images of that Sunday morning in Leicester. Is my mind playing tricks with me? Is this an example of what Ian McEwen labelled 'false memory' when describing how he convinced himself that he had written a novella, the manuscript of which was lost in a house move? I remain sceptical of McEwen's story (would there not have been a file on his hard drive and/or memory stick?), and yet I do wonder if my experience is not that dissimilar. This complex act of self-deception is not a consequence of ageing as I have regularly recounted the episode over the years.

Extending his expertise from popular music to historiography, *Rolling Stone*'s Rich Cohen has found history to be, 'not what happened, but what remains when everything else is forgotten.' Beware the post-modernist rock critic, and yet maybe Cohen is right, in that the reconstruction of past experience given permanence in preceding essays will over time become 'the memory', like a fresh, more vivid layer of recollection on the canvas of consciousness. The irony is that a memory thus fixed – and renewed in my mind whenever I reread what I've written – can embrace an event I recall vividly but which all evidence suggests never took place, namely the dawn visit to De Montfort. These problems of recollection, record, and interpretation preoccupied historian and epistemologist R.G. Collingwood, who in turn inspired Simon Schama to write *Dead Certainties (Unwarranted Speculations)*, a deliberately provocative merger of 'fact' and fiction. My imaginary trip to Leicester would be meat and drink to Schama and McEwen, but is there a more banal explanation? Could it be that my case of 'false memory' is in itself false, and I did drive to the De Montfort Hall because nominated box offices up and down the country had been designated ticket outlets for the Earls Court gigs? In this version of events I was in the right city but at the wrong box office (to date I've found it impossible to discover where ticket outlets for the 1978 tour were located).

Unlike today, when the Never Ending Tour encompasses these islands at least once a year, Bob Dylan's London dates constituted a major event. He hadn't played in Britain since August 1969, and his concerts would coincide with the release of *Street Legal*: given the critical and commercial success of *Blood On The Tracks* and *Desire*, his new album was much anticipated. Nor had Dylan's reputation suffered to any great extent as punk brutally swept aside the old, the over-inflated, and the self-indulgent. On the strength perhaps of his 1965-66 'fuck you' image, Dylan never seriously pissed off stroppy punks with attitude – they had easier targets to take on. Irrespective of what Mick Jones or Steve Jones might think of the man from Minnesota there remained legions of fans eager to see Dylan live – and in June and July 1978 they got their opportunity.

The irony is that, while I can recall the trip I did or didn't make to Leicester, my memories of Bob Dylan playing at Earls Court are near non-existent. I can remember being struck by the irony of hearing the writer of 'All Along the Watchtower' dutifully cover Hendrix's cover; that cover of a cover in due course being covered by Neil Young and then by Eddie Vedder. Had I, a month later, been in Surrey at Blackbushe aerodrome, where Dylan entertained a festival crowd with a lengthy run through his back catalogue, then I would probably have a clearer idea of how well he was playing at the time: by all accounts, Dylan and his *Street Legal* backing band followed a soporific set by Eric Clapton with a storming session that sent two hundred thousand fans home happy. If Dylan had done so the night I saw him at Earls Court then I would surely have remembered (the tour's live album, recorded in Japan, is a demoralising combination of bombast and ennui). I didn't spend a day at the 'Blackbushe Picnic' sitting cross-legged on an abandoned runway because I was out of the country. However, given my aversion to festivals I was unlikely to have attended anyway – never the Dylan fanatic, seeing one show a year was enough.

I dutifully returned to Earls Court in June 1981 despite my fear that Bob the born-again Christian would preach hell, fire, and damnation halfway through his set. Thankfully we were spared the sermon, and many in the audience roared their approval of a raucous performance, driven along by hot gospellers and supercharged session men. However, nothing that night dissuaded me from the opinion that Dylan's second born again offering, *Shot of Love*, was his most mediocre album to date – it was, but across the 1980s far worse was to come. Over twenty years would pass before I next saw Bob Dylan, at Wembley Arena in May 2002. Arthritis prevented the star of the show from playing the guitar, and his croaking voice became ever more grating. Not even guitar maestro Charlie Sexton and a hot-shot backing band could rescue the deliberate mauling of so many great songs. In short, Dylan was awful, such that I vowed never to see him again.

That vow was broken on 12 July 2019 when I saw a septuagenarian Bob Dylan share top billing with Neil Young in Hyde Park. To my surprise and delight Dylan and his top-of-their-game sidemen (after several years away, Sexton was back to orchestrate proceedings) performed as if in a cabaret bar at two in the morning, entertaining an audience of sixty not sixty thousand. I may see Dylan again, I may not; but if I don't then that's fine. Far better to remember Hyde Park 2019 than Wembley Arena 2002 – and at least I can remember these two shows, albeit without the sharpness of recall that marks my memories of the Isle of Wight 1969.

All in all, I have seen Bob Dylan perform five times, which many would contend disqualifies me from writing with any authority about the man and his music. All around the world there are fans who make plans to see their hero five times on one tour (dedicated devotees are phlegmatic, viewing one poor show as an acceptable price if in their eyes the next half dozen constitute confirmation of the great man's genius). Digital communication has seen Dylan's global fan base consolidate and expand, with every aspect of his career up to and including this very moment logged and analysed – no detail is too small to be scrutinised and discussed. This is why I found it so strange that, having heard 'Dear Mrs Roosevelt' for the first time in 1982, it took me twenty years to find a Dylan enthusiast who knew the song – and they were Americans who sang and wrote about the music of Woody Guthrie: Joel Raphael and Will Kaufman. Even now, a decade later, I have never met anyone in Britain who declares how much they like Bob Dylan, and then says 'yes' when I ask if they know of Guthrie's panegyric to FDR. The podcast 'Dylan, Guthrie, and Roosevelt – the story of a song' is slowly raising Dylan fans' awareness of the Guthrie cover he has performed only twice in his career. Publication of this slim volume will hopefully increase the numbers further. Thankfully we have aural evidence of Dylan and The Band-to-be's performance that cold January day in New York city over half a century ago. Their set isn't a 'false memory', as my 1978 expedition to Leicester seems to be, but a real life event that occurred, not once but twice.

Not long before the Carnegie Hall concerts Dylan dashed off the words to 'Open The Door, Homer', a rewrite of an old Louis Jordan song; however hastily written, the lyrics contain wise words: 'Take care of all your memories…For you cannot relive them.' It's unlikely Bob Dylan spends much if any time recalling the afternoon and evening he entertained a cross-generational audience of New York folkies and radicals. Yet you can be sure that anyone present on 20th January 1968, and still alive, won't have forgotten the day Bob and his boys resurrected a long lost lament for the president who won the peace and then won the war – as the Nobel laureate later advised the whole wide world, and not just an audience of five in a basement in West Saugerties: 'If you want to keep your memories, you first have to live them.'

Acknowledgements

I'm grateful for the help and advice of Frank Cogliano (University of Edinburgh); James Jordan, David Dunn, and Chris Prior (University of Southampton); Will Kaufman (University of Central Lancashire); Bob Clark (Franklin D. Roosevelt Library and Museum); Tiffany Colannino (formerly of the Woody Guthrie Center); and Joel Rafael (Inside Recordings). Like Frank Cogliano, Mike Hammond (University of Southampton) offered an invaluable American perspective. Assuming his alter ego as the Dodge Brothers' songwriter/vocalist/guitarist, Mike performed the full, uncensored version of 'Dear Mrs Roosevelt' for my podcast *Dylan, Guthrie, and Roosevelt – the story of a song*. This is the first recording of the complete song, and my sincere thanks to Mike for his consummate performance.

Above all, I have to say a heartfelt thank you to Rob Joy (University of Southampton) for his encyclopaedic knowledge of Bob Dylan, forensic scrutiny of the original text, and technical assistance in creating *Dylan, Guthrie, and Roosevelt – the story of a song*; also, to David Kynaston, who from the outset has been extraordinarily helpful and encouraging. Together, Rob and David provided invaluable advice, and they bear no responsibility for any faults – they are all mine. I'm similarly grateful to Steve Hodder of Takahe Publishing for rendering publication such a stress-free and pleasant experience – how great to have a book published in your home town!

This book is shorter by about twenty thousand words than its previous incarnation, but it's a lot better for it. My thanks to Dan Franklin, Simon Fox, and Roy Foster for highlighting weaknesses in the original book and convincing me to start again. An important influence at the outset was *The Blue Moment*, Richard Williams' partly autobiographical exploration of *A Kind Of Blue*'s enduring legacy. A debt remains, but

221

it's shared now with Joan Didion's earliest collections of essays. Even though I could never match their author's style, wit, and perspicacity, *Slouching Towards Bethlehem* and *The White Album* showed me how I could organise and structure my material.

The representatives of Bob Dylan and Robbie Robertson require no thanks as they ignored my letters and e-mails requesting access and information. Thank you to TRS Music for their tacit agreement, following three unanswered approaches to the company, to use Woody Guthrie's words and music for purely academic purposes in this book and in the podcast *Dylan, Guthrie, and Roosevelt – the story of a song*.

When my mother had a bad fall, my cousin Maryrose Bodycote, and her husband Ron, put me up for a fortnight in Coventry, for which I am extremely grateful; not least as between waiting times I could continue work on the original book courtesy of the hospital library. Another close cousin, Lyn Clark, and her husband Roger, deserve a special mention for enabling me in 1982 to hear 'Dear Mrs Roosevelt' for the first time, on an album bought within spitting distance of FDR's Hyde Park home.

The book is dedicated to Mary Smith, who is always wonderfully supportive – and patient, and to our daughter-in-law Georgia McDonald. They share this dedication with a loving and courageous son and husband, who in December 2016 died far too young. This is the second book written in Adam Smith's memory – given his love of The Band I hope that he would have enjoyed reading it had he lived.

I still ask myself why I began writing the first version of this book so soon after finishing its predecessor. With the loss of Adam still fresh and raw, the pleasure and satisfaction derived from working on a project so different from the day job (writing about the music you love – what could be better?) was both a distraction and a therapy. The grief never goes away, and time is a slow and only partial healer. Yet walking the dog on the sea wall or in the New Forest, while reflecting upon what to write or on what has just been written, helped move the book along; and, more importantly, it calmed me down. Witnessing, day after day, a world gone wrong had compounded my grief, as I fell victim to an anger-inducing synthesis of the personal and the political. A laid-back chocolate lab, and a determination to complete – and then to rewrite – a book which, were it written by someone else, I would be keen to read, has proved a powerful combination. This book has without doubt left the writer in a better frame of mind. For everyone who reads it I hope the same proves true.

Select Sources

There are no footnotes, but any request(s) for specific references can be made via Adrian Smith's University of Southampton staff profile:

www.southampton.ac.uk/history/about/staff/as5.page

Podcast accompanying the book

To hear the Dodge Brothers' Mike Hammond perform the full version of 'Dear Mrs Roosevelt' listen to episode 13 of the podcast *Dylan, Guthrie, and Roosevelt – the story of a song*:

Apple/iTunes: https://podcasts.apple.com/gb/podcast/dylan-guthrie-and-roosevelt-the-story-of-a-song/id1473733233 OR

Android/Google Play Music: https://play.google.com/music/listen#/ps/Iangwibvf7jtkqj4hsbs4l5d 654 OR

PodBean: https://dylanguthrieandroosevelt.podbean.com

The text of 'Dylan, Guthrie, and Roosevelt' is essentially the same as the podcast narrative in episodes 1-12.

Select Recordings

To hear Bob Dylan and 'The Crackers' perform a shortened version of 'Dear Mrs Roosevelt' in Carnegie Hall on 20th January 1968 simply type in the title of the song on YouTube or Spotify – otherwise hear their full set on CDs of the 1968 and 1970 Woody Guthrie tribute concerts: *A Tribute to Woody Guthrie* (Warner Brothers, USA/UK, 1989) or the box set *Woody Guthrie The Tribute Concerts: Carnegie Hall 1968 Hollywood Bowl 1972* (Bear Family, Germany, 2017).

Details re relevant Bob Dylan recordings to be found on his official website:

www.bobdylan.com

Details re relevant recordings by The Band to be found on the relevant Wikipedia website:

www.en.wikipedia.org/wiki/The_Band_discography

Details re relevant recordings by Woody Guthrie to be found on the website of the Woody Guthrie website:

www.woodyguthriecenter.org/archives

The Almanac Singers, *Songs of Protest* (Prism, UK, 2001) CD

Various Artists, Folkways: *A Vision Shared – A Tribute to Woody Guthrie and Lead Belly* (Folkways, USA/UK, 1988) CD

Various Artists, *Roosevelt's Blues: African-American Blues and Gospel Songs on FDR* (Agram Blues, Netherlands, 1998) CD

Select Bibliography

Lester Bangs, *Mainlines, Blood Feasts and Bad Taste A Lester Bangs Reader,* John Northland, ed. (Serpent's Tail, London, 2003)

Billy Bragg, *Roots, Radicals, and Rockers: How Skiffle Changed the World* (Faber & Faber, London, 2017)

David Caute, *The Great Fear The Anti-Communist Purge Under Truman and Eisenhower* (Secker and Warburg, London, 1978)

Sue C. Clark, 'Bob Dylan Turns Up for Woody Guthrie Memorial', *Rolling Stone*, 24 February 1968.

Neil Corcoran, ed., *Do You Mr Jones? Bob Dylan with the Poets and Professors* (Pimlico, UK, 2003)

Robert Cohen, ed., *Dear Mrs Roosevelt Letters from Children of the Great Depression* (University of South Carolina Press, Columbia SC, 2006)

Ronald Cohen, *Woody Guthrie Writing America's Songs* (Routledge, London, 2012)

Jonathan Cott, ed., *Bob Dylan: The Essential Interviews* (Wenner Books, New York, 1996)

Ed Cray, *Ramblin' Man The Life and Times of Woody Guthrie* (W.W. Norton, New York, 2004)

Cameron Crowe, liner notes and interview with Bob Dylan in Bob Dylan, *Biograph* (Columbia/CBS, USA/UK, 1985)

Don Delillo, *Great Jones Street* (Houghton Miflin, Boston, 1973/Picador, London, 1992)

Kevin J.H. Dettmar, ed., *The Cambridge Companion to Bob Dylan* (Cambridge University Press, Cambridge, 2009)

Joan Didion, *Live and Learn* (Harper Perennial, London, 2005)

Bob Dylan, *Tarantula* (Scribner, New York, 1971/Macmillan, London, 1971)

Bob Dylan, *Writings and Drawings by Bob Dylan* (Jonathan Cape, London, 1973)

Bob Dylan, *Chronicles: Volume One* (Simon and Schuster, New York/London, 2004)

Marc Eliot, *Phil Ochs Death of a Rebel* (Omnibus Press, London, 1990)

Daniel Mark Epstein, *The Ballad of Bob Dylan A Portrait* (Souvenir Press, UK, 2011)

Allen Ginsberg, *Collected Poems 1947-1980* (Harper and Row, New York, 1984)

Michael Gray, *Song and Dance Man The Art of Bob Dylan* (Abacus, London, 1973)

Michael Gray, *The Bob Dylan Encyclopaedia* (London, Continuum, 2006)

Thom Gunn, *The Sense of Movement* (Faber, London, 1959)

Woody Guthrie, *Bound For Glory* (E.P. Dutton, New York, 1943/Penguin, London, 2004)

Woody Guthrie, *Woody Guthrie Folk Songs: A Collection of Songs by America's Foremost Balladeer*, Howard S. Richmond, Harold Lebinovitz, Pete Seeger et al, eds. (Ludlow/Essex Music, New York, 1961)

Woody Guthrie, *The Nearly Complete Collection of Woody Guthrie Folk Songs: A Collection of Songs by America's Foremost Balladeer*, Pete Seeger, ed. (Ludlow Music, New York, 1963)

Woody Guthrie, *Born To Win: Nitty-Gritty Songs and Snatches from the boss Father/Hero of Bob Dylan, Joan Baez, Donovan, The Lovin' Spoonful, The Mamas and the Papas and Everyone else in the Mainstream of Pop Sound Today*, Robert Shelton, ed. (Macmillan, UK, 1965)

Woody Guthrie, *Pastures of Plenty A Self-portrait*, Dave Marsh and Harold Leventhal, eds. (Harper Perennial, London, 1992)

Benjamin Hedin, ed., *Studio A The Bob Dylan Reader* (W.W. Norton & Company, New York/London, 2004)

Levon Helm, with Stephen Davis, *This Wheel's On Fire Levon Helm and the Story of the Band* (Plexus, London, 1994)

Clinton Heylin, *Bob Dylan: The Complete Recording Sessions: 1960-1994* (St Martin's Press, New York, 1997)

Barney Hoskins, *Across the Great Divide The Band and America* (Pimlico, London, 2003)

Barney Hoskins, *Small Town Talk: Bob Dylan, The Band, Van Morrison, Janis Joplin, Jimi Hendrix & Friends in the Wild Years of Woodstock* (Da Capo Press, Boston Mass., 2016)

Langston Hughes, 'Ballad of Roosevelt', *New Republic*, 31, 14 November 1934

Will Kaufman, *Woody Guthrie American Radical* (University of Illinois Press, Urbana, 2011)

Robert Klara, *FDR's Funeral Train: A Betrayed Widow, A Soviet Spy, and a Presidency in the Balance* (Palgrave Macmillan, New York, 2010)

Joe Klein, *Woody Guthrie A Life* (Alfred A. Knopf, New York, 1980/Faber & Faber, London, 1988)

Millard Lampell, liner notes in Various Artists, *A Tribute to Woody Guthrie* (Warner Brothers, USA/UK, 1976)

Millard Lampell and Hally Wood, eds., *A Tribute to Woody Guthrie* (TRO/Woody Guthrie Publications, New York, 1972) in Various Artists, *Woody Guthrie The Tribute Concerts: Carnegie Hall 1968 Hollywood Bowl 1972* (Bear Family, Germany, 2017)

Robert Lieberman, *"My Song Is My Weapon" People's Songs, American Communism, and the Politics of Culture, 1930-1950* (University of Illinois Press, Urbana and Chicago, 1995)

Alan Lomax, ed., *The Folk Songs of North America* (Doubleday, New York, 1960)

Alan Lomax, Woody Guthrie, and Pete Seeger, eds., *Hard Hitting Songs for Hard-hit People* (Oak Publications, New York, 1967)

John A. Lomax, ed., *Cowboy Songs and Other Frontier Ballads* (Sturgis and Walton, New York, 1911)

John A. Lomax and Alan Lomax, eds., *Our Singing Country A Second Volume of American Ballads and Folk Songs* (Macmillan, New York, 1941)

Dorian Lynskey, *33 Revolutions Per Minute A History of Protest Songs* (Faber & Faber, London, 2010)

Greil Marcus, *Mystery Train Images of America in Rock 'n' Roll Music*, fourth revised edition (Plume, New York, 1997)

Greil Marcus, *Invisible Republic Bob Dylan's Basement Tapes* (Picador, London, 1997)

Greil Marcus, *Bob Dylan by Greil Marcus Writings 1968-2010* (Faber & Faber, London, 2010)

Phil Ochs, 'The Guthrie Legacy', *Broadside*, 16, August 1963.

John S. Partington, ed., *The Life, Music and Thought of Woody Guthrie A Critical Appraisal* (Ashgate, Farnham, 2011)

Robbie Robertson, *Testimony* (William Heinemann, London, 2016)

Eleanor Roosevelt and Frances Cooke Macgregor, *This Is America* (G.P. Putnam's and Sons, New York, 1942)

William G. Roy, *Reds, Whites, and Blues: Social Movements, Folk Music, and Race in the United States* (Princeton University Press, Princeton/Oxford, 2010)

Philip Roth, *The Plot Against America* (Houghton Mifflin, New York, 2004/Jonathan Cape, London, 2004)

Robert Santelli, *This Land Is Your Land Woody Guthrie and the Journey of an American Folksong* (Running Press, Philadelphia, 2012)

Anthony Scaduto, *Bob Dylan* (Abacus, London, 1973)

Robert Shelton, 'Bob Dylan: a distinctive folk-song stylist', *New York Times*, 29 September 1961.

Robert Shelton, 'Tribute to the Life and Legend of Woody Guthrie', *New York Times*, 22 January 1968.

Robert Shelton, *No Direction Home The Life and Music of Bob Dylan*, Elizabeth Thomson and Patrick Humphries, eds. (Omnibus Press, London, 2011)

Sam Shepard, *Rolling Thunder Logbook* (Penguin, London, 1977)

Jean Edward Smith, *FDR* (Random House, New York, 2007)

John Steinbeck, *The Grapes of Wrath* (The Viking Press-James Lloyd, New York, 1939/Penguin, London, 2014)

John Steinbeck, *Cannery Row* (The Viking Press, New York, 1945/Penguin, London, 2017)

Guido van Rijn, *Roosevelt's Blues: African-American Blues and Gospel Songs on FDR* (University Press of Missouri, Columbia MO, 1997)

Graham White and John Maze, *Henry A. Wallace His Search for a New World Order* (University of North Carolina Press, Chapel Hill/London, 1995)

Richard Williams, *The Blue Moment: Miles Davis's A Kind of Blue and the Remaking of Modern Music* (Faber & Faber, 2010)

Select Documentaries and Websites

Arena – Woody Guthrie (Paul Lee, BBC, 1988)

Roll On Columbia: Woody Guthrie and the Bonneville Power Administration (Michael Majic and Dennis Matthews, University of Oregon, USA, 2000)

'My Day by Eleanor Roosevelt':
www2.gwu.edu/~erpapers/myday/browsebyyear.cfm

Theme Time Radio Hour Archive:
www.themetimeradio.com

CPSIA information can be obtained
at www.ICGtesting.com
Printed in the USA
LVHW082138010820
662082LV00006B/106

9 781908 837141